The Magic of Children's Gardens

The Magic of Children's Gardens

INSPIRING THROUGH CREATIVE DESIGN

Lolly Tai

With a Foreword by Jane L. Taylor

TEMPLE UNIVERSITY PRESS

Philadelphia · Rome · Tokyo

Frontispiece: Square Maze at Longwood Gardens' Indoor Children's Garden

TEMPLE UNIVERSITY PRESS
Philadelphia, Pennsylvania 19122
www.temple.edu/tempress

Library of Congress Cataloging-in-Publication Data

Names: Tai, Lolly, author.
Title: The magic of children's gardens : inspiring through creative design / Lolly Tai ; with a foreword by Jane L.
    Taylor.
Description: Philadelphia, Pennsylvania : Temple University Press, 2017. | Includes bibliographical references and
    index.
Identifiers: LCCN 2016042660 | ISBN 9781439914472 (cloth : alk. paper)
Subjects: LCSH: Children's gardens—United States.
Classification: LCC SB457 .T24 2017 | DDC 635.083—dc23 LC record available at https://lccn.loc.gov/2016042660

♾ The paper used in this publication meets the requirements of the American National Standard for Information
Sciences—Permanence of Paper for Printed Library Materials, ANSI Z39.48-1992

Printed in the United States of America

9 8 7 6 5 4 3 2 1

To the parents and teachers who have worked tirelessly to instill a love of nature in children, planting the seed for future generations who will conserve our natural landscapes and create more outdoor learning places for children. With special tribute to my loving and nurturing parents, Rev. Dr. Kuang Ming Tai and Kuo Hua Li Tai, who facilitated discovery and fostered my appreciation of nature when I was a child.

Hershey Children's Garden at
Cleveland Botanical Garden

Contents

Michigan 4-H Children's Garden
at Michigan State University

Foreword

More than a century ago, Liberty Hyde Bailey, the father of American horticulture and an early proponent of nature study for children, said that learning about nature should "open the child's mind by direct observation to a knowledge and love of the common things and experiences in the child's life and environment" (Dorf 1956, 110). Throughout years of visiting public gardens in the United States and Europe, I had the opportunity to observe parents interacting with their children, and the parents' words mirrored what signs posted in the garden already said: Do not touch. Stay on the path. No running. The plant identification signs were not written for children; the sculptures, seating, steps, and so forth were not to their scale. Instead of teaching about plants, adults spent more time trying to control their children. Not surprisingly, bored children could not wait to leave. The message seemed to be that allowing children hands-on interaction with plants was to be discouraged.

I would see crops on display in long straight rows with no mention of a child's morning cereal or daily bread. There would be fiber and dye garden theme areas with no connection to T-shirts and blue jeans. Components of kids' favorite foods were all displayed in boring arrangements. References to the plants mentioned in their favorite childhood storybooks to bring the tales to life were nonexistent. To quote Liberty Hyde Bailey, the "love of the common things" in a child's environment was being ignored.

In the early 1900s, public gardens such as the Brooklyn Botanic Garden (1914) and Cleveland Botanic Garden (1936) initiated marvelous teaching programs for kids in which the enrolled children had a small plot and could visit to care for their vegetables and flowers. These gated and restricted areas reached these participating children exceptionally well. But what about the young children accompanying hundreds of casual visitors to public gardens who were being ignored?

As our world grew more technically advanced, as our population suffered from plant blindness, and as our access to natural environments became more limited, our children were experiencing the consequences. Children were lacking outdoor playtime, had little or no knowledge of where food comes from, and were struggling with childhood obesity. It was time for public gardens to take heed and add a new focus: children and families.

It is my belief that science is best taught as the student learns to see, touch, taste, hear, and smell the common things. The plants and the part they play in a child's life and environment are the starting point. Children will learn to care for what they first learn to love. The explosion of gardens for children and families across the country in the past twenty-three years speaks to the popularity of visiting public garden spaces. Garden membership increases, outreach to local schools and community gardens expands, and a new sense of garden ownership is enhanced because of the feeling of inclusiveness. Gardens are truly for everyone!

It is my hope that the gardens displayed in this book will enliven your imagination, stimulate your curiosity, and awaken your own childhood sense of wonder to encourage the creation and fostering of these very special enchanted spaces for children and families. We have entered an age when nature no longer occurs naturally for children. The pages that follow are essential for anyone embarking on the critical mission of designing spaces that provide opportunities for children to explore and experience nature. Now more than ever, our children deserve the very best green spaces.

Jane L. Taylor, Founding Curator
Michigan 4-H Children's Garden
Michigan State University

Acknowledgments

This book was made possible through the help of so many people. I acknowledge and thank four groups of people.

First, I thank Sara Cohen, Nikki Miller, Ann-Marie Anderson, and Kate Nichols at Temple University Press, who made this book a reality. I am honored to share my research about children's garden designs through this publication.

Second, I thank garden administrators, staff, and designers for graciously sharing their stories and knowledge about their gardens, as well as for their support and enthusiasm about this book. Special thanks go to the following:

Brooklyn Botanic Garden's Children's Garden: Jenine Osbon and Ashley Gamell
Brooklyn Botanic Garden's Discovery Garden: Ashley Gamell, Paul Seck, Tyler Rob,
    Elizabeth Reina-Longoria, and Rachel Dobkin
Paul Smith Children's Village at Cheyenne Botanic Gardens: Shane Smith, Herb Schaal,
    Aaron Sommers, and Mark Kosmos
Chicago Botanic Garden's Regenstein Learning Campus:
    Grunsfeld Children's Growing Garden: Eileen Prendergast, Kathy Johnson, and Scott
      Byron
    Kleinman Family Cove: Stacilyn Feldman and Lisa Delplace
    Learning Campus Garden: Mikyoung Kim and Terry Ryan
Children's Garden at Hershey Gardens: Anthony Haubert, Crystal Huff, and Jane Taylor
Helen and Peter Bing Children's Garden at Huntington Botanical Gardens: James Folsom,
    Katie Chiu, Scott Kleinrock, Todd Bennitt, and Ned Kahn
Ithaca Children's Garden: Erin Marteal, Harriet Becker, and Marcia Eames-Sheavly
Luci and Ian Family Garden at Lady Bird Johnson Wildflower Center: Gary Smith and
    Andrea Delong-Amaya
Longwood Gardens' Indoor Children's Garden: Marnie Conley, Patricia Evans, Tres
    Fromme, Mary Allinson, and Abigail Palutis
Michigan 4-H Children's Garden at Michigan State University: Jane Taylor, Lee Taylor,
    Norm Lownds, Jessica Wright, and David Cavagnaro
Morton Arboretum Children's Garden: Herb Schaal, Susan Jacobson, Andrew Howard,
    and Hanna Rennard
Vicky C. and David Byron Smith Children's Garden at Naples Botanical Garden: Herb
    Schaal, Brian Holley, Chad Washburn, Mark Kosmos, and Ellin Goetz
Everett Children's Adventure Garden at New York Botanical Garden: James Boyer, Allen
    Juba, Fred Charles, and Natalie Andersen

Childhood's Gate Children's Garden in the Arboretum at Pennsylvania State University: Emmanuel Didier, Kim Steiner, Judy Larkin, and Shari Elderson

Children's Garden at River Farm: Tom Underwood and David Ellis

Ann Goldstein Children's Rainforest Garden at Marie Selby Botanical Gardens: Tom Buchter, Herb Schaal, Emmanuel Didier, Mischa Kirby, Jeannie Perales, Judi Cox, Mike McLaughlin, and Angelo Randaci

United States Botanic Garden Children's Garden: Nick Nelson, Allan Summers, Rodney Robinson, and Holly Shimizu

Children's Discovery Garden at Wegerzyn Gardens MetroPark: Cindy Tyler and Gita Michulka

Enchanted Woods at Winterthur Museum, Garden, and Library: Linda Eirhart, Gary Smith, and Denise Magnani

Third, I thank Karen Langhauser for reviewing my book and for providing invaluable feedback and Eva Monheim for reviewing the plant lists.

Finally, I thank my husband, Joseph Michael Kelly, and my siblings, Lois, Noah, and Luther, for their love, encouragement, and boundless support.

The Magic of Children's Gardens

Hershey Children's Garden
at Cleveland Botanical Garden

Introduction

Designing outdoor spaces that are attractive to children requires a thoughtful landscape design process that incorporates key considerations of what appeals to children. The following pages embark on an exploration of inspiring ideas for creating magical children's spaces in garden settings. Nineteen case studies of outstanding children's outdoor environments in public gardens are described in detail. The examples provided are intended to serve as a broad platform to inspire the creation of more well-designed children's outdoor spaces and as a resource for anyone planning to design and build such spaces. Through a comprehensive collection of drawings, sketches, and photographs of successful children's outdoor environments, what follows is an explanation of both the design process and criteria for designing children's outdoor spaces.

The primary goal, concept, and design for each garden are evaluated. Within this context, the landscape design process (research, program development, site inventory and analysis, design and construction) and the special considerations relevant for creating children's outdoor environments are also detailed. Design concepts involving scale, water, plants, wildlife, heights, retreat or enclosure, make-believe, creative and active play, and stimulation of the five senses are highlighted. Educational and sustainable landscape concepts unique to each garden are also covered. Educational elements help children learn and appreciate various aspects of the natural environment, and in many gardens the educational component is tied to school curriculum. Sustainable landscape concepts expose children to nature and instill in them environmental stewardship at an early age.

Creating children's outdoor environments is critical in today's society as more and more children grow up in cities. Children no longer have ready access to natural environments, which are important to their physical, mental, and emotional development. Just over half the world now lives in cities, and by 2050, over 70 percent of people will be urban dwellers (United Nations 2014). Children are spending less time outdoors. Sedentary lifestyles are contributing to obesity and other health problems, as well as a sense of disconnection from nature, for today's urban children (Louv 2005).

Children's contact with nature is critical for their healthy development. Research shows that green environments support attention functioning, cooperative behavior, and physical health. Data suggest that childhood experiences of green space bestow strong physical and the emotional benefits (Kellert and Derr 1998). Children's mental and emotional needs must be met to ensure healthy childhood development, but maintaining places where children can be physically active is also crucial (Moore 1997).

When nature no longer occurs naturally for children, it is imperative that we collectively work to design spaces that provide opportunities for children to explore and experience nature.

Children cultivating
in the garden, 1928

Brooklyn Botanic Garden's Children's Garden

BROOKLYN, NEW YORK

GOAL

Brooklyn Botanic Garden, founded in 1910, is an internationally recognized leader and innovator in environmental education programs. The Children's Garden program, established in 1914, is the oldest children's garden in continuous use in the world. It was founded in part by Ellen Eddy Shaw, a trailblazing educator and advocate of hands-on learning. According to Brooklyn Botanic Garden, "A botanical institution [can] do important work in both research and display and at the same time connect with its local community through . . . education" (Peters 2014).

CONCEPT

Brooklyn Botanic Garden first opened garden plots to the community on May 2, 1914. Today, it offers various gardening programs for children from two to eighteen years old to assist them in planting their own crops and flowers and harvesting them under the guidance of garden instructors. For the youngest children, between ages two and three, and their parents, the Trees and Saplings program is available. The Seeds program is for four- to six-year-olds entering pre-kindergarten or kindergarten. These programs also combine planting activities with craft making, food preparation, and creative play. Older children in grades one through eight can garden and learn about science, urban ecology, and cooking in the City Farmers program. "Once children are in the eighth grade, they can apply to become an apprentice in the Garden Apprentice Program, which offers internships for students up to grade twelve or eighteen years old to learn and mentor younger children in the Children's Garden," explains Jenine Osbon, coordinator of the Children's Garden.

DESIGN

In 1914, the garden began with 150 garden plots, each 5 by 7 feet (1.5 by 2.1 meters), planted with a variety of vegetables. Flowerbeds were planted along the boundaries, and larger plants were accommodated in larger sections.

Today, the Children's Garden is 1 acre (0.4 hectare) and is delineated within a fenced area. The plant beds range from 3 by 12 feet (0.9 by 3.7 meters) for Trees and Saplings classes and up to 4 by 15 feet (1.2 by 4.6 meters) for City Farmers classes. Children plan, plant, and harvest crops of lettuce, tomatoes, squash, onions, peppers, and other vegetables and companion plants, such as herbs and flowers. Adjacent to the garden area are the Deborah Reich Courtyard Green, Frances M. Miner Children's House, and an outdoor covered activity area. Built in 1917 for educational programs and tool storage, the Children's House was later named for Frances Miner, who educated children at Brooklyn Botanic Garden from 1930 to 1973.

CONCLUSION

The original goals and ideals are still an integral part of Brooklyn Botanic Garden's Children's Garden and are embraced by both educators and environmentalists. Today, Brooklyn Botanic Garden fosters greening the urban environment through education, sustainable practices, and stewardship. Every year, over a thousand children engage with the Children's Garden. The garden continues to encourage young people to be participants, not just spectators, in community horticulture and conservation.

Opposite top: Harvesting the first crop, 1914
Opposite bottom: Harvesting in the garden, 2015
Top: Tending the garden in the 1930s and in 2015

Cucurbita pepo (pumpkin)

Lablab purpureus (purple hyacinth bean)

Citrullus lanatus (watermelon)

Children's Garden typical crop list, 2015

Scientific name	Cultivar	Common name
Allium ampeloprasum	'King Richard'	Leek
Allium cepa	'Stuttgarter'	Onion
Apium graveolens	'Tango'*	Celery
Beta vulgaris	'Chioggia'	Beet
	'Golden Detroit'	Beet
	'Bright Lights'*	Chard
	'Golden'*	Chard
Brassica cretica	'Charming Snow'	Cauliflower
Brassica rapa var. *rosularis*	—	Tatsoi
Brassica oleracea	'Limba'*	Broccoli
	'Vates'*	Collard
	'Lacinato'*	Kale
	'Vates Dwarf Blue'*	Kale
	'Early White'*	Kohlrabi
	'Kolibri'*	Kohlrabi
Brassica rapa	'Gold Ball'	Turnip
	'White Egg'	Turnip
Capsicum annuum	'Purple Beauty'	Pepper
Cucumis sativus	'Lemon'*	Cucumber
Cucurbita pepo	'Black'*	Squash (summer)
	'Costata Romanesca'*	Squash (summer)
	'New England Pie'	Pumpkin
	'Waltham Butternut'	Squash (winter)
Daucus carota ssp. *sativus*	'Mokum'	Carrots
	'Red Cured Chantenay'	Carrots
Eruca sativa	'Astro'	Arugula
Helianthus annuus	'Mammoth Grey Stripe'	Sunflower
Lactuca sativa var. *longifolia*	'Black Seeded Simpson'	Lettuce (head)
	'Blushed Butter'	Lettuce (head)
	'Green Deer Tongue'	Lettuce (loose)
	'Hyper Red'	Lettuce (loose)
	'Plato II'	Lettuce (romaine)
	'Speckled Amish'	Lettuce (head)
	'Tom Thumb'	Lettuce (head)
Phaseolus vulgaris	'Provider'*	Bean
Pisum sativum var. *macrocarpon*	'Sugar Ann'	Snap pea
Raphanus sativus	'Easter Egg'*	Radish
	'French Breakfast'	Radish
Solanum melongena	'Diamond'	Eggplant
Solanum tuberosum	'Desiree OG'	Potato
	'German Butterball'	Potato
Solanum lycopersicum	'Cherokee Purple'*	Tomato
	'Goldie'*	Tomato
	'Principe Borghese'	Tomato (cherry)
Spinacia oleracea	'Space'	Spinach
Tagetes patula	'Sparky Mix'	Marigold

* Crops that were the most productive in 2015 in terms of their yield

Brooklyn Botanic Garden's Children's Garden

1000 Washington Avenue, Brooklyn, NY 11225

718-623-7200   http://www.bbg.org/collections/gardens/childrens_garden

Opening date: May 2, 1914

Project size: 1 acre (0.4 hectare) within Brooklyn Botanic Garden's 52-acre (21-hectare) site

Design

Ellen Eddy Shaw

Current Contacts

Brooklyn Botanic Garden director of communications: Elizabeth Reina-Longoria
Brooklyn Botanic Garden Children's Garden coordinator: Jenine Osbon

Interviews and Personal Communications

Ashley Gamell, November 9, 2015; Jenine Osbon, December 7, 2015; Elizabeth Reina-Longoria, January 21, 2016

Physalis philadelphica (tomatillo)

Rubus idaeus (raspberry)

Beta vulgaris subsp. *cicla* 'Bright Lights' (Swiss chard)

Opposite top left: Harvesting the crop, 1930

Opposite top center: Harvesting the crop, 2015

Opposite top right: Children's Garden delineated within fenced area

Top left and center: Learning in the Garden Apprentice Program

Top right: Deborah Reich Courtyard Green and Frances M. Miner Children's House

Winding path through the meadow
toward the marsh

2

Brooklyn Botanic Garden's Discovery Garden

BROOKLYN, NEW YORK

GOAL

The new Discovery Garden is designed for the next generation of naturalists. This garden embraces Brooklyn Botanic Garden's mission "as an urban botanic garden that connects people to the world of plants, fostering delight and curiosity while inspiring an appreciation and sense of stewardship of the environment" (Brooklyn Botanic Garden 2013). "A major goal is to encourage children of all ages to build science skills as they play and explore the natural world," states Ashley Gamell, manager of the Discovery Garden. The 1-acre (0.4-hectare) Discovery Garden, designed to engage children ages two to twelve, has woodland, meadow, and marsh habitats found in the greater New York area, as well as vegetable gardens. The new garden is four times the size of the previous 10,500-square-foot (975-square-meter) Discovery Garden, which was designed for smaller groups of three- to six-year-old children and emphasized sensory exploration through touching and smelling plants, playing on a nature trail, and participating in special programs.

CONCEPT

The overall design process took ten years. Initial conceptual planning began in 2005 with W. Gary Smith Design and Argyle Design. Brooklyn Botanic Garden held many focus groups and conducted interviews and surveys to solicit input from the community. The garden's educators and staff also provided invaluable insights from observing children's interactions with the original Discovery Garden for fifteen years. After a great deal of consideration during the initial planning phase, the garden's current site, along Flatbush Avenue, was chosen. In 2010, the landscape architecture firm Michael Van Valkenburgh Associates was selected to design the new Discovery Garden, which opened in 2015, along with the adjacent Water Garden and Water Conservation project, which opened in September 2016. Brooklyn Botanic Garden's education exhibits team worked with Metcalfe Architecture and Design and Art Guild Museums and Environments from schematic design through project completion. Following the cues from the previous Discovery Garden, the main concept for the new garden focuses on the natural environment, with an emphasis on plant ecosystems.

Design process sketch,
July 19, 2010

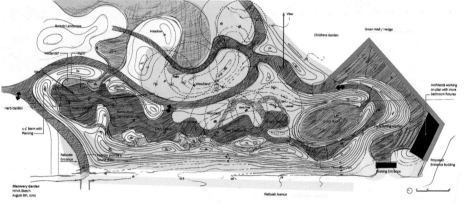

Design process sketch,
August 6, 2010

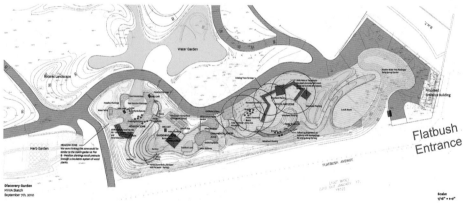

Design process sketch,
September 7, 2010

Flatbush
Entrance

Design process sketch,
November 12, 2010

DESIGN

Design process sketch,
February 8, 2011

The new Discovery Garden is designed with a network of winding trails that weave in and out of woodland, meadow, and marsh plant communities. Visitors arrive from the garden's southwest entry at the woodland or from the northeast entry at the four seasons garden. The meadow is in the middle. Near the marsh are two distinct gardens: the four seasons garden and the fruit and vegetable garden. This area includes the Hamm Children's Learning Courtyard, the discovery pavilion for educational programs, and a service building.

Along the path, interpretive signs, interactive sound boxes (echoing wildlife sounds), and activity stations and science tables provide educational opportunities and experiences for visitors of all ages about plant ecosystems and wildlife habitats. Field guides are available to use in the garden and change seasonally. Environmental art in the garden such as the giant bird's nest and the insect hotel add another interesting dimension in the garden. Large split logs and wooden benches throughout the garden provide seating and storage. A berm along Flatbush Avenue provides a visual buffer, topographic interest, and sound attenuation. A portion of this undulating berm also serves as a rolling lawn.

Key areas of the Discovery Garden

Key area	Features
Marquard Family Woodland and Vanneck Bailey Tree Platform	Giant bird's nest, marimba, and raised deck under a large interactive space
Meadow	Water pump with metal troughs for watering plants and play, as well as boulder seating arranged for small groups
Marsh	Marsh/pond exploration
Fruit and vegetable garden	Plant beds and hands-on horticultural experience with soils, composting, and planting and harvesting fruits and vegetables
Four seasons garden	Nonnative showy sensory plants selected for interesting texture, scent, shape, and color throughout the year
Hamm Children's Learning Courtyard and discovery pavilion	Space for educational sessions equipped with large tables and seating
Service building	Space for tool storage

Hand pump and movable water troughs

Large round wood pavers through the meadow

Exploring the marsh area

Giant bird's nest in the woodland area

ren's Discovery Garden & Spring Garden

Water Garden

Oak Hill

Meadow

Gardeners'
Pavilion

Outdoor
Classroom

Evergreen
Entry

Orientation Area

Deciduous
Forest

Entry Arch

Flatbush Avenue

Illustrative plan

Exploring plant characteristics
at a science station

Make your own bird's nest station

Woodland sign with field guide

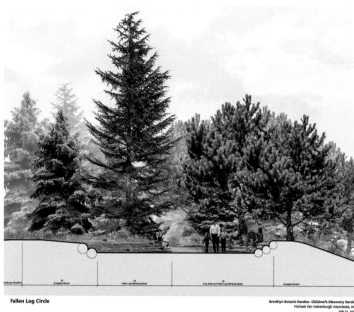

Fallen Log Circle

Brooklyn Botanic Garden- Children's Discovery Garden
Michael Van Valkenburgh Associates, Inc.
July 12, 2013

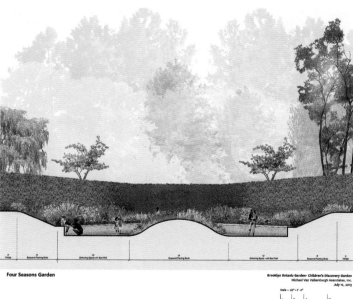

Four Seasons Garden

Brooklyn Botanic Garden- Children's Discovery Garden
Michael Van Valkenburgh Associates, Inc.
July 12, 2013

Top left and right: Fallen log circle at southwest entrance

Bottom left: Fruit and vegetable garden

Bottom right: Four seasons garden

Opposite top: Meadow

Opposite bottom left and right: Garden during and after construction

Meadow

Brooklyn Botanic Garden- Childrens Discovery Garden
Michael Van Valkenburgh Associates, Inc.
July 11, 2013

Brooklyn Botanic Garden's Discovery Garden

Deciduous trees

Acer pensylvanicum 'Erythrocladum'
Acer rubrum 'Frank Jr.'
Acer saccharum 'Bailsta'
Asimina triloba
Betula lenta
Betula papyrifera
Carpinus caroliniana
Cercidiphyllum japonicum
Cercis canadensis
Cercis chinensis
Cladrastis kentukea
Diospyros kaki
Diospyros virginiana
Fagus grandifolia
Fagus sylvatica
Ginkgo biloba 'Autumn Gold'
Gleditsia triacanthos f. *inermis*
Gymnocladus dioicus 'Espresso'
Liriodendron tulipifera
Liquidambar styraciflua
Magnolia grandiflora
Magnolia macrophylla
Magnolia virginiana 'Henry Hicks'
Malus domestica 'Liberty'
Malus domestica 'Freedom'
Malus floribunda
Ostrya virginiana
Poncirus trifoliata
Prunus armeniaca 'Mormon'
Prunus avium 'Black Tartarian'
Prunus cerasus 'Montmorency'
Prunus subhirtella 'Pendula'
Quercus alba
Quercus acutissima
Quercus macrocarpa
Quercus rubra
Sassafras albidum
Stewartia monadelpha
Stewartia pseudocamellia
Tilia americana

Evergreen trees

Cedrus deodara
Chamaecyparis obtusa
Chamaecyparis obtusa 'Magnifica'
Chamaecyparis obtusa 'Wells Special'
Chamaecyparis obtusa 'Gracilis Compacta'
Chamaecyparis obtusa 'Gracilis'
Chamaecyparis obtusa 'Kosteri Fast Form'
Chamaecyparis obtusa var. *formosana*
Cryptomeria japonica
Ilex 'Nellie R. Stevens'
Picea abies 'Pendula'
Pinus strobus
Pinus wallichiana
Sciadopitys verticillata

Shrubs

Aesculus pavia
Amelanchier × *grandiflora* 'Autumn Brilliance'
Callicarpa americana
Calycanthus floridus 'Edith Wilder'
Camellia hybrids
Camellia japonica
Camellia sinensis
Cephalanthus occidentalis
Chionanthus virginicus
Clethra alnifolia 'Hummingbird'
Cornus officinalis 'Kintoki'
Corylopsis glabrescens
Corylopsis pauciflora
Corylopsis spicata
Corylus cornuta
Edgeworthia chrysantha
Hamamelis mollis 'Wisley Supreme'
Hamamelis virginiana
Ilex glabra 'Compacta'
Ilex × *aquipernyi* 'Meschick' Dragon Lady
Ilex verticillata 'Winter Red'
Ilex verticillata 'Southern Gentleman'
Itea virginica 'Henry's Garnet'
Kalmia latifolia
Leucothoe axillaris
Lindera benzoin
Lindera glauca var. *salicifolia*
Morella pensylvanica 'Silver Sprite'
Prunus laurocerasus 'Otto Luyken'
Rhododendron maximum
Rhododendron catawbiense 'Roseum Elegans'
Rhododendron chionoides 'Lemon Ice'
Rhus glabra
Ribes rubrum 'Pink Champagne'
Ribes rubrum 'Red Lake'
Ribes rubrum 'White Pearl'
Salix discolor
Salix gracilistyla 'Melanostachys'
Vaccinium corymbosum
Viburnum × *burkwoodii* 'Mohawk'
Viburnum × *rhytidophylloides* 'Alleghany'

Vines

Campsis radicans
Parthenocissus quinquefolia
Parthenocissus vitacea

Four Seasons Mix

Perennials

Acanthus mollis
Alchemilla mollis
Amsonia hubrichtii
Anemone × *hybrida* 'Honorine Jobert'
Angelica archangelica
Aster novae-angliae
Astrantia major 'Moulin Rouge'
Baptisia australis
Bergenia cordifolia
Campanula persicifolia 'Telham Beauty'
Crambe maritima
Cynara cardunculus
Dahlia 'Park Princess'
Dahlia 'Night Queen'
Digitalis parviflora
Echinacea pallida 'Hula Dancer'
Geranium sanguineum 'Max Frei'
Helleborus argutifolius
Hemerocallis flava
Kirengeshoma palmata
Onopordum acanthium
Platycodon grandiflorus 'Perlmutterschale'
Tricyrtis formosa 'Sinonome'

Bulbs

Allium holandicum
Lycoris squamigera
Narcissus actea
Narcissus 'Pheasant's Eye'

Wetland Mix

Asclepias incarnata
Aster puniceus
Carex bebii
Carex vulpinoidae
Chelone glabra
Equisetum hyemale
Eupatorium perfoliatum
Eupatorium purpureum
Filipendula rubra
Hibiscus moscheutos
Iris versicolor
Juncus effusus
Lobelia cardinalis
Lobelia siphilitica
Mimulus regens
Pontederia cordata
Sagitaria latifolia
Scirpus cyperihus
Symplocarpus foetidus

Ferns

Matteuccia struthiopteris
Onoclea sensibilis
Osmunda regalis var. *spectabilis*

Meadow Mix Grasses

Bouteloua curtipendula
Bouteloua gracilis
Bromus kalmii
Carex bicknellii
Diarrhena americana
Elymus hystrix
Eragrostis spectibilis
Schizachyrium scoparium
Sporobolis heterolepsis

Forbs

Asclepias purpurescens
Asclepias tuberosa
Allium cernuum
Aster azureus
Callirhoe bushii
Coreopsis tinctoria
Dalea purpurea
Echinacea pallida
Eryngium yuccifolium
Geum triflorum
Heliopsis helianthoides
Liatris aspera
Lilium michiganense
Parthenium integrifolium
Phlox paniculata
Pycnanthemum muticum
Rudbeckia maxima
Silphium terebinthinaceum
Solidago caesia
Zizia aurea

Fern

Dennstaedtia punctilobula

Woodland Mix

Perennials

Anemone canadensis
Aquilegia canadensis
Arisaema triphyllum
Aruncus dioicus
Asarum canadense
Carex albicans
Carex flaccosperma
Carex pensylvanica
Cypripedium acaule
Dicentra cucullaria
Dicentra eximia
Erythronium americanum
Gaultheria procumbens
Heuchera villosa 'Autumn Bride'
Mitchella repens
Oxalis montana
Polygonatum odoratum 'Variegatum'
Smilacina racemosa
Tiarella cordifolia
Trillium grandiflorum
Uvularia perfoliata
Viola pubescens

Top and bottom: A diverse array of plants being installed in the woodland area

Ferns

Adiantum pedatum
Athyrium filix-femina
Dryopteris intermedia
Polystichum acrostichoides
Thelypteris noveboracensis

Bulb

Anemone blanda

Discovery Edge Mix

Ferns

Dryopteris marginalis
Polystichum acrostichoides

Groundcover

Asarum europaeum

Shrub

Comptonia peregrina

Spring Garden Mix

Perennials

Helleborus 'Apricot Blush'
Helleborus argutifolius
Helleborus 'Cherry Blossom'
Hemerocallis flava
Helleborus foetidus
Helleborus 'Josef Lemper'
Helleborus niger 'Potter's Wheel'
Helleborus niger 'Praecox'
Helleborus × *hybridus* 'Pine Knot
    Select'
Helleborus × *hybridus* 'PK Select
    White'
Sarcococca hookeriana var. *humilis*

Ferns

Dryopteris marginalis
Polystichum acrostichoides

Bulbs

Galanthus elwesii
Narcissus actaea
Narcissus 'Avalanche'
Narcissus 'Hawera'
Narcissus 'Jack Snipe'
Narcissus 'Petrel'
Narcissus 'Stint'
Scilla pratensis
Tulipa 'Ice Stick'
Tulipa orphanidea var. *flava*

Groundcover

Asarum europaeum

Brooklyn Botanic Garden's Discovery Garden

Top: Insect hotel by Lisa Lee Benjamin

Bottom: Fall view of meadow to marsh

Opposite top left: Four seasons garden

Opposite top right: Fruit and vegetable garden within Hamm Children's Learning Courtyard

CONCLUSION

Brooklyn Botanic Garden's Discovery Garden is a sophisticated garden emphasizing the complexities within three ecosystems. Larger than the previous Discovery Garden and designed for children up to twelve years old, the garden attracts families, school and camp groups, and adult visitors alike. Visitors are immersed in the garden while playing, exploring, and learning about the diverse landscape and habitats around them. The Discovery Garden exemplifies Brooklyn Botanic Garden's mission to "inspire[] people of all ages through the conservation, display, and enjoyment of plants . . . with educational programs that emphasize learning by doing . . . and with research focused on understanding and conserving regional plants and plant communities" (Brooklyn Botanic Garden 2013).

Brooklyn Botanic Garden's Discovery Garden

1000 Washington Avenue, Brooklyn, NY 11225

718-623-7200   http://www.bbg.org/collections/gardens/discovery_garden

Opening date: June 6, 2015, Public Opening Festival
Project size: 1 acre (0.4 hectare) within Brooklyn Botanic Garden's 52-acre (21-hectare) site

Design and Construction Team
Brooklyn Botanic Garden:
     President: Scot Medbury
     Manager of Discovery Garden and family programs: Ashley Gamell
Landscape architects:
     Early 2005 concept: W. Gary Smith Design
     Landscape architect of record: Michael Van Valkenburgh Associates Inc. (Paul Seck, project manager)
Architect: Architecture Research Office
Contractors: Kelco Landscaping and Construction, E. W. Howell Co. Inc.
Environmental designer of the insect hotel: Lisa Lee Benjamin
Exhibition planner for early 2005 concept: Argyle Design
Interpretation signs and exhibits: Metcalfe Architecture and Design LLC, Art Guild Museums and
          Environments Inc.

Current Contacts
Manager of Discovery Garden and family programs: Ashley Gamell
Communications associates: Rachel Dobkin, Jeffrey Walkowiak

Interviews and Personal Communications
Ashley Gamell, November 9, 2015; Tyler Krob, November 19, 2015; Elizabeth Reina-Longoria, January 21, 2016; Paul Seck, November 13, 2015; Jeffrey Walkowiak, October 22, 2015

Paul Smith Children's Village at Cheyenne Botanic Gardens

CHEYENNE, WYOMING

GOAL

The goal of the Paul Smith Children's Village grew out of Cheyenne Botanic Garden's long history as a proponent of energy conservation. The garden has the first public solar greenhouse opened in the nation. The theme of the Children's Village is to teach concepts of sustainability from the past, present, and future. It was named in honor of Paul Smith, a long-time resident of Cheyenne and a business owner, philanthropist, and enthusiastic supporter of the garden. The village site, located on 0.75 acre, used an existing stone building and stone walls surrounding a courtyard that was originally constructed in the 1930s by the Works Progress Administration program. The building was converted to the solar- and wind-powered Lowe's Discovery Lab, and the grounds were transformed into the Children's Village. A small historic greenhouse was also included on the site.

CONCEPT

The Children's Village is designed primarily to foster the interest and understanding of children ages four through twelve about the natural environment and sustainable systems through fun hands-on demonstrations and interactive experiences in the garden.

The design involved an iterative and collaborative process among the landscape architecture firm EDAW (Herb Schaal, principal landscape architect, and Mark Kosmos, associate landscape architect); Cheyenne Botanic Gardens (garden director Shane Smith, the garden staff, and the garden's board of directors); and community members that began in August 2005. The work included the development of the purpose and theme, program and key elements, budget, and relationship to Cheyenne Botanic Gardens' overall master plan. Construction drawings were completed in August 2008. Construction commenced in January 2009, and the project was completed in September 2009.

Pond and water works

The six sustainability themed areas

Sustainable community

1 Lowe's Discovery Lab with solar heating system
2 Village square with a color-coded geodesic dome and birthday butterfly sunrise-sunset calculator

Sustainable agriculture and greenhouse

3 Greenhouse with energy-conserving materials and courtyard
4 Lath house and world food garden (refreshment area and restrooms)

Sustainable water

5 Gravity-powered waterworks with many water features
6 Archimedes's screw
7 Farmer windmill
8 Natural wetlands

Sustainable nature

9 Prairie discovery area with Native American teepees
10 Picnic area

Sustainable habitation

11 Picnic orchard
12 Historic sheepherder's wagon
13 Russ, the guide dog with a green-roof doghouse
14 Mother Goose story circle

Sustainable art

15 Garden arts plaza
16 Kinetic plaza and basalt fountain
17 Puppet theater
18 Secret garden
19 Sustainable energy wind turbine
20 Peek-a-boo patch

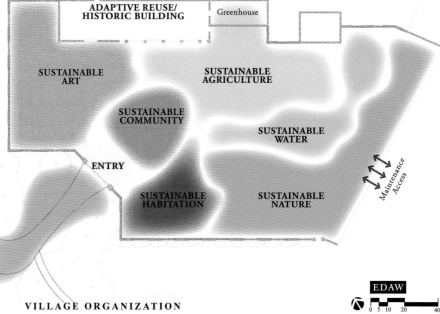

VILLAGE ORGANIZATION

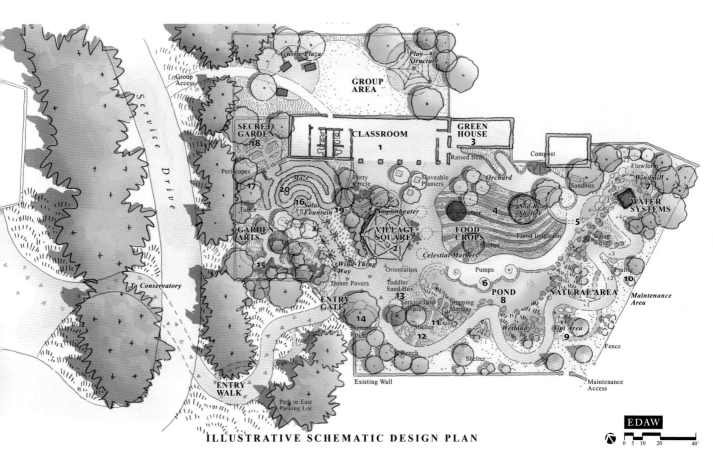

ILLUSTRATIVE SCHEMATIC DESIGN PLAN

DESIGN

The Children's Village was designed with six themed areas focused on sustainability: sustainable community, agriculture, water, nature, habitation, and garden arts. The village is lush with landscape. Interpretive signs in select locations help parents explain the details of the garden to their children. The design aims to enable children to experience the sights and sounds in the garden, which are key to discovery.

Visitors enter the Children's Village through an ornamental rainbow gate and a pathway with quotes about sustainable living inscribed in the paving. They experience the sustainable landscapes through the six theme areas:

1 **Community:** Directly across from the main entrance area is the village square, the central organizing space of the Children's Village and adjacent to the Lowe's Discovery Lab. Featured in this space is a color-coded geodesic dome and a sheltered amphitheater for community events. Inlaid in the pavement is a decorative pattern of a butterfly that serves as an interesting alternative to a sundial. Called the "birthday butterfly," this is a celestial device that points to where on the horizon the sun rises and sets on any given birthday or day of the year. The right and left wings of the butterfly have inlaid metal lines that graphically show the sunrise and sunset points. It also depicts the hours of night on each day of the year. It is fun for children to compare the sun paths and length of the night for different birthdays with family members and friends. This is an innovative way for children to learn about how the sun moves and how it changes through the seasons, and it could easily fit within lesson plans and curricula related to astronomy, seasons, and solar power. A copyrighted design by Shane Smith, the birthday butterfly was constructed into an art piece by Joe McGrane.

Opposite top: Village organization
Opposite bottom: Design plan
Top and bottom: Main entrance gate

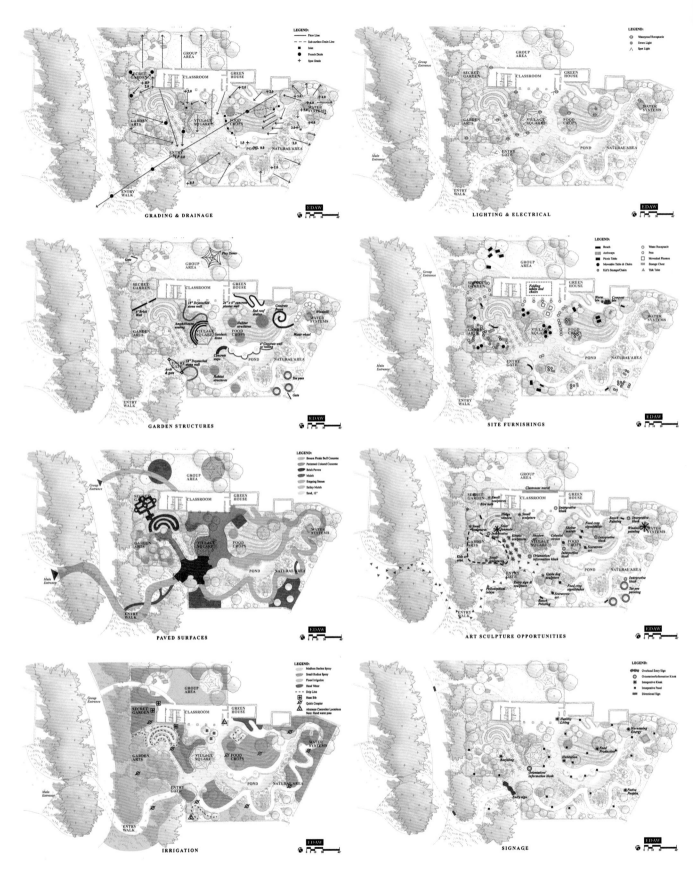

GRADING & DRAINAGE

LIGHTING & ELECTRICAL

GARDEN STRUCTURES

SITE FURNISHINGS

PAVED SURFACES

ART SCULPTURE OPPORTUNITIES

IRRIGATION

SIGNAGE

Opposite: Conceptual design drawings

Right: Flow form descending from high point

2 Agriculture: The food crops area is immediately adjacent to the village square and the greenhouse. Plant beds here use irrigation techniques such as drip, flood, and spray and sustainable growing methods such as permaculture, companion plantings, crop rotation, and composting. The area also includes a solar court where healthy food preparation using solar and adobe ovens is demonstrated.

3 Water: The water area and water system are dominant elements in the landscape and can be seen from nearly anywhere in the village. Techniques for improving water quality, including flow forms, aeration, and biofiltration with wetlands, are featured. A portion of the site was built five feet above the existing grade to illustrate how to create energy to recirculate water. A windmill pumps water from a pond to the high point. As the water moves from the low to high points, children operate a water wheel, gates, siphons, and pumps to irrigate the crops.

4 Natural wetlands and prairie: The naturally sustaining plant communities of the High Plains prairie and marshland contrast with human-made landscapes where wetlands have been drained and prairie destroyed.

5 Habitation: Structures that demonstrate the use of sustainable materials and methods of construction include teepees used by Native Americans in the High Plains, shade trellises in the food crops area, and a green-roof doghouse, which is covered with vegetation.

6 Garden arts: The garden arts area consists of intimate spaces where children can engage in creative play, such as an art plaza, the Secret Garden, and a puppet theater. Art elements in this garden include artful kinetic objects and a solar-powered fountain.

The landscape design incorporates water conservation principles that reduce water use by 55 percent and permeable pavers that capture and retain storm water runoff. Recycled building materials were used, and the windmill is a reused object.

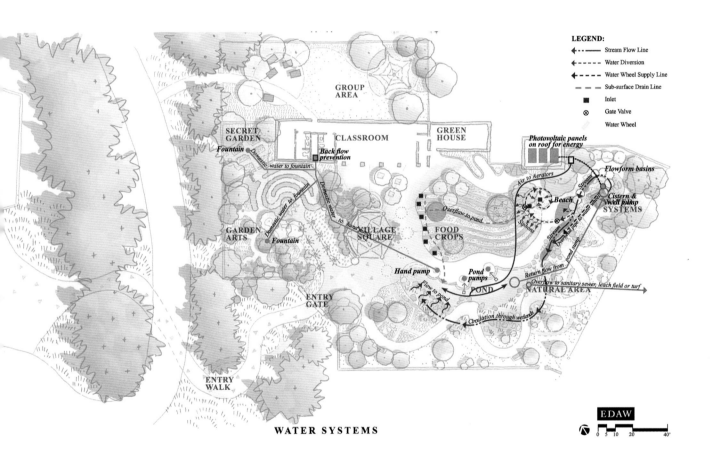

LEGEND:

Stream Flow Line
Water Diversion
Water Wheel Supply Line
Sub-surface Drain Line
■ Inlet
⊗ Gate Valve
Water Wheel

GROUP AREA

SECRET GARDEN
Fountain

CLASSROOM

GREEN HOUSE

Back flow prevention

Photovoltaic panels on roof for energy

Flowform basins

Domestic water to fountain

Air to Aerators

Beach

Cistern & well pump **SYSTEMS**

GARDEN ARTS

Domestic water to fountain

Domestic water to hand pump

VILLAGE SQUARE

FOOD CROPS

Overflow to pond

Siphons

Stream

Stream

Downfall pipe to water wheel

Fountain

Hand pump

Pond pumps

Return flow from pond pump

Overflow to sanitary sewer, leach field or turf

ENTRY GATE

Flow to pond

POND

NATURAL AREA

Circulation through wetland

ENTRY WALK

WATER SYSTEMS

EDAW

0 5 10 20 40'

Top left and right: Playing at the water wheel

Bottom: Water systems

Opposite top left: Flow form basins adjacent to the windmill

Opposite top right: Archimedes's screw

Opposite bottom: Bird's-eye perspective from high point at the windmill

Windmill pumping system

Wood trough to water wheel

Panning for minerals

Water wheel

Flowforms & stream

Bird Habitats

Water Transfer Devices

Food Crop Ditch Irrigation

Pond

Concrete Flume

Tipi

Wetland

Water Wheel Energy

High Point

Water Source

Top left: Prairie discovery area

Top right: Geodesic lath house

Bottom and opposite bottom: Lowe's Discovery Lab and a sustainable agriculture area featuring a village square, farmer's market, and amphitheater. A solar court demonstrates healthy food preparation methods with fresh produce.

Opposite top left: Sedum planter bed

Opposite top middle: Demonstration of sod used as a sustainable building material by early settlers of High Plains

Opposite top right: Food production area

Stepping stones

Pond edge

Bird houses

Water source

Food Production

Solar Fountain

Water Wheel

Tipi

Wetland

Prairie

Rabbit Trails

Existing Cedar Fence

Selected permanent native annuals and perennials featured in the prairie landscape

Deciduous trees

Acer tataricum 'GarAnn'
Alnus tenuifolia
Amelanchier × grandiflora
  'Autumn Brilliance'
Amelanchier lamarckii
Betula occidentalis
Betula platyphylla 'Whitespire'
Fraxinus americana 'Jeffnor'
Populus × acuminata
Populus tremuloides 'Erecta'
Prunus fontanesiana
Malus 'Radiant'
Malus 'Red Barron'
Malus 'Sentinel'
Malus 'Thunderchild'
Salix alba var. *vitellina*
Syringa pekinensis 'Summer
  Charm'

Evergreen trees

Juniperus scopulorum 'Medora'
Juniperus scopulorum 'Skyrocket'
Juniperus scopulorum 'Wichita
  Blue'
Picea glauca 'North Star'
Picea pungens 'Iseli Fastigiate'

Deciduous shrubs

Artemisia tridentata
Cercocarpus montanus
Chrysothamnus nauseosus
Cotoneaster lucidus
Philadelphus lewisii 'Cheyenne'
Potentilla fruticosa 'Pink Beauty'
Rhus aromatica 'Gro-Low'
Rhus glabra 'Laciniata'
Rosa 'MEldomonac' Bonica
Rosa 'Nearly Wild'
Salix exigua
Shepherdia argentea
Syringa meyeri 'Palibin'
Viburnum × burkwoodii
Viburnum opulus var. *america-
  num* 'Compactum'

Evergreen shrubs

Juniperus horizontalis 'Hughes'
Picea glauca 'Conica'

Grasses

Calamagrostis acutiflora 'Karl
  Foerster'
Helictotrichon sempervirens
Miscanthus sinensis 'Gracillimus'
Panicum virgatum 'Heavy Metal'

Perennials

Achillea 'Coronation Gold'
Agastache aurantiaca 'PO12S'
  Coronado
Agastache barberi
Agastache 'Blue Fortune'
Agastache cana
Aquilegia chrysantha
Aster novae-angliae 'Purple
  Dome'
Echinacea purpurea 'Ruby Star'
Hemerocallis 'Hyperion'
Heuchera 'Chocolate Ruffles'
Heuchera micrantha 'Palace
  Purple'
Heuchera sanguinea 'Snow
  Angel'
Hosta × fortunei 'Patriot'
Hosta 'Honeybells'
Hosta sieboldiana 'Elegans'
Hosta × undulata
  'Mediovariegata'
Iris × germanica 'Steller Lights'
Iris pallida 'Variegata'
Lamium maculatum 'Beacon
  Silver'
Lavandula angustifolia 'Hidcote'
Leucanthemum × superbum
  'Alaska'

Liatris spicata 'Kobold'
Lilium 'Stargazer'
Lilium 'Sunray'
Monarda 'Cambridge Scarlet'
Monarda 'Petite Delight'
Nepeta × faassenii 'Walker's Low'
Oenothera speciosa 'Rosea'
Penstemon 'Red Rocks'
Penstemon strictus
Perovskia atriplicifolia
Rudbeckia fulgida 'Goldsturm'
Thalictrum aquilegifolium
Thymus praecox
  'Pseudolanuginosus'
Tradescantia andersoniana 'Red
  Cloud'
Veronica spicata 'Goodness
  Grows'

Wetlands

Caltha palustris
Persicaria maculata
Polypogon monspeliensis
Sagittaria latifolia
Schoenoplectus lacustris
Sparganium eurycarpum
Verbena hastada

CONCLUSION

The Paul Smith Children's Village began as a grassroots initiative in the small town of Cheyenne. The project was realized through remarkable fund-raising efforts, including $2 million from the community. The theme of the Children's Village, "Sustainability: Past, Present and Future," complements the mission of Cheyenne Botanic Gardens to "inspire[], beautif[y], and enrich[] the greater High Plains community through gardening, volunteerism, education, and stewardship" (Cheyenne Botanic Gardens, n.d., "About"). The garden exposes children and families to sustainable concepts focused on the natural ecosystems of the High Plains in Cheyenne. Details in the garden provide visitors with the contrast of natural and urban components. The sustainable measures in the garden result in an annual energy budget that is energy neutral.

Top left: Color-coded geodesic dome
Top middle: Activities under the geodesic dome
Top right: Birthday butterfly sunrise-sunset calculator

The Children's Village earned the Leadership in Energy and Environmental Design (LEED) program Platinum certification, the highest possible rating, in 2010 from the U.S. Green Building Council. LEED is an international green building certification program promoting responsible and efficient environmental practices for design, construction, operation, and maintenance of green buildings and sites. According to Cheyenne Botanic Gardens, "Achieving a LEED Platinum rating for remodeled buildings and landscape is usually more difficult than for new construction because of restrictions imposed by the existing designs. This was the second site to have achieved a LEED Platinum rating in Wyoming and is the first public children's garden to receive this designation" (Cheyenne Botanic Gardens, n.d., "Paul Smith").

Top left: Garden arts plaza
Top middle: Puppet theater
Top right: Pretty water fountain

Paul Smith Children's Village at the Cheyenne Botanic Gardens

616 S. Lions Park Drive, Cheyenne, WY 82001

307-637-6349   http://www.botanic.org/discover/childrens-village

Opening date: September 23, 2009
Project size: 0.75 acre (0.3 hectare) within Cheyenne Botanic Gardens' 9-acre (3.6-hectare) site

Design and Construction Team
Cheyenne Botanic Gardens:
    Director: Shane Smith
    Associate director: Claus Johnson
    Development director: KellyAnne Terry
Landscape architects: EDAW/AECOM (Herb Schaal, principal landscape architect and planner; Mark
        Kosmos, associate landscape architect and lead on computer graphics construction
        documents and reviews)
Architect: The Design Studio Inc. (Randy Byers)
General contractor: Dohn Construction Inc.

Current Contacts
Director: Shane Smith
Education director: Aaron Sommers

Interviews and Personal Communications
Mark Kosmos, December 7, 2015; Herb Schaal, July 10, 2013; Shane Smith, August 11, 2014; Aaron Sommers, August 28, 2014

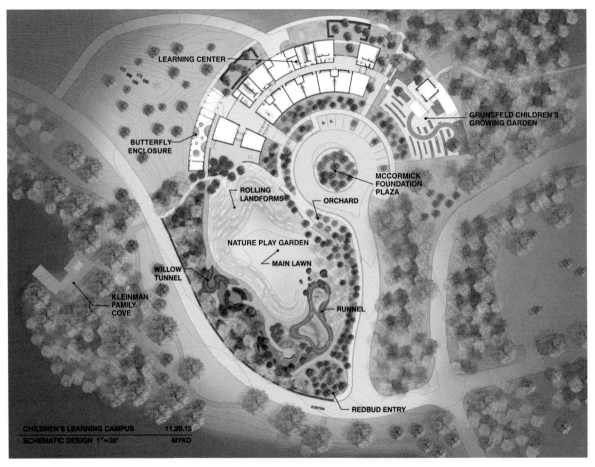

LEARNING CENTER

GRUNSFELD CHILDREN'S GROWING GARDEN

BUTTERFLY ENCLOSURE

ROLLING LANDFORMS

MCCORMICK FOUNDATION PLAZA

ORCHARD

NATURE PLAY GARDEN

MAIN LAWN

WILLOW TUNNEL

KLEINMAN FAMILY COVE

RUNNEL

REDBUD ENTRY

CHILDREN'S LEARNING CAMPUS   11.20.13
SCHEMATIC DESIGN 1"=30'   MYKD

Model and drawing of the Regenstein Learning Campus
building and garden

4

Chicago Botanic Garden's Regenstein Learning Campus

GLENCOE, ILLINOIS

GOAL

The Chicago Botanic Garden's 7-acre Regenstein Learning Campus was designed to attract children of all ages and educate them about plants and nature and the importance of protecting the natural environment. The 385-acre (155.8-hectare) Chicago Botanic Garden features twenty-six gardens and four natural areas on and around nine islands, with 6 miles (9.6 kilometers) of lake shoreline. Visitors come for the garden's spectacular displays as well as its educational programming.

CONCEPT

The existing components of the Regenstein Learning Campus opened between 2011 and 2013, including the Robert R. McCormick Foundation Plaza and entry drive, the Grunsfeld Children's Growing Garden, the Kleinman Family Cove, and the Butterflies and Blooms exhibition. The final two components—the Nature Play Garden and the 25,000-square-foot (2,323-square-meter) Learning Center—opened to the public on September 10, 2016.

The Grunsfeld Children's Growing Garden offers guided learning activities to students and families. "We know that children need to play, but we want to offer an elegant play space that is compatible with the level of design found throughout the rest of the garden," explains Kathy Johnson, youth education director.

The design of the Learning Campus began with extensive research of children's gardens. The Chicago Botanic Garden sought advice and consultation from experts from the Chicago Children's Museum, the Erikson Institute, the Kohl Children's Museum, and the Chicago Park District.

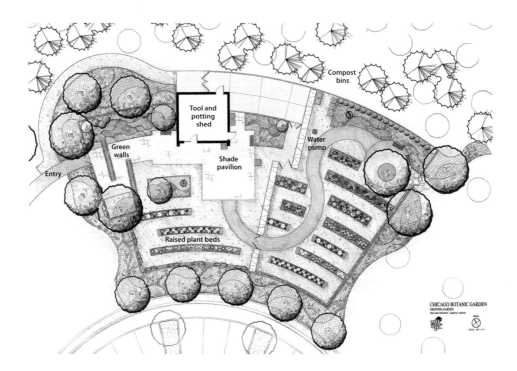

Tool and
potting
shed

Compost
bins

Green
walls

Water
pump

Entry

Shade
pavilion

Raised plant beds

CHICAGO BOTANIC GARDEN
GROWING GARDEN

Top: Grunsfeld Children's Growing Garden plan

Bottom: Double green sedum entry wall

Opposite left and right: Tool and potting shed with solar
panels and shade trellis—in winter and spring

DESIGN

Grunsfeld Children's Growing Garden

The 0.23-acre (0.09-hectare) Grunsfeld Children's Growing Garden was designed "for children to actively engage in the garden and learn by doing as they dig, plant, water, weed, and harvest. While planting, children observe and learn about wildlife in the garden and the important role wildlife plays in nature," says Eileen Prendergast, director of education. "The children love digging worms out of the worm compost bins."

The garden is filled with colorful and showy plants. Through low-mounted interpretive signs, expert instructors, and parents, children learn about key ingredients to plant life: water, sun, wind, animals, and soil. Children participate in camp programs and engage in creative play by pretending to collect bees and butterflies "pollinating" flowers, exploring insect anatomy using large-scale models, carting vegetables in wheelbarrows, and cooking as chefs.

The Children's Growing Garden space, designed by landscape architect Scott Byron, is intimate and inviting. The approach into the garden is through two living green walls covered in different species of sedum. The space inside the garden is arranged with raised plant beds at just the right height for little arms to reach the soil, in-ground demonstration beds, display beds, and roll-under planting trays for ADA accessibility.

The garden incorporates sustainable design principles. It is equipped with a tool and potting pavilion that includes a teaching space and shade, a water-harvesting system for the entire site, and a rain barrel. It has compost bins, porous paving, and solar panels on the tool and potting shed roof. An open-weave fence covered with different varieties of climbing and espaliered plants surrounds the garden, creating a safe, enclosed space for children. Planted pathways direct visitors from the Growing Garden to the next garden.

Southeast section of the Grunsfeld
Children's Growing Garden

Top: ADA-accessible roll-under planting trays

Bottom: Tool and potting shed with solar panels and shade pavilion

Top left: Entry gate

Top right: Building sign

Bottom left: Carting fruits and vegetables in a wheelbarrow

Bottom right: Interpretive sign on a small chalkboard asks, "Which pollinates what?" and is easily changeable to accommodate new information

Opposite top left: Interpretive sign conveys how the sun "heats things up, powers the tool shed, turns plants green, and powers photosynthesis"

Opposite top right: Washing fruit at the water pump

Opposite bottom left: Interpretive sign conveys how animals help plants as they spread and collect seeds and aerate soil

Opposite bottom right: Hands-on planting activity under the shade pavilion

Plants in the Children's Growing Garden, 2015

Antirrhinum majus 'Potomac Early Yellow'
Apium graveolens 'Tango'
Capsicum annuum 'Gourmet'
Citrullus lanatus 'Crimson Sweet'
Ipomoea batatas 'Illusion Emerald Lace'
Ipomoea batatas 'Sweetheart Purple'
Lactuca sativa 'Nevada Summer Crisp'
Lantana camara 'Ms Huff'
Ocinum basilicum 'Dark Opal'
Pelargonium hortorum 'Bullseye Scarlet'
Raphanus sativus 'Crunchy Royale'
Solanum lycopersicum 'Matt's Wild Cherry'
Tagetes erecta 'Inca Gold'

Kleinman Family Cove

Opposite: Plan by Oehme, van Sweden and Associates

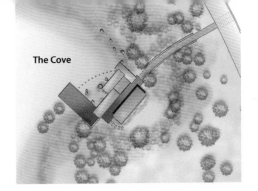

The Cove

Kleinman Family Cove

The Kleinman Family Cove is on the garden's North Lake. It was part of a larger project to re-store 800 feet (243.8 meters) of shoreline around the lake. The primary foci of the cove are water, aquatic plants, and animals. The objective is to teach children about the importance of water to plants and all living creatures.

The cove, designed by Oehme, van Sweden, and Associates, includes a canopied outdoor amphitheater pavilion built into the natural grade with a boardwalk and an aquatic demonstra-tion garden. Lisa Delplace, landscape architect and designer, explains that "the design intent of the cove was to engage children in experiential rather than didactic environmental education."

The amphitheater overlooks a small bay where students wear waders and use nets to analyze aquatic animal life. They assess water quality and discover why water is important to human and environmental health. On a wide boardwalk, students view aquatic plants at different depths, perform shallow- and deep-water tests for turbidity and pH levels, and take water sam-ples to look for and identify macroinvertebrates (typically the larval state of insects like dragon flies) and other small aquatic creatures, such as tadpoles, crayfish, and water scorpions, says Prendergast. Interpretive signs provide clues for visitors to observe and understand aquatic wildlife and habitat.

Aquatic explorations at the Kleinman Family Cove

Sketch of Kleinman Family Cove by Oehme,
van Sweden and Associates

Kleinman Family Cove under construction

Interpretive signage along railing

Observing aquatic wildlife in winter

Exploring aquatic wildlife in summer

Sketch of Kleinman Family Cove
by Oehme, van Sweden and Associates

Sporobolus heterolepis (prairie dropseed)   *Taxodium distichum* (bald cypress)   *Iris siberica* 'Caesar's Brother'

Plants in Kleinman Family Cove

Terrestrial planting

Trees
Amelanchier canadensis
Nyssa sylvatica
Salix alba 'Trista'
Taxodium distichum

Shrubs
Aesculus parvifolia
Aralia spinosa
Aronia melanocarpa 'Nero'
Cornus sericea 'Cardinal'
Cornus sericea 'Silver and Gold'
Hamamelis virginiana
Lindera benzoin
Rosa rugosa
Salix integra 'Flamingo'
Sambucus canadensis 'Maxima'
Spiraea alba
Viburnum dentatum 'Crpuzam'
Viburnum nudum 'Brandywine'
Viburnum trilobum 'Spring Green Compact'

Planted rock swale

Perennials
Achillea millefolium × 'Citronella'
Acorus calamus
Acorus gramineus 'Variegatus'
Asclepias incarnata
Iris siberica 'Caesar's Brother'
Iris virginica var. *shrevei*
Gaura lindheimeri 'Whirling Butterflies'
Liatris spicata 'Kobold'
Scirpus pendulus

Grasses
Hakonechloa macra 'Nicolas'
Molinia caerulea 'Moorhexe'
Molinia litoralis 'Transparent'
Panicum virgatum 'Heiliger Hain'
Pennisetum villosum

Shoreline plants

Shrub
Cephalanthus occidentalis

Grasses
Carex aquatilis
Carex comosa
Carex hystericina
Carex lacustris
Carex lupulina
Carex stricta
Glyceria striata
Juncus effusus
Panicum virgatum
Scirpus atrovirens
Scirpus cyperinus

Perennials
Acorus calamus
Aquilegia canadensis
Asclepias incarnata
Boltonia latisquama
Filipendula rubra
Heracleum maximum
Hibiscus palustris
Iliamna remota
Iris virginica var. *shrevei*
Lobelia siphilitica
Oligoneuron riddelli
Peltandra virginica
Rudbeckia subtomentosa
Sagittaria latifolia
Saururus cernuus
Schoenplectus pungens
Silene regia
Sium suave
Verbena hastata
Vernonia fasciculata

Aquatic plants

Grasses
Carex aquatilis
Carex comosa
Juncus effusus

Perennials
Acorus calamus
Caltha palustris
Decodon verticillatus
Iris virginica var. *shrevei*
Lobelia cardinalis
Nuphar variegatum
Nymphaea odorata
Peltandra virginica
Pontederia cordata
Sagittaria latifolia
Saururus cernuus
Scirpus pendulus
Schoenoplectus acutus
Sparganium eurycarpum

Perennial planting (alternate)

Perennials
Achillea millefolium 'Citronella'
Anemone canadensis
Asclepias incarnata
Asclepias tuberosa
Aster azureus
Aster ericoides
Astible chinensis 'Superba'
Baptisia 'Carolina Moonlight'
Baptisia 'Solar Flare'
Boltonia asteroides
Echinacea purpurea
Eupatorium maculatum 'Gateway'
Filipendula rubra 'Venusta'
Gentiana 'True Blue'
Hemerocallis 'Butterscotch'
Hemerocallis 'Ginger'
Hemerocallis 'Starlight'

Heuchera richardsonii
Hibiscus 'Lord Baltimore'
Iris virginica var. *shrevei*
Liatris spicata
Monarda fistulosa
Papaver turkenlouis
Patrinia scabiosifolia
Penstemon digitalis
Perovskia atriplicifolia 'Little Spire'
Persicaria amplexicaulis 'Rosea'
Phlox paniculata
Phlox pilosa
Physostegia speciosa
Sanguisorba officinalis
Sanguisorba canadensis
Solidago speciosa
Solidago canadensis 'Little Lemon'

Grasses
Calamagrostis brachytricha
Carex alata
Carex bicknellii
Carex pendula 'Fresh Look'
Juncus dudleyi
Molinia caerulea 'Hedebrant'
Panicum virgatum
Schizachyrium scoparium
Sporobolus heterolepis
Stipa gigantea
Stipa pulcherrima

Nature Play Garden

The Chicago Botanic Garden completed construction of the new, 1-acre outdoor self-guided Nature Play Garden in September 2016. The initial concept design was developed in 2012 by landscape architect Mikyoung Kim. From 2014 to 2015, Jacobs/Ryan Associates, a Chicago-based landscape architecture firm with Terry Warriner Ryan as the lead landscape architect, completed the design and construction documents.

The new garden is just west of the Growing Garden in a small bowl-shaped valley. Kim explains, "Our work encourages direct engagement with plant life and the natural cycles of nature in order to reconnect our youth to the ecological world. We designed this garden to highlight process, transformation, and creative discovery in this four-season landscape experience." Discovery and imagination are emphasized, offering children and families fertile ground for the expansion of the mind and self-definition.

The programmatic components introduce children of all ages to environments that highlight renewal and decay and give a multisensory experience. Features in the garden allow for a variety of ways to engage with plants and stimulate a child's curiosity about nature. This diversity also lets children exercise their bodies and minds and develop physically, socially, emotionally, and cognitively. The design captures the essence of self-guided play in nature, and the plantings emphasize the full range of diversity, seasonal color, texture, fragrance, and fruits to give a rich experience of nature.

In the garden, visitors delight in the following spaces:

1 Butterfly House, with the Butterflies and Blooms exhibition for learning and discovery (a new Butterflies and Blooms exhibition will open Memorial Day weekend in 2017 and will replace the current Butterfly House)
2 Evergreen room for sitting and relaxation
3 Fire pit and picnic grove for group and family gatherings
4 Grass-covered amphitheater for group events
5 Grass-covered hillocks for rolling and resting
6 Hornbeam room for sitting and relaxation
7 Logs and boulders for climbing and hiding
8 Maples for potential syrup tapping
9 Runnel and boulders that invite little hands and toes
10 Willow tunnel for hiding

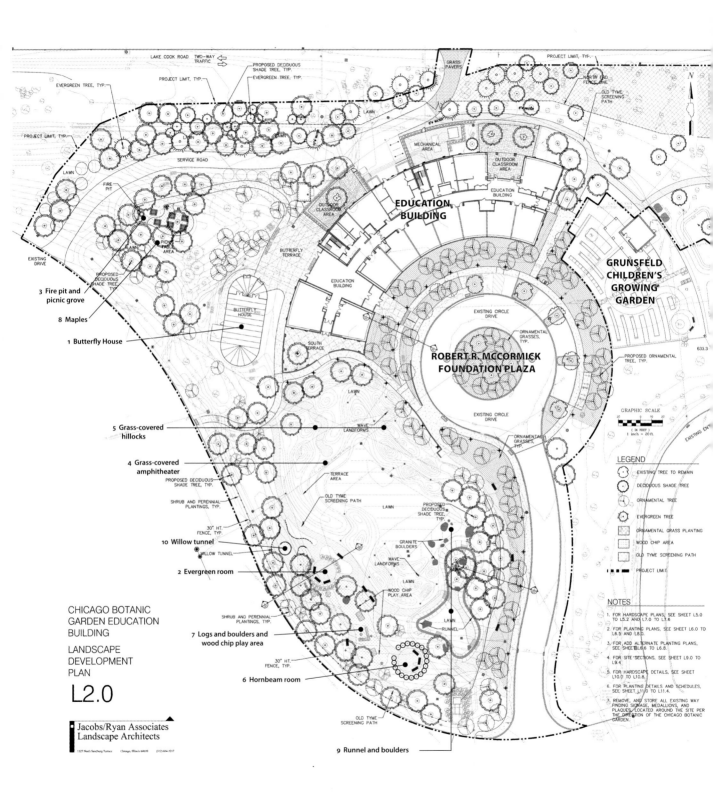

LAKE COOK ROAD TWO-WAY TRAFFIC

PROPOSED DECIDUOUS SHADE TREE, TYP.

PROJECT LIMIT, TYP.

EVERGREEN TREE, TYP.

NORTH END FENCE LINE

GRASS PAVERS

PROJECT LIMIT, TYP.

OLD TYME SCREENING PATH

EVERGREEN TREE, TYP.

PROJECT LIMIT, TYP.

LAWN

LAWN

N

SERVICE ROAD

LAWN

LAWN

LAWN

MECHANICAL AREA

OUTDOOR CLASSROOM AREA

EDUCATION BUILDING

EDUCATION BUILDING

GRUNSFELD CHILDREN'S GROWING GARDEN

EXISTING DRIVE

FIRE PIT

OUTDOOR CLASSROOM AREA

ORNAMENTAL GRASSES, TYP.

3 Fire pit and picnic grove

PICNIC TABLE AREA

BUTTERFLY TERRACE

8 Maples

PROPOSED DECIDUOUS SHADE TREE, TYP.

EDUCATION BUILDING

PROPOSED ORNAMENTAL TREE, TYP.

1 Butterfly House

BUTTERFLY HOUSE

EXISTING CIRCLE DRIVE

633.3

SOUTH TERRACE

ROBERT R. MCCORMICK FOUNDATION PLAZA

ORNAMENTAL GRASSES, TYP.

LAWN

GRAPHIC SCALE

EXISTING CIRCLE DRIVE

EXISTING EN

5 Grass-covered hillocks

WAVE LANDFORMS

ORNAMENTAL GRASSES, TYP.

(IN FEET)
1 inch = 20 ft.

4 Grass-covered amphitheater

TERRACE AREA

PROPOSED DECIDUOUS SHADE TREE, TYP.

OLD TYME SCREENING PATH

LEGEND

PROPOSED DECIDUOUS SHADE TREE, TYP.

SHRUB AND PERENNIAL PLANTINGS, TYP.

LAWN

EXISTING TREE TO REMAIN

DECIDUOUS SHADE TREE

30" HT. FENCE, TYP.

GRANITE BOULDERS

ORNAMENTAL TREE

10 Willow tunnel

WILLOW TUNNEL

WAVE LANDFORMS

EVERGREEN TREE

2 Evergreen room

LAWN

ORNAMENTAL GRASS PLANTING

WOOD CHIP AREA

WOOD CHIP PLAY AREA

OLD TYME SCREENING PATH

CHICAGO BOTANIC GARDEN EDUCATION BUILDING

LAWN

RUNNEL

PROJECT LIMIT

LANDSCAPE DEVELOPMENT PLAN

SHRUB AND PERENNIAL PLANTINGS, TYP.

NOTES

L2.0

7 Logs and boulders and wood chip play area

1. FOR HARDSCAPE PLANS, SEE SHEET L5.0 TO L5.2 AND L7.0 TO L7.6

2. FOR PLANTING PLANS, SEE SHEET L6.0 TO L6.5 AND L8.0.

30" HT. FENCE, TYP.

3. FOR ADD ALTERNATE PLANTING PLANS, SEE SHEET L6.6 TO L6.8.

Jacobs/Ryan Associates
Landscape Architects

6 Hornbeam room

4. FOR SITE SECTIONS, SEE SHEET L9.0 TO L9.4

5. FOR HARDSCAPE DETAILS, SEE SHEET L10.0 TO L10.8.

1527 North Sandbury Terrace   Chicago, Illinois 60610   (312) 664-9217

6. FOR PLANTING DETAILS AND SCHEDULES, SEE SHEET L11.0 TO L11.4.

7. REMOVE, AND STORE ALL EXISTING WAY FINDING SIGNAGE, MEDALLIONS, AND PLAQUES LOCATED AROUND THE SITE PER THE DIRECTION OF THE CHICAGO BOTANIC GARDEN.

9 Runnel and boulders

OLD TYME SCREENING PATH

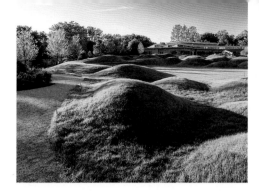

Grass-covered hillocks

Ryan interpreted Kim's concept design, copying the locations of elements, landforms, and plants and respecting the basic framework of the design. She carefully revised the design based on the client's requests and reviewed the progress during construction. According to Ryan, "Some of the adjustments made to the plan include accessibility features, safety precautions, creating a more challenging rolling landform and infinity-shaped runnel, incorporating seasonal displays and plants for the garden's collection, matching stone and boulder colors to the rest of the botanic garden areas, and focusing special attention to the site's southern floodplain area, which experiences periodic inundation."

This garden uses materials that are regionally available as well as materials that have historically been used elsewhere in the Chicago Botanic Garden. Ryan says, "We are using Marshfield fieldstone, a quartzite from the middle of Wisconsin, for boulders in the wood chip area. [It] is used in other areas at Chicago Botanic Garden. We have selected a variety of shapes and sizes, many with moss and lichens on them."

The project, including the building and site, was designed for LEED Platinum certification.

CONCLUSION

The Chicago Botanic Garden features many display gardens, and the spaces created for children align with this garden concept. Spatially, the Chicago Botanic Garden children's gardens are near each other but in separate gardens within one Learning Campus. This is an excellent way to share resources and enable children to experience a variety of gardens with easy access.

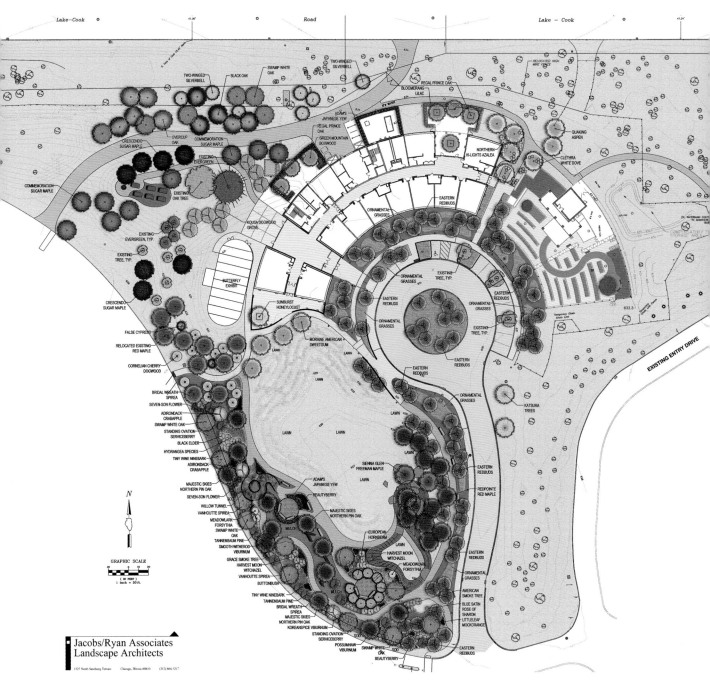

Planting plan

Shade trees

Acer freemanii 'Autumn Blaze'
Acer freemanii 'Autumn Fantasy'
Acer rubrum 'Frank Jr.'
Acer saccharum 'Commemoration'
Acer saccharum 'Green Mountain'
Acer saccharum 'Morton'
Carpinus caroliniana 'JN Select'
Catalpa speciosa
Cercidiphyllum japonicum
Diospyros virginiana
Fagus grandiflora
Gymnocladus dioicus
Liriodendron tulipifera 'Emerald City'
Liquidambar styraciflua 'Moraine'
Populus tremuloides
Quercus bicolor
Quercus elipsoidalis
Quercus lyrata
Quercus velutina
Tilia americana 'American Sentry'
Ulmus 'Frontier'

Ornamental trees

Acer griseum
Amelanchier alnifolia 'Obelisk'
Cercis canadensis 'Burgundy Hearts'
Cercis canadensis 'Cascading Hearts'
Cercis canadensis 'Columbus Strain'
Cercis canadensis 'Northern Strain'
Cercis canadensis 'Rubye Atkinson'
Cornus kousa 'Satomi'
Cornus kousa 'Wolf Eyes'
Cornus mas
Cotinus coggygria 'Daydream'
Cotinus obovatus
Crataegus crusgalli 'Crusader'
Halesia diptera var. magniflora
Hamamelis virginiana 'Harvest Moon'
Magnolia denudata 'Forest Pink'
Magnolia 'Galaxy'
Magnolia macrophylla
Malus 'Adirondack'

Evergreen trees

Picea abies
Pinus mugo 'Tannenbaum'
Thuja plicata 'Green Giant'

Evergreen shrubs

Buxus 'Green Mountain'
Rhododendron 'Orchid Lights'
Taxus cuspidata 'Adams'

Shrubs

Aronia melanocarpa 'Hugin'
Buddleja 'Blue Chip' Lo and Behold

Callicarpa americana
Cephalanthus occidentalis 'Sugar Shack'
Clethra alnifolia 'White Dove'
Cornus sericea 'Farrow'
Forsythia 'Meadowlark'
Heptacodium miconioides
Hibiscus moscheutos 'Luna Red'
Hydrangea quercifolia 'Munchkin'
Hydrangea quercifolia 'Ruby Slippers'
Hydrangea paniculata 'Rensun'
Hypericum kalmianum 'SMHKBF'
Ilex verticillata 'Nano Red Sprite'
Leptodermis oblonga
Paeonia suffruticosa 'Double Pink'
Philadelphus coronarius 'Romanizam'
Physocarpus opulifolius 'Lemon Candy'
Physocarpus opulifolius 'Tiny Wine'
Potentilla fruiticosa 'Happy Face Pink Paradise'
Rhododendron 'Rosy Lights'
Rhododendron 'White Lights'
Rubus idaeus 'Fall Gold'
Salix spp.
Sambucus nigra 'Gerda'
Spiraea tomentosa
Spiraea vanhouttei
Syringa hyanthiflora 'Mount Baker'
Syringa × 'Penda'
Symphoricarpos orbiculatus
Vaccinium corymbosusm 'Bluecrop'
Viburnum bracteatum 'All That Glitter'
Viburnum carlesii 'JN Select'
Viburnum cassinoides
Viburnum nudum 'Pink Beauty'
Viburnum nudum 'Winterthur'
Viburnum sargentii 'Onondaga'
Weigela florida 'Rainbow Sensation'

Ornamental grasses

Andropogon gerargii 'Dancing Wind'
Andropogon gerardii 'Nondhwr'
Carex flacca
Panicum virgatum 'Cheyenne Sky'
Panicum virgatum 'Northwind'
Pennisetum alopecuroides 'Ginger Love'
Schizachyrium scoparium 'Jazz'
Schizachyrium scoparium 'Little Arrow'
Schizachyrium scoparium 'The Blues'
Sesleria autumnalis
Sorghastrum nutans 'Indian Steel'
Sporobolus heterolepis 'Tara'

Groundcovers/perennials

Adiantum pedatum
Agastache rugosa 'Golden Jubilee'
Alchemilla mollis 'Thriller'
Allium cernum 'Wine Drop'
Allium tanguticum 'Balloon Bouquet'
Amsonia hubrichtii 'Halfway to Arkansas'
Anemone × hybrida 'Cinderella'
Anemone hupehensis 'Pamina'
Asarum canadense
Asclepias incarnata 'Hello Yellow'
Asclepias incarnata 'Ice Ballet'
Baptisia australis 'Blue Mound'
Baptisia 'Dutch Chocolate'
Baptisia 'Lemon Meringue'
Bergenia cordifolia 'Winterglut'
Boltonia asteroides 'Snowbank'
Campanula poscharskyana 'Blue Waterfall'
Chelone obliqua 'Alba'
Chelone obliqua 'Tiny Tortuga'
Cimicifuga ramosa 'Hillside Black Beauty'
Clematis 'H. F. Young'
Coreopsis 'Full Moon'
Darmera peltata
Conoclinium coelestinum
Dodecatheon meadia 'Aphrodite'
Dicentra formosa 'Aurora'
Dicentra 'Luxuriant'
Dryopteris erythorosa 'Brilliance'
Dryopteris intermedia
Echinacea 'Pixie Meadowbrite'
Echinacea 'Red Knee High'
Eupatorium fistulosum 'Gateway'
Eupatorium perfoliatum 'Milk and Cookies'
Geranium 'Brookside'
Geranium cantabrigiense 'Karmina'
Geranium 'Johnson's Blue'
Geranium maculatum 'Espresso'
Geum 'Cosmopolitan'
Geum fragarioides
Geum 'Limoncello'
Helleborus niger 'HGC Jacob'
Helleborus 'Winter Thriller Red Racer'
Helianthus salicifolius 'Low Down'
Heuchera 'Big Top Gold'
Heuchera 'Carnival Rose Granita'
Heuchera 'Hercules'
Heuchera longiflora
Heuchera 'Sugar Berry'
Hibiscus 'Kopper King'
Hibiscus 'Robert Fleming'
Hosta 'Blue Mammoth'
Hosta 'Candy Hearts'
Hosta 'Fire Island'
Hosta 'Humpback Whale'
Hosta 'Sum and Substance'

Iris cristata 'Tennessee White'
Iris versicolor 'Gerald Darby'
Lamium maculatum 'Beacon Silver'
Meehania cordata
Monarda didyma 'Marshall's Delight'
Nepeta × faassenii 'Junior Walker'
Pachysandra procumbens
Penstemon 'Prairie Twilight'
Phlox carolina 'Miss Lingard'
Phlox divaricata 'Blue Moon'
Phlox divaricata 'May Breeze'
Phlox paniculata 'Blue Paradise'
Phlox paniculata 'Jeana'
Phlox pilosa 'Bungalow Blue'
Phlox subulata 'Fort Hill'
Physostegia virginiana 'Miss Manners'
Platycodon grandiflorus 'Hakone Blue'
Polemonium reptans 'Heaven Scent'
Rudbeckia subtomentosa 'Little Henry'
Salvia nemorosa 'Blueberry Beret'
Sedum 'T-Rex'
Stachys byzantina 'Big Ears'
Stachys officinalis 'Pink Cotton Candy'
Stokesia laevis 'Blue Danube'
Symphyotrichum 'Vibrant Dome'
Syneilesis aconitifolia
Veronia lettermannii 'Iron Butterfly'
Veronica 'Waterperry Blue'
Veronicastrum virginicum 'Cupid'

Bulbs

Allium aflatunense 'Purple Sensation'
Allium 'Globemaster'
Anemone nemorosa 'Alba'
Camassia quamash 'Blue Melody'
Colchicum bornmuelleri
Crocus speciosus 'Conquerer'
Crocus tommasinianus 'Ruby Giant'
Cycloman coum
Cycloman hederafolium
Erythronium 'Pagoda'
Hyacinthoides non-scripta 'White'
Lycoris squamigera
Muscari armeniacum 'Blue Spike'
Narcissus 'Baby Boomer'
Narcissus cantibricus
Narcissus cassata
Narcissus 'King Alfred'
Narcissus 'Tiny Bubbles'
Narcissus 'White Medal'
Scilla bifolia 'Rosea'
Scilla siberica 'Spring Beauty'
Tulipa humilis 'Helena'

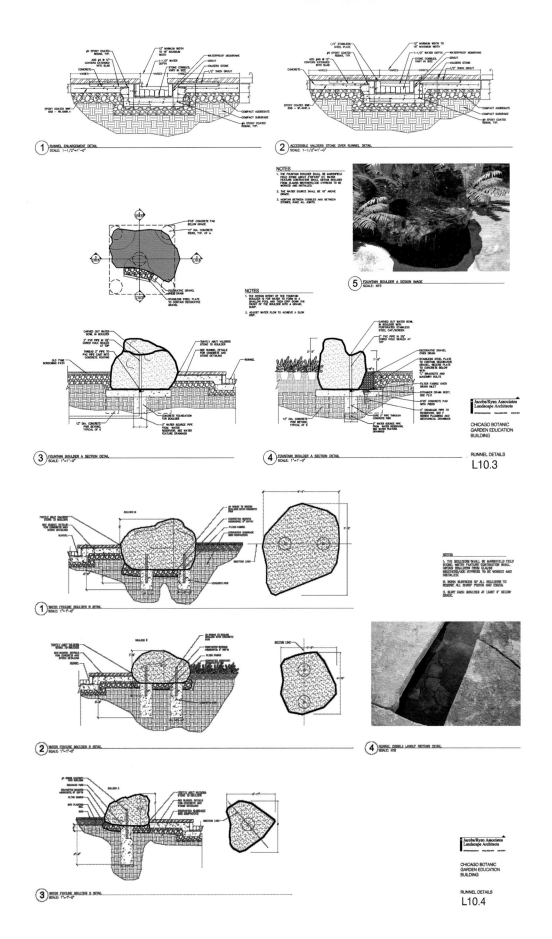

Opposite: Runnel details

Top left: The largest Marshfield fieldstone in the garden; unloading the largest boulder with a crane

Top right and bottom: Runnel and boulders

Chicago Botanic Garden's Regenstein Learning Campus

Aerial view of Regenstein Learning Campus

Chicago Botanic Garden

Regenstein Foundation Learning Campus

1000 Lake Cook Road, Glencoe, IL 60022

847-835-5440   http://www.chicagobotanic.org/gardens/growinggarden

http://www.chicagobotanic.org/gardens/cove   http://www.chicagobotanic.org/education/campus

Opening date: Grunsfeld Children's Growing Garden opened 2012; Kleinman Family Cove opened 2012; Nature Play Garden opened 2016

Project size: 7 acres (2.8 hectares) within Chicago Botanic Garden's 385-acre (156-hectare) site: Grunsfeld Children's Growing Garden, 0.23 acre (0.09 hectare); Kleinman Family Cove, 0.5 acre (0.2 hectare); Nature Play Garden, 1 acre (0.4 hectare)

Design and Construction Team

Chicago Botanic Garden:

    Teacher and student programs director: Kathy Johnson

    Youth and family programs director: Eileen Prendergast

Grunsfeld Children's Growing Garden:

    Landscape architect: Scott Byron

    Architect: Bruce F. Klein

    Contractor: Scott Byron and Co.

Kleinman Family Cove:

    Landscape architect: Oehme, van Sweden and Associates Inc.

    Architect: Lukasik and Associates Ltd.

    Civil engineer: Conservation Design Forum

    Structural engineer: Sowlat Structural Engineers

    Construction management: Brown and Associates Inc.

    General contractor: Featherstone Inc.

Nature Play Garden:

    Landscape architect:

        Concept design: Mikyoung Kim Design

        Design development and construction drawings: Jacobs/Ryan Associates (Terry Ryan)

    Architect: Booth Hansen

    Civil engineer: Gewalt Hamilton Associates Inc.

    Construction: Turner Construction

    Landscape contractor: Clauss Brothers Inc.

Current Contacts

Chicago Botanic Garden director of education: Eileen Prendergast

Youth education director: Kathy Johnson

Interviews and Personal Communications

Lisa Delplace, May 19, 2014; Stacilyn Feldman, May 19, 2014; Kathy Johnson, April 14, 2014; Mikyoung Kim, May 19, 2014; Eileen Prendergast, April 14, 2014; Terry Ryan, November 24, 2015

5

Children's Garden at Hershey Gardens

HERSHEY, PENNSYLVANIA

GOAL

The 1.5-acre (0.6-hectare) Children's Garden was designed as a "garden to sweeten the imagination," where children of all ages discover the wonder of plants through hands-on learning in different theme gardens. Interactive curriculum-based programs are conducted throughout the theme gardens, enabling children to learn through active rather than passive participation.

As early as in 1909, Milton S. Hershey, of Hershey's Chocolate fame, acknowledged the importance of agricultural education with the establishment of the Hershey Industrial School for orphan boys. The deed of trust states that one of the objectives of the school was to teach and instruct in agriculture, horticulture, and gardening.

More recently, public schools in Pennsylvania are required by the state board of education to provide planned instruction in agriculture or agricultural science annually to every child from kindergarten through twelfth grade. In addition, emphasis is placed on active learning experiences, or hands-on education. The Children's Garden at Hershey Gardens is an excellent educational resource, providing programs that fulfill this requirement.

Rose Compass Court
at main entrance

THE MAGIC OF CHILDREN'S GARDENS

CONCEPT

A brainstorming session of a committee of community members, advisory board members, and staff working with a horticulturist, Jane L. Taylor, and a landscape architect, Deborah Kinney, was held in November 1999 to determine what to include in the garden's master plan. The committee believed that the garden should represent Hershey's Chocolate and the central Pennsylvania culture.

When Taylor and Kinney embarked on the design, they made sure to incorporate ideas that were fitting to Hershey's Chocolate and the local region. They reviewed their design with the committee and incorporated comments from them to develop the final master plan in April 2001. At that time, only a handful of children's gardens existed in the United States, but Taylor and Kinney provided a solid foundation for the project, as they had designed the successful 4-H Children's Garden at Michigan State University in 1993. Derck and Edson Associates, a local landscape architecture firm, created construction drawings. Hershey Trust Company managed the project. Construction of the Children's Garden commenced in late 2001, and the garden opened in June 2003.

DESIGN

The Children's Garden at Hershey Gardens is designed for children to touch, smell, and interact with plants. Thirty-two unique theme gardens provide opportunities for hands-on learning, self-discovery, and fun with water features, hideaways, creatures, surprises, and whimsical features. Over five hundred plant species are showcased throughout the garden. Many unusual plants delight children.

Interactive elements such as chocolate bars showing fractions, a human sundial, a pretzel maze, a Native American longhouse and grinding stone, and a walkway with a globe painted on the pavement allow children to learn about math, science, cultures, geography, and history. In addition, dance chimes, a xylophone, an alligator drum, and misters shaped like huge Hershey's Kisses provide interactive experiences throughout the garden.

Opposite: Kisses Fountain Plaza
Top: Chocolate Bar Lane

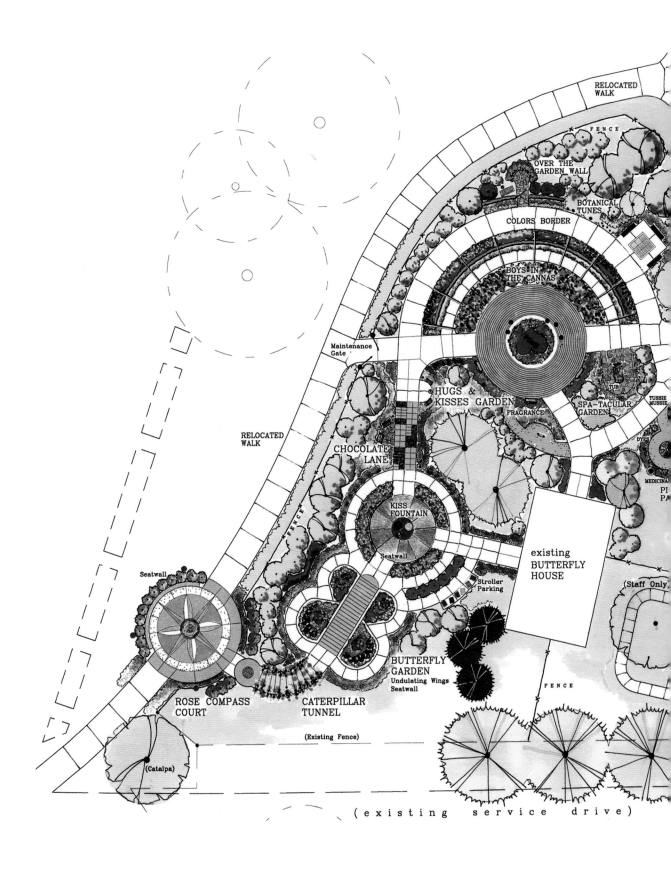

RELOCATED WALK

FENCE

OVER THE GARDEN WALL

BOTANICAL TUNES

COLORS BORDER

BOYS IN THE CANNAS

Maintenance Gate

HUGS & KISSES GARDEN

FRAGRANCE

SPA-TACULAR GARDEN

TUB

TUSSIE MUSSIE

RELOCATED WALK

CHOCOLATE LANE

DYES

FENCE

KISS FOUNTAIN

MEDICINAL

PI PA

Seatwall

existing BUTTERFLY HOUSE

(Staff Only

Stroller Parking

Seatwall

Seatwall

BUTTERFLY GARDEN
Undulating Wings Seatwall

FENCE

ROSE COMPASS COURT

CATERPILLAR TUNNEL

(Existing Fence)

(Catalpa)

(existing service drive)

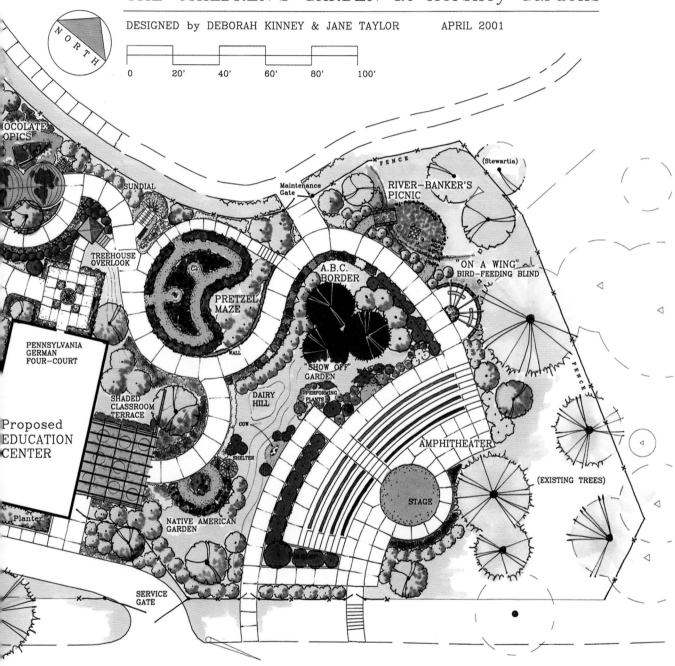

MASTER PLAN
THE CHILDREN'S GARDEN at Hershey Gardens

DESIGNED by DEBORAH KINNEY & JANE TAYLOR   APRIL 2001

NORTH

0   20'   40'   60'   80'   100'

OCOLATE
OPICS

SUNDIAL

TREEHOUSE
OVERLOOK

PENNSYLVANIA
GERMAN
FOUR-COURT

Proposed
EDUCATION
CENTER

SHADED
CLASSROOM
TERRACE

Planter

PRETZEL
MAZE

WALL

DAIRY
HILL

COW

SHELTER

NATIVE AMERICAN
GARDEN

Planter

SERVICE
GATE

Maintenance
Gate

FENCE

RIVER-BANKER'S
PICNIC

(Stewartia)

A.B.C.
BORDER

"ON A WING"
BIRD-FEEDING BLIND

"SHOW OFF"
GARDEN

PERFORMING
PLANTS

AMPHITHEATER

STAGE

FENCE

(EXISTING TREES)

Theme gardens and their plants and special features

Garden	Plants and special features
Rose Compass Court	A colorful entrance with a compass motif in the pavement.
Caterpillar Tunnel and Butterfly Garden	A tunnel located at the entrance of the Children's Garden. The body of the caterpillar is fiveleaf akebia, also known as chocolate vine. On the other side of the Caterpillar Tunnel, the caterpillar transforms into a butterfly. The wings of the butterfly are planted with an assortment of colorful annuals.
Kisses Fountain Plaza	Home to misting fountains. The fountains, shaped like Hershey's Kisses, spray a cool mist with playful whistle, which surprises guests as they walk by. The Kisses Fountain Plaza also has an ample display of colorful candy-themed plants, such as chocolate mint.
Chocolate Lane	A path with Hershey's Milk Chocolate Bar pavers also helps kids learn about fractions. Preserving the history of Milton Hershey and the Hershey community is important to the Hershey Gardens. The Children's Garden has many historical items on display, such as the 4-Pot Conch rollers that were used in the process of chocolate making. The gardens also have a few historical photographs on display, including the "Breakfast at the Mansion" and "The Cart and Pony Ride" at Hershey Park. Chocolate Lane features Hot Cocoa roses, White Chocolate crape myrtles, and a few tropical chocolate copper leaf plants.
Hugs and Kisses Garden	A circular plaza with a heart-shaped pond and a floating ball fountain modeled after a similar fountain at Milton Hershey's Lancaster home.
Boys in the Cannas	A half-moon trellis with cannas and a wall behind.
Colors Border	Flowers arranged in the colors of a rainbow.
Over the Garden Wall	A limestone garden wall and gate. Features plants native to the United States, such as oakleaf hydrangea and a weeping hemlock. The oakleaf hydrangea, a native plant, is also a multiseason plant. The weeping hemlock is a cultivated variety of the native eastern hemlock, which is Pennsylvania's state tree.
Botanical Tunes	A place to play music on dance chimes.
Spa-Tacular Garden	A living willow curtain.
Fragrance Garden	A place of fragrant flowers and leaves.
Chocolate Tropics	A sidewalk that illustrates the world and chocolate-producing countries.
Tree House Overlook	A perch to view the entire garden.
Sundial Garden	A place to tell time by raising one's hand.
Pretzel Maze	A green maze of arborvitae.
Pennsylvania German Four-Court	A courtyard with four raised planters.
Pioneer Patch	An herb garden.
Native American Garden	A display of native flowers and vegetables.
River-Banker's Picnic	A picnic spot that leads to other places.
On-a-Wing Garden	A structure that is half a silo that doubles as the perfect spot to bird watch. The silo also features another vine, the cardinal vine.
ABC Border	Plants starting with each of the twenty-six letters of the alphabet.
Show-Off Garden	A display of unusual plants.
Dairy Hill	Maisy, the friendly cow sculpture represents a very important ingredient used in chocolate! Got milk?

Butterfly Garden

MASTER PLAN
THE CHILDREN'S GARDEN at Hershey Gardens

DESIGNED by DEBORAH KINNEY & JANE TAYLOR   APRIL 2001

0   20'   40'   60'   80'   100'

JAPANESE GARDEN

existing BUTTERFLY HOUSE

Proposed EDUCATION CENTER

Top: Butterfly House and Garden

Bottom: Rose Compass Court

Top: They have spotted a butterfly
Bottom: Butterfly cage in Butterfly House

Children's Garden at Hershey Gardens

THE MAGIC OF CHILDREN'S GARDENS

Opposite top: Magical Ball, Hugs and Kisses Garden's Heart-Shaped Fountain

Opposite middle and bottom: Dancing Pig sculpture and Dance Chimes in Hugs and Kisses Garden

Top: Boat in Chocolate Tropics

Bottom: Tree House Overlook

Children's Garden at Hershey Gardens

THE MAGIC OF CHILDREN'S GARDENS

Opposite top: Native American Garden
Opposite middle: Maisy, the dairy cow
Opposite bottom: Amphitheater
Bottom: Bridge at River-Banker's Picnic

Children's Garden at Hershey Gardens

Acmella oleracea (eyeball plant)

Berlandiera lyrata (chocolate flower)

Selected plants in the garden

Caterpillar Tunnel
Akebia quinata
Amelanchier × grandiflora 'Autumn Brilliance'
Rudbeckia fulgida 'Goldsturm'

Butterfly wings/Butterfly waystation
Assorted annuals
Asclepias tuberosa
Buddleja davidii 'Nanho Blue'
Eutrochium purpureum
Lindera benzoin

Kisses Fountain Plaza
Assorted annuals with candy-themed names
Mentha piperita
Lagerstroemia indica 'White Chocolate'

Chocolate Lane
Ajuga 'Chocolate Chip'
Rosa 'WEKpaltlez' Hot Cocoa
Papaver orientalis 'Royal Chocolate Distinction'
Solenostemon scutellarioides 'Chocolate Mint'

Botanical Tunes
Hemerocallis 'Miss Tinkerbell'
Styrax japonicus 'Pink Chimes'
Weigela florida 'Minuet'

Heart-Shaped Fountain
Canna 'Tropicanna'
Sisyrinchium angustifolium 'Lucerne'

Color Border
Assorted annuals matching the colors of the rainbow
    including white, gray, and black

Fragrance Garden
Calycanthus floridus
Chionanthus virginicus
Paeonia 'Renata'
Phlox divaricata 'May Breeze'
Viburnum carlesii

Over the Garden Wall
Betula nigra 'Cully' Heritage
Eupatorium rugosum 'Chocolate'
Hydrangea quercifolia
Pinus strobus 'Fastigiata'
Polygonatum odoratum 'Variegatum'
Vernonia glauca

Chocolate Tropics
Assorted tropical-like annuals
Calamagrostis × acutifolia 'Karl Foerster'
Hibiscus 'Kopper King'

Human Sundial
Ipomoea spp.
Magnolia stellata 'Royal Star'

Pioneer Patch
*Achillea × 'Moonshine'
Artemisia dracunculus
Foeniculum vulgare dulce 'Rubrum'
Melissa officinalism
Pycnanthemum muticum
Sambucus canadensis

Show-Off Garden
Chelone lyonii 'Hot Lips'
Miscanthus sinensis 'Zebrinus'
Physostegia virginiana 'Vivid'

Wind in the Willows
Salix arenaria 'Curly Scarlet'
Salix integra 'Hakuro Nishiki'
Salix melanostachys
Stewartia pseudocamellia

Vigna unguiculata (pretzel bush bean)   *Proboscidea louisianica* (unicorn plant)

CONCLUSION

The Children's Garden at Hershey Gardens was carefully designed to be unique but also a customized fit for Hershey and central Pennsylvania. Very few of its elements can be found anywhere else in the world. Chocolate Lane, Kisses, Fountain Plaza, Hugs and Kisses, and Chocolate Tropics can be found only at this garden.

The Children's Garden at Hershey Gardens

170 Hotel Road, Hershey, PA 17033

717-534-3492   http://www.hersheygardens.org/attractions/childrens-garden

Opening date: June 14, 2003
Project size: 1.5 acres (0.6 hectare, including Butterfly House and Education Center) within Hershey Gardens' 23-acre (9.3-hectare) site

Design and Construction Team
The M. S. Hershey Foundation:
  Hershey Gardens director of visitor services: Crystal Huff
  Hershey Gardens director of horticulture: Barbara J. Whitcraft
  Hershey Trust Co. project management: Sue Bingeman
Landscape architect:
  Concept design and codesigner: Deborah Kinney
  Landscape architect of record: Derck and Edson Associates LLP (John Hershey)
  Horticulturist, codesigner, and founding curator of Michigan 4-H Children's Garden, Michigan State University: Jane L. Taylor
Architect: Cox Evans Architects LLC (Bruce Evans)
Structural engineer: Greenebaum Structures PC (Edward Greenebaum)
Electrical engineer: Consolidated Engineers (Steve Gribb)
Construction consultant: Strata Development Services Inc. (Tobie Wolf)

Current Contact
M. S. Hershey Foundation communications and public relations specialist: Anthony Haubert

Interviews and Personal Communications
Anthony Haubert, August 11, 2014; Crystal C. Huff, September 24, 2015; Jane L. Taylor, September 15, 2015

WATER: Vortex and water bells

Helen and Peter Bing Children's Garden
at the Huntington Botanical Gardens

SAN MARINO, CALIFORNIA

GOAL

The Helen and Peter Bing Children's Garden is a sophisticated, interactive garden designed primarily to teach children two to seven years old that plants need light, air, water, and nutrients to grow. This message is conveyed through hands-on experiences that demonstrate scientific principles related to earth, air, fire, and water, which form the main garden themes. Constructed on a 0.4-acre (0.16-hectare) site, the garden embraces the mission of the Huntington Library, Art Collections, and Botanical Gardens with its "devotion to research, education, and beauty" (The Huntington, n.d., "About").

CONCEPT

The idea of a children's garden began in 1995 under the leadership of James Folsom, director of the Huntington Botanical Gardens. The objective was to appropriately integrate a playful children's garden into the main garden, an estate garden with exotic plants as well as a serious research institution with many programs for library-based research. After extensive planning, in 2002, the Conservatory—a plant science center for families—was built, modeled after Henry Huntington's former Lath House.

What followed was a natural progression of a program that included a space for children as well. Folsom says, "The design process took two years, but [the garden] took less than a year to build." Important to the design was scale and fitting a small garden within the context of the 120-acre (48.6-hectare) Huntington Botanical Gardens. The children's garden was envisioned to offer engagement, surprise, play, and delight but not be a playground or amusement park. It was also designed for parents to have an enjoyable garden experience. The design goal and program led to a formal axial garden design that incorporated the theme of classical elements—earth, air, fire, and water. "The Bing Children's Garden design is an expression and interpretation of these four elements," explains Folsom. Designed by landscape architect Todd Bennitt, a variety of whimsical garden features were integrated throughout the garden spaces. Kinetic artist Ned Kahn incorporated the ability to interact with traditional garden basins, statuary, trellises, walls, and pavement. These artful kinetic pieces proved to be highly effective interactive points of wonder for children and adults.

AIR: Fog grotto

AIR: Fog grotto

THE MAGIC OF CHILDREN'S GARDENS

During the research and design process, Folsom visited other gardens, such as the Atlanta Botanical Garden and Red Butte Garden in Salt Lake City. He observed how children interacted in these gardens. He sought the advice of Jane Taylor, designer of the Michigan 4-H Children's Garden. Inspired by the Montessori method, Folsom wanted to create an environment of self-directed activities for children. The design team developed ideas for how to interpret the four elements and determined the specific details for each space. For example, four to five children can cluster around each of the central garden features and twenty-five to thirty children can gather in the patio areas.

Children actively engage in all parts of the Bing Children's Garden from the moment they enter through the blue entry gate. Children love water, climbing, and discovery. Thus, most popular are activities that take place at the fog grotto, rainbow room, vortex and water bells, magnetic sand, sonic pool, and juniper mound. Children shout, "It's on!" as they pack in to the fog grotto and rainbow room in anticipation of magical moments. As they explore the garden, they discover the wonder in subtle elements such as the pebble chimes and prism tunnel.

FIRE: Prism tunnel

FIRE: Topiary volcano

FIRE: Rainbow room

AIR: Fragrance garden

Blue entry gate

DESIGN

The Bing Children's Garden is conveniently located near the main garden entrance and parking. It is secure, having only one entry and one exit. The garden is flanked on three sides by buildings that make up the Frances L. Brody Botanical Center, including the Botanical Center building, the Conservatory, and the teaching greenhouse. The children's garden entrance is well defined and welcomes the visitor through an arbor in the shape of a whimsical house facade, clad with climbing roses, a blue wooden gate scaled for children (inspired by *Alice in Wonderland*), and a radial paving pattern at the doorway. Marble jets, sonic pool, and prism tunnel compose the central spine of the garden. Immediately at the entrance of the marble jets, children find delight in the grape-sized water droplets jumping from one basin to another as they run to catch them. Visitors meander through the gardens along both sides of the central spine to find wonder and surprise in each garden. Fog lifted into the air beckons visitors to the fog grotto. Aromatic herbs and fruit trees draw visitors to the fragrance garden. Brilliantly colored plants attract curious visitors to the topiary volcano. In the Bing Children's Garden, plants "frame" the landscape.

The concepts of earth, air, fire, and water were integrated early in the design process. Huntington Gardens describes each element as follows:

- Earth is soil, rock, pebbles, stone, and metal. The earth is where plants root and where they get their nutrients.
- Air is a forgotten substance—until it is made visible by fog or smoke. But the atmosphere is the greatest nutrition source on Earth, providing all the carbon dioxide that plants require for food.
- Fire yields light and heat, demonstrated through the power of sunlight, whose energy plants use to create their food.
- Water gives movement to our lives and the world around us. Plants take water in through their roots and lose it through their leaves. (The Huntington, n.d., "Children's Garden")

Illustrative plan and bird's-eye
perspective by Lisa Pompelli

Restrooms

Topiary volcano

Magnetic sand

Prism tunnel

Rainbow room

Self-centered globe

Pebble chimes

Teaching greenhouse

Greenhouse

Sonic pool

Fragrance garden

Terrace

Marble jets

Vortex and water bells

Fog grotto

POMPELLI

Terrace

Terrace

Lawn

Entrance and blue door

Lawn

Conservatory

Helen and Peter Bing Children's Garden at the Huntington Botanical Gardens

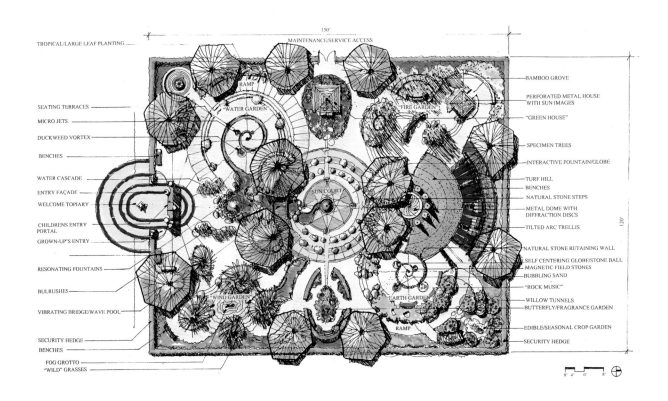

TROPICAL/LARGE LEAF PLANTING

150'

MAINTENANCE/SERVICE ACCESS

RAMP

"WATER GARDEN"

"FIRE GARDEN"

SEATING TERRACES

MICRO JETS

DUCKWEED VORTEX

BENCHES

SUN COURT

WATER CASCADE

ENTRY FAÇADE

WELCOME TOPIARY

CHILDRENS ENTRY PORTAL

GROWN-UP'S ENTRY

RESONATING FOUNTAINS

BULRUSHES

VIBRATING BRIDGE/WAVE POOL

"WIND GARDEN"

"EARTH GARDEN"

RAMP

SECURITY HEDGE

BENCHES

FOG GROTTO

"WILD" GRASSES

BAMBOO GROVE

PERFORATED METAL HOUSE WITH SUN IMAGES

"GREEN HOUSE"

SPECIMEN TREES

INTERACTIVE FOUNTAIN/GLOBE

TURF HILL

BENCHES

NATURAL STONE STEPS

METAL DOME WITH DIFFRACTION DISCS

TILTED ARC TRELLIS

NATURAL STONE RETAINING WALL

SELF CENTERING GLOBE/STONE BALL MAGNETIC FIELD STONES

BUBBLING SAND

"ROCK MUSIC"

WILLOW TUNNELS

BUTTERFLY/FRAGRANCE GARDEN

EDIBLE/SEASONAL CROP GARDEN

SECURITY HEDGE

120'

8' 4' 0' 8'

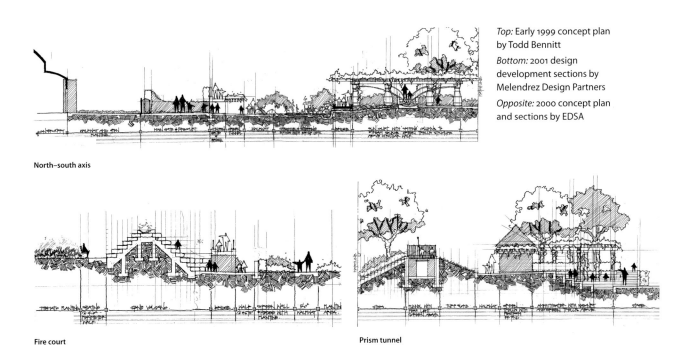

North–south axis

Fire court

Prism tunnel

Top: Early 1999 concept plan by Todd Bennitt

Bottom: 2001 design development sections by Melendrez Design Partners

Opposite: 2000 concept plan and sections by EDSA

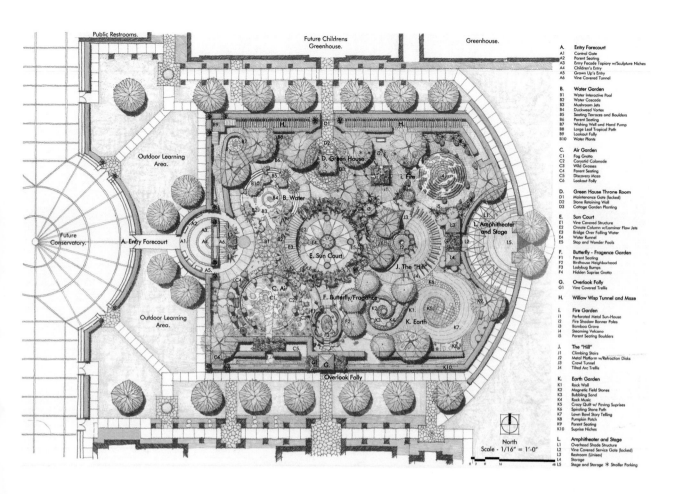

Public Restrooms.

Future Childrens Greenhouse.

Greenhouse.

Outdoor Learning Area.

Future Conservatory.

A. Entry Forecourt

Outdoor Learning Area.

D. Green House

i. Fire

B. Water

L. Amphitheater and Stage

E. Sun Court

J. The "Hill"

C. Air

F. Butterfly/Fragrance

K. Earth

G. Overlook Folly

North
Scale - 1/16" = 1'-0"

A.	**Entry Forecourt**
A1	Control Gate
A2	Parent Seating
A3	Entry Facade Topiary w/Sculpture Niches
A4	Children's Entry
A5	Grown Up's Entry
A6	Vine Covered Tunnel
B.	**Water Garden**
B1	Water Interactive Pool
B2	Water Cascade
B3	Mushroom Jets
B4	Duckweed Vortex
B5	Seating Terraces and Boulders
B6	Parent Seating
B7	Wishing Well and Hand Pump
B8	Large Leaf Tropical Path
B9	Lookout Folly
B10	Water Plants
C.	**Air Garden**
C1	Fog Grotto
C2	Caryatid Colonade
C3	Wild Grasses
C4	Parent Seating
C5	Discovery Maze
C6	Lookout Folly
D.	**Green House Throne Room**
D1	Maintenance Gate (locked)
D2	Stone Retaining Wall
D3	Cottage Garden Planting
E.	**Sun Court**
E1	Vine Covered Structure
E2	Ornate Column w/Laminer Flow Jets
E3	Bridge Over Falling Water
E4	Water Runnel
E5	Stop and Wonder Pools
F.	**Butterfly - Fragance Garden**
F1	Parent Seating
F2	Birdhouse Neighborhood
F3	Ladybug Bumps
F4	Hidden Suprise Grotto
G.	**Overlook Folly**
G1	Vine Covered Trellis
H.	**Willow Wisp Tunnel and Maze**
i.	**Fire Garden**
i1	Perforated Metal Sun-House
i2	Fire Shadow Banner Poles
i3	Bamboo Grove
i4	Steaming Volcano
i5	Parent Seating Boulders
J.	**The "Hill"**
J1	Climbing Stairs
J2	Metal Platform w/Refraction Disks
J3	Crawl Tunnel
J4	Tilted Arc Trellis
K.	**Earth Garden**
K1	Rock Wall
K2	Magnetic Field Stones
K3	Bubbling Sand
K4	Rock Music
K5	Crazy Quilt w/ Paving Suprises
K6	Spiraling Stone Path
K7	Lawn Bowl Story Telling
K8	Pumpkin Patch
K9	Parent Seating
K10	Suprise Niches
L.	**Amphitheater and Stage**
L1	Overhead Shade Structure
L2	Vine Covered Service Gate (locked)
L3	Restroom (Unisex)
L4	Storage
L5	Stage and Storage ✱ Stroller Parking

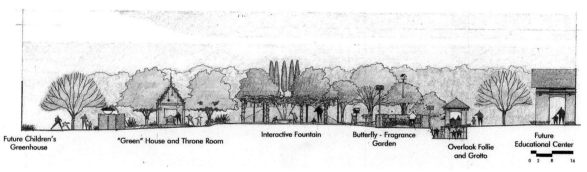

Future Children's Greenhouse

"Green" House and Throne Room

Interactive Fountain

Butterfly - Fragrance Garden

Overlook Follie and Grotto

Future Educational Center

East–west elevation

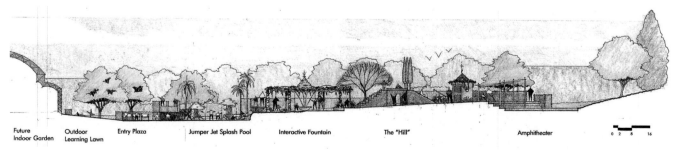

Future Indoor Garden

Outdoor Learning Lawn

Entry Plaza

Jumper Jet Splash Pool

Interactive Fountain

The "Hill"

Amphitheater

North–south elevation

Helen and Peter Bing Children's Garden at the Huntington Botanical Gardens

EARTH: Magnetic sand

THE MAGIC OF CHILDREN'S GARDENS

Element-themed gardens keep children engaged for hours at the Bing Children's Garden. Plants with interesting characteristics, such as topiary animals, vines covering a house, weeping mulberry trees, papyrus, and ponytail palms, create a whimsical atmosphere in the garden. Shaded benches in the center of the garden and rocking chairs in the overlook offer seating.

The components and intricacies within each themed garden are as follows:

Earth

- **Magnetic sand:** Visitors learn about the interaction of force fields. Magnetic sand is attracted to the two powerful magnets and provides an opportunity to create interesting shapes.
- **Self-centered globe:** Visitors look and feel for evidence of the earth's sunrise and sunset, shadows, and surface heat. With Los Angeles positioned at the top, the globe shows how the sun is striking the earth at this very moment.
- **Pebble chimes:** Visitors compose their own sound of music. A musical instrument is played by dropping pebbles through a matrix of stainless steel nails embedded inside a perforated stainless steel structure. The leaf-shaped structure acts as a resonator to amplify the water-like sounds.

Air

- **Fragrance garden:** Visitors smell gentle aromas of citrus, rosemary, lavender, and other fragrance-rich plants.
- **Fog grotto:** Visitors experience the swirl of clouds and the constant currents that surround them. Fog, generated by nearly one hundred high-pressure nozzles, flows in and fills the grotto. A sudden breeze sweeps it away.

WATER: Marble jets

THE MAGIC OF CHILDREN'S GARDENS

Fire

- **Prism tunnel:** Visitors experience the tunnel illuminated by intricate patterns of colored light from diffraction gratings in the ceiling. The light patterns change with the time of day and with the seasons.
- **Topiary volcano:** Visitors view flame-colored leaves of New Zealand flax growing atop the volcano that is "fueled" by sunlight. Rampant vines form a shady refuge. Mist is emitted from the volcano, which represents volcanic eruption.
- **Rainbow room:** Visitors feel pulses of mist that break sunlight into a circular rainbow that shimmers against the background of miniature Bull Bay magnolias.

Water

- **Sonic pool:** Visitors reach into the water and feel the water ripples. Vibrations at the rim of the basin create waves that interfere with each other to produce this dynamic effect.
- **Vortex and water bells:** Visitors change the flow of water in the vortex and watch the effects of the water as it swirls through the funnel. At the water bells, water forms umbrella-like shapes, only to be pierced and reshaped by small hands.
- **Marble jets:** Visitors catch grape-sized spurts of water in the air that are propelled by jets.

CONCLUSION

The Helen and Peter Bing Children's Garden was created as a teaching garden, to complement the mission of the Huntington Botanical Gardens and to attract families and children. It focuses on four ancient elements—fire, water, earth, and air. These are the raw elements that fuel the plant world and, through plant growth, give rise to the oxygen, food resources, and habitats that sustain human life. Learning about the natural elements of the world at a young age influences children to appreciate nature and the natural world. The Helen and Peter Bing Children's Garden reached its tenth anniversary in June 2014, having touched the lives of thousands of children in its first decade.

FINISH SCHEDULE

KEY	MATERIAL	COLOR	FINISH	COMMENT
C1	CONC.	INT. COLOR— MIAMI BUFF	MED. SANDBLAST	COLOR AND FIN. TO MATCH EXISTING CONCRETE
C2	CONC.	INT. COLOR— L.M. SCOFIELD CLASS 2	MED. SANDBLAST	LATEX SKINS WITH LEAF AND PLANT IMPRESSION, 1 12x12 IMPRESSION PER 20SF OF PAVING
C3	CONC.	INT. COLOR— MIAMI BUFF	MED. SANDBLAST	2X2 CHECKER, HANDPRINTS, FOUND ELEMENTS, SHELLS, BOLTS, HANDS ETC.
C4	CONC.	INT. COLOR— MIAMI BUFF	MED. SANDBLAST	4" BAND
C5	CONC.	INT. COLOR— L.M. SCOFIELD CLASS 2	MED. SANDBLAST	4" BAND
M1	WD. MULCH	NAT.	N/A	"WOOD CARPET WOOD MULCH BY ZEAGER BROS, INC 888-358-8524
ST2	ACADEMY GRANITE	BLACK	CLEFT FACE	COLD SPRINGS GRANITE, 320-685-3621
ST3	MEXICAN BEACH PEBBLE	BLACK	4" — 8" DIA.	AMERICAN BUILDING SUPPLY (ABS), 661-255-5300
ST4	PENNSYLVANIA BLUESTONE	FULL-RANGE	NATURAL	(ABS)
ST5	STONE	NAT.	—	RUBBLE WALL, PER EDWIN HAMILTON
ST6	MALIBU BOULDERS	NAT.	—	(ABS)
ST7	PENNSYLVANIA BLUESTONE	FULL-RANGE	—	LEDGER — STACKED STONE SEAT WALLS WITH CAP (ABS)
ST8	PENNSYLVANIA BLUESTONE	FULL-RANGE	—	4" x 4" TILES
ST9	MALIBU BOULDERS	NAT.	—	A 24"-30"x24"-30" B 30"-42"x30"-42" C 42"-48"x42"-48"
ST10	MALIBU BOULDERS	NAT.	—	BOULDERS SEAT HT. +/—18", FLAT TOP; (ABS)
W1	CMU BLOCK	INT. COLOR, "NEW WHITE"	SPLIT FACE	12"x8" BLOCK, MANUF. BY ORCO BLOCK
W2	CMU BLOCK	INT. COLOR, "NEW WHITE"	SMOOTH	8"x8" BLOCK, MANUF. BY ORCO BLOCK
W3	PRECAST CONC. CAP	INT. COLOR—TO MATCH BLOCK	—	M01-10 3/8" MANUF. BY CDI
W4	PRECAST CONC. CAP	INT. COLOR—TO MATCH BLOCK	—	PC MC1-18" MANUF. BY CDI, FIELD CUT TO FIT CMU.
CO-1	CONC. COL.	INT. COLOR		CTB-15" DIA. — MANUF. BY CDI
CO-2	CONC. COL.	INT. COLOR		CL-8-SP48 — MANUF. BY CDI
CO-3	CONC. COL.	INT. COLOR— L.M. SCOFIELD CLASS 2		CL-7-18" DIA. — MANUF. BY CDI

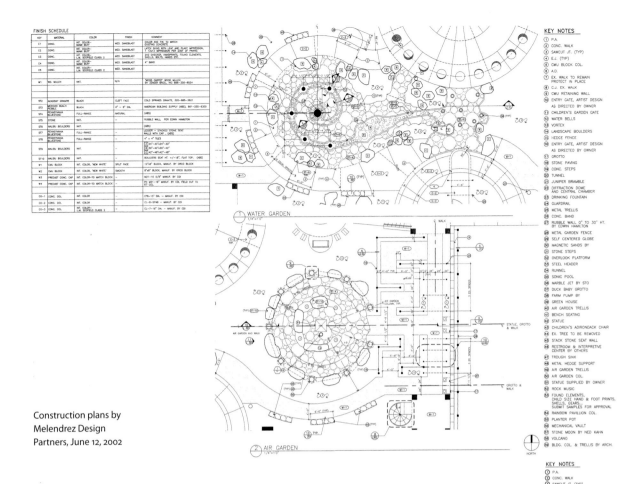

1 WATER GARDEN

2 AIR GARDEN
1/4"=1'-0"

**Construction plans by
Melendrez Design
Partners, June 12, 2002**

KEY NOTES

1. P.A.
2. CONC. WALK
3. SAWCUT JT. (TYP)
4. E.J. (TYP)
5. CMU BLOCK COL.
6. A.D.
7. EX. WALK TO REMAIN PROTECT IN PLACE
8. C.J. EX. WALK
9. CMU RETAINING WALL
10. ENTRY GATE, ARTIST DESIGN AS DIRECTED BY OWNER
11. CHILDREN'S GARDEN GATE
12. WATER BELLS
13. VORTEX
14. LANDSCAPE BOULDERS
15. HEDGE FENCE
16. ENTRY GATE, ARTIST DESIGN AS DIRECTED BY OWNER
17. GROTTO
18. STONE PAVING
19. CONC. STEPS
20. TUNNEL
21. JUNIPER BRAMBLE
22. DIFFRACTION DOME AND CENTRAL CHAMBER
23. DRINKING FOUNTAIN
24. GUARDRAIL
25. METAL TRELLIS
26. CONC. BAND
27. RUBBLE WALL 0" TO 30" HT. BY EDWIN HAMILTON
28. METAL GARDEN FENCE
29. SELF CENTERED GLOBE
30. MAGNETIC SANDS BY
31. STONE STEPS
32. OVERLOOK PLATFORM
33. STEEL HEADER
34. RUNNEL
35. SONIC POOL
36. MARBLE JET BY STO
37. DUCK BABY GROTTO
38. FARM PUMP BY
39. GREEN HOUSE
40. AIR GARDEN TRELLIS
41. BENCH SEATING
42. STATUE
43. CHILDREN'S ADIRONDACK CHAIR
44. EX. TREE TO BE REMOVED
45. STACK STONE SEAT WALL
46. RESTROOM & INTERPRETIVE CENTER BY OTHERS
47. TROUGH SINK
48. METAL HEDGE SUPPORT
49. AIR GARDEN TRELLIS
50. AIR GARDEN COL.
51. STATUE SUPPLIED BY OWNER
52. ROCK MUSIC
53. FOUND ELEMENTS, CHILD SIZE HAND & FOOT PRINTS, SHELLS, GEARS... SUBMIT SAMPLES FOR APPROVAL
54. RAINBOW PAVILLION COL.
55. PLANTER POT
56. MECHANICAL VAULT
57. STONE MOON BY NED KAHN
58. VOLCANO
59. BLDG. COL. & TRELLIS BY ARCH.

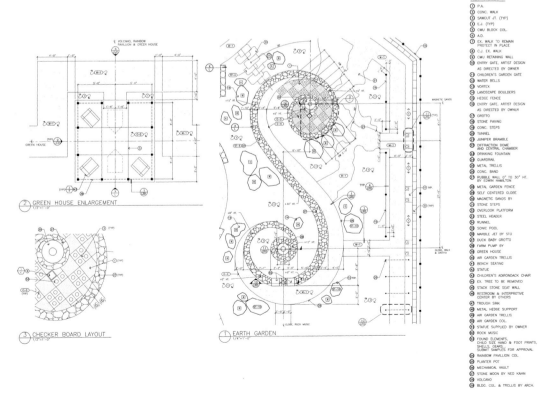

2 GREEN HOUSE ENLARGEMENT
1/2"=1'-0"

3 CHECKER BOARD LAYOUT
1/2"=1'-0"

1 EARTH GARDEN
1/4"=1'-0"

KEY NOTES

1. P.A.
2. CONC. WALK
3. SAWCUT JT. (TYP)
4. E.J. (TYP)
5. CMU BLOCK COL.
6. A.D.
7. EX. WALK TO REMAIN PROTECT IN PLACE
8. C.J. EX. WALK
9. CMU RETAINING WALL
10. ENTRY GATE, ARTIST DESIGN AS DIRECTED BY OWNER
11. CHILDREN'S GARDEN GATE
12. WATER BELLS
13. VORTEX
14. LANDSCAPE BOULDERS
15. HEDGE FENCE
16. ENTRY GATE, ARTIST DESIGN AS DIRECTED BY OWNER
17. GROTTO
18. STONE PAVING
19. CONC. STEPS
20. TUNNEL
21. JUNIPER BRAMBLE
22. DIFFRACTION DOME AND CENTRAL CHAMBER
23. DRINKING FOUNTAIN
24. GUARDRAIL
25. METAL TRELLIS
26. CONC. BAND
27. RUBBLE WALL 0" TO 30" HT. BY EDWIN HAMILTON
28. METAL GARDEN FENCE
29. SELF CENTERED GLOBE
30. MAGNETIC SANDS BY
31. STONE STEPS
32. OVERLOOK PLATFORM
33. STEEL HEADER
34. RUNNEL
35. SONIC POOL
36. MARBLE JET BY STO
37. DUCK BABY GROTTO
38. FARM PUMP BY
39. GREEN HOUSE
40. AIR GARDEN TRELLIS
41. BENCH SEATING
42. STATUE
43. CHILDREN'S ADIRONDACK CHAIR
44. EX. TREE TO BE REMOVED
45. STACK STONE SEAT WALL
46. RESTROOM & INTERPRETIVE CENTER BY OTHERS
47. TROUGH SINK
48. METAL HEDGE SUPPORT
49. AIR GARDEN TRELLIS
50. AIR GARDEN COL.
51. STATUE SUPPLIED BY OWNER
52. ROCK MUSIC
53. FOUND ELEMENTS, CHILD SIZE HAND & FOOT PRINTS, SHELLS, GEARS... SUBMIT SAMPLES FOR APPROVAL
54. RAINBOW PAVILLION COL.
55. PLANTER POT
56. MECHANICAL VAULT
57. STONE MOON BY NED KAHN
58. VOLCANO
59. BLDG. COL. & TRELLIS BY ARCH.

Vortex and water bells

Self-centered globe

Helen and Peter Bing Children's Garden at the Huntington Botanical Gardens

Greenhouse

Opposite: Construction details by Melendrez
Design Partners, June 12, 2002

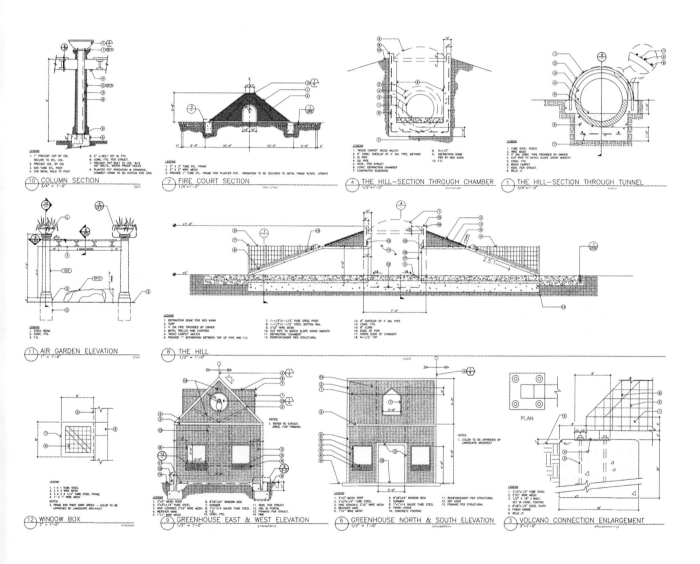

WATER: Sonic pool

Opposite: Construction details by
Melendrez Design Partners, June 12, 2002

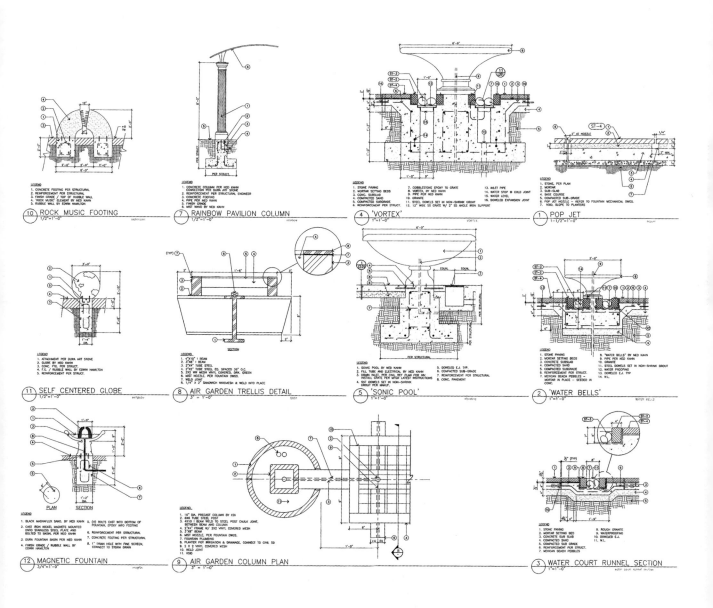

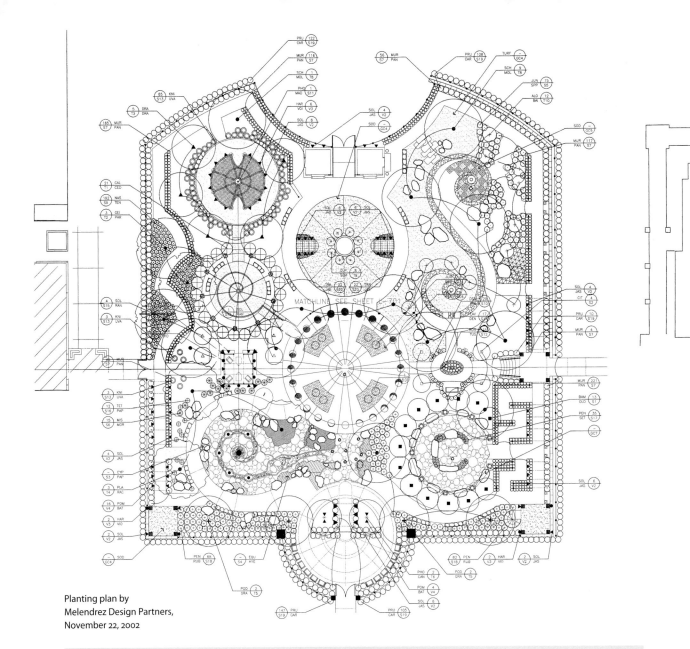

Planting plan by
Melendrez Design Partners,
November 22, 2002

Selected plants in the garden

Trees
Aloe bainesii
Calocedrus decurrens
Cupressus sempervirens
Dracaena draco
Geijera parviflora
Juniperus spp.
Phoenix canariensis
Platanus racemosa
Podocarpus gracilior
Schinus molle

Shrubs
Bambusa oldhamii
Citrus spp.
Cyprus papyrus
Equisetum hyemale
Juniperus spp.
Kniphofia uvaria
Lavendula dentata
Miscanthus sinensis 'Morning
    Light'
Murraya paniculata
Myoporum parvifolium
Nassella tenuissima

Osmanthus fragrans
Pennisetum rubrum
Pennisetum setaceum
Phormium tenax 'Maori Chief'
Rosmarinus officinalis 'Tuscan
    Blue'
Solanum rantonnetii
Tetrapanax papyriferus
Trachelospermum jasminoides

Groundcovers
Acorus gramineus
Acorus gramineus 'Variegatus'

Cynodon dactylon ×
    C. transvaalensis Tifgreen
Sedum brevifolium
Stenotaphrum secundatum
    hybrid

Vines
Ficus pumila
Hardenbergia violacea
Pomoea batatas
Solanum jasminoides

Details in the garden

Helen and Peter Bing Children's Garden at the Huntington Library, Art Collections, and Botanical Gardens

1151 Oxford Road, San Marino, CA 91108

626-405-2100   http://www.huntington.org/WebAssets/Templates/general.aspx?id=16566

Opening date: Father's Day 2004

Project size: 0.4 acre (0.16 hectare) within Huntington Botanical Gardens' 120-acre (48.6-hectare) site

Design and Construction Team

Huntington Botanical Gardens:

Director: James P. Folsom

Staff: Gail Shair, Laurie Sowd

Landscape architects:

Initial concept (1999): Bennitt Design Group (Todd Bennitt)

Concept development (2000): EDSA

Landscape architect of record (2001): Melendrez Design Partners (Todd Bennitt and Willie Nishizawa)

Architects: Offenhauser Associates Inc. (Bob Ray Offenhauser, Jim Fry)

Artist: Ned Kahn Studios

Hardscape contractor: ValleyCrest Landscape Development

Greenhouse: Mastercraft Iron Co. Inc.

Rainbow room columns: Dura Art Stone

Water features: Aquatic Creations Inc.

Current Contacts

Huntington Botanical Gardens director: James P. Folsom

Interviews and Personal Communications

Todd Bennitt, April 6, 2011; Katie Chiu, April 7, 2011; James P. Folsom, April 2, 2011; Ned Kahn, April 5, 2011; Scott Kleinrock, November 7, 2014

Ithaca Children's Garden

ITHACA, NEW YORK

GOAL

Ithaca Children's Garden is a unique and whimsical garden that inspires, empowers, and connects youths with the wonders of the natural environment. The garden provides a wide variety of educational opportunities for children, families, schools, and the community in addition to rich experiences for casual visitors. Ithaca Children's Garden was cofounded by Harriet Becker, Monika Roth, and Mary Alyce Kobler in 1997. They were inspired to create a children's garden in Ithaca after hearing a presentation by Jane Taylor, codesigner of the Michigan 4-H Children's Garden. In 1998, Ithaca Children's Garden began as a nonprofit entity, and in the following year funding was secured for a part-time director and education program assistant. Through cooperative partnerships, in 2004, a twenty-five-year lease for a three-acre parcel in the southern portion of Cass Park was granted by the City of Ithaca for the children's garden.

CONCEPT

Ithaca Children's Garden is a remarkable grassroots initiative, made possible through the efforts of the local community, hundreds of volunteers, generous donations, and grants each year. The original design involved significant input from children and the community. In 1998, every second grader in Ithaca contributed ideas for the garden through drawings. These drawings were made into quilt blocks that were used for developing conceptual designs of the garden. On November 1, 2001, an Ithaca Children's Garden Design Day was held to capture the best skills, insights, and ideas from parents, artists, teachers, gardeners, and community leaders to determine key elements for the garden—special features in the garden, types of gardens and plants, educational emphasis areas, age groups, and development phases. Participants considered gardens with water, earth sculptures covered with plants, specific habitats and structures, and hiding spaces. Since 2011, Ithaca Children's Garden has increased its focus on practicing and demonstrating permaculture principles in action. The garden has also become internationally recognized as a champion for children's free play through its leadership in adventure play and playwork.

Gaia the giant snapping turtle

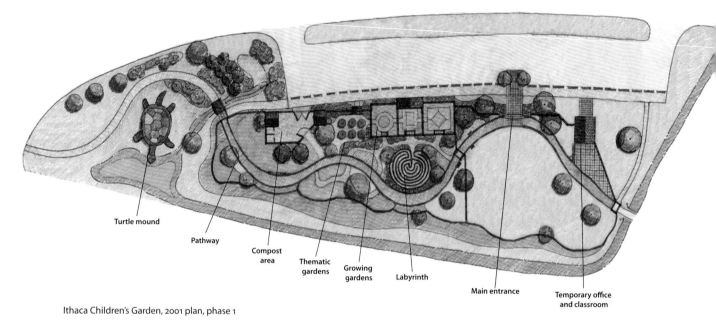

Turtle mound

Pathway

Compost
area

Thematic
gardens

Growing
gardens

Labyrinth

Main entrance

Temporary office
and classroom

Ithaca Children's Garden, 2001 plan, phase 1

Selected plants in the garden

Wildflower meadow plan
Myosotis spp. (forget-me-nots)
Spring bulbs

Middle–late spring (May)
Lychnis flos-cuculi (ragged robin)
Ranunculus acris (tall buttercup)

Early summer (June–July)
Centaurea montana (mountain
   bluets)
Geranium endresii (cranesbill
   geranium)
Leucanthemum vulgare (oxeye
   daisy)
Malva moschata (musk mallow)

Summer (July–August)
Asclepias syriaca (common
   milkweed)
Baptisia spp. (wild false indigo)
Echinacea purpurea (purple
   coneflower)
Liatris spp. (blazing star)
Linaria vulgaris (butter and eggs)

Monarda didyma (red beebalm)
Oenothera fruticosa (sundrops)
Rudbeckia hirta (black-eyed Susan)

Late summer–fall
Schizachyrium scoparium (little
   bluestem)
Symphyotrichum novi-angliae (New
   England aster)

Wetlands
Agastache foeniculum (anise
   hyssop)
Aronia melanocarpa (black choke-
   berry)
Asclepias incarnata (swamp
   milkweed)
Baptisia australis (blue false indigo)
Baptisia leucantha (white wild
   indigo)
Cephalanthus occidentalis (but-
   tonbush)
Cornus alternifolia (pagoda
   dogwood)
Cornus amomum (silky dogwood)

Filipendula rubra (Queen-of-the-
   Prairie)
Ilex verticillata (winterberry)
Liatris spicata (blazing star)
Lindera benzoin (spice bush)
Lobelia cardinalis (cardinal flower)
Monarda didyma (bee balm)
Morella pensylvanica (bayberry)
Panicum virgatum (switchgrass)
Penstemon calycosus (long-sepal
   beardtongue)
Sambucus canadensis (American
   elder)
Schizachyrium scoparium (little
   bluestem)
Sporobolus heterolepis (prairie
   dropseed)
Vernonia noveboracensis (New York
   ironweed)
Veronicastrum virginicum (Culver's
   root)
Yucca filamentosa (Adam's needle)

Stringing plants in the growing garden

DESIGN

The original design concept plan (formulated in 2001) and kitchen garden plan (formulated in 2007) by Rick Manning, landscape architect, guided the garden development. Daniel Krall, landscape architect, also contributed significantly through the years to the evolution and implementation of the designs in the landscape. Unique garden features throughout the garden provide vast opportunities for education and learning. Key components of the garden include the following:

- Gaia (completed in 2005), the giant thirty-by-sixty-foot snapping turtle sculpture, designed by Bo Atkinson, is a signature piece in the garden. On Gaia's back, visitors discover a variety of plants and a lunar calendar, designed by Victoria Romanoff, with thirteen central shields representing the thirteen moons, or lunar months, in a year and twenty-eight outer shields representing the twenty-eight days in each lunar month. Young visitors also learn about the Haudenosaunee creation story while playing on Gaia's back.
  - Pond, wetland, and swale, which Gaia looks over, represents her native habit. In the stream, crossed by boulders and bridge, children explore and find tadpoles, frogs, and even baby snapping turtles.
  - Sod salamander sculpture (2008) is a sod-covered salamander-shaped mound near Gaia for children to climb on that was installed by Teen Urban Farmers.
- Wildflower meadow (2006–2007), full of flowers, rushes, chicory, ironweed, and false indigo, provides a rich habitat for birds and insects.
  - Recycled bottle house (2009), across from the wildflower meadow, serves as the garden's Nature Museum. Campers and visitors can display natural treasures they discover during their visits to the garden, including feathers, bones, insect wings, stones, fossils, and seedpods.

Recycled bottle house

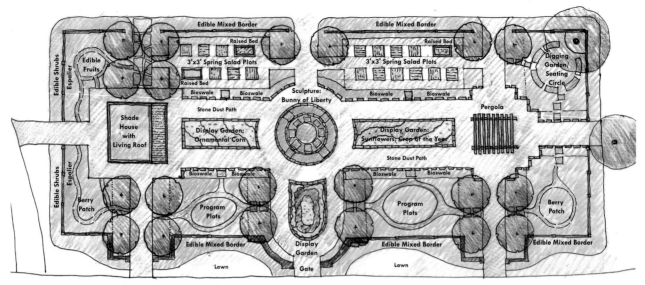

Kitchen garden sketch plan by Rick Manning, landscape architect, October 30, 2007

Selected plants in the kitchen garden

Digging garden
Helianthus annuus (sunflower)
Zinnia elegans (zinnia)

Herb garden
Anethum graveolens (dill)
Coriandrum sativum (cilantro)
Matricaria chamomilla (chamomile)
Ocimum basilicum (basil)
Petroselinum crispum (parsley)
Rosmarinus officinalis (rosemary)

Central Circle bed
Abelmoschus esculentus 'Clemson Spineless' (green okra)
Abelmoschus esculentus 'Red Burgundy' (red okra)
Brassica oleracea 'Romanesco' (broccoli)
Ipomoea batatas (sweet potato)
Tropaeolum majus (nasturtium)

Central Shield
Lactuca sativa var. *longifolia* 'Red Salad Bowl' (romaine lettuce)

Underground garden
Beta vulgaris (beet)
Solanum tuberosum 'Adirondack Blue' (potato)
Apium graveolens var. *rapaceum* (celeriac)
Solanum tuberosum (fingerling potato)
Allium ampeloprasum (leek)
Allium fistulosum (onion)
Brassica napobrassica (rutabaga)
Brassica rapa (turnip)

Daucus carota 'Rainbow Mix F1' (carrot)
Raphinus sativus (radish)

Three Sisters garden
Cucurbita maxima 'Sunshine' (squash)
Phaseolus vulgaris (pole bean)
Zea mays ssp. *mays* 'Strawberry' (popcorn)

TUF market garden
Ocimum basilicum (basil)
Lycopersicum cerasiforme (cherry tomato)
Brassica oleracea (collard)
Lactuca sativa (lettuce mix)
Allium spp. (onions/scallions)
Capsicum annuum (pepper)
Solanum tuberosum (potato)
Solanum lycopersicum (tomato)

Home veggie demo garden
Ocimum basilicum (basil)
Apium graveolens (celery)
Solanum lycopersicum (cherry tomato)
Solanum melongena 'Jewel Neon' (eggplant)
Phaseolus vulgaris 'French Filet' (haricot bush bean)
Cucumis sativus 'Lemon' (cucumber)
Cucurbita pepo 'Patty Pan' (squash)
Capsicum annuum 'Lipstick' (pepper)
Solanum lycopersicum 'Sweet Aroma' (sauce tomato)

Cucumis sativus 'Green Apple' (slicing cucumber)
Lycopersicon esculentum 'Porterhouse' (slicing tomato)
Citrullus lanatus 'Moon and Stars' (watermelon)
Pyrus spp. (yellow pear)
Cucurbita pepo (zucchini)

Pickle garden
Cucumis sativus 'Cool Breeze' (cucumber)
Cucumis sativus 'N. Pickling' (cucumber)
Anethum graveolens (dill)
Capsicum annuum 'Pizza Pepper' (hot pepper)
Abelmoschus esculentus (okra)
Phaseolus vulgaris (bush bean)
Phaseolus vulgaris (pole bean)
Raphanus sativus (radish)

Latin American garden
Allium cepa (onion)
Capsicum annuum (pepper)
Capsicum annuum 'Pizza Pepper' (hot pepper)
Coriandrum sativum (cilantro)
Phaseolus vulgaris 'Black Coco' (black bean)
Physalis philadelphica (tomatillo)
Solanum lycopersicum (tomato)

Herb garden
Matricaria chamomilla (chamomile)
Rosmarinus officinalis (rosemary)

European garden
Brassica oleracea 'Early Golden Acre' (cabbage)
Brassica oleracea 'Diablo' (brussels sprouts)
Brassica oleracea (kohlrabi)
Brassica raab (broccoli raab)
Chicorium endivia (Belgian endive)
Cucumis melo 'Charentais' (French melon)
Cucurbita spp. (squash)
Cynara spp. (artichoke)
Eruca sativa 'Rocket' (arugula)
Ocimum basilicum (basil)
Phaseolus vulgaris 'Dragon Tongue' (flat bean)
Solanum tuberosum (potato)

Asian garden
Basella alba (Malabar spinach)
Brassica oleracea (greens)
Brassica rapa 'Shuko' (bok choy)
Brassica rapa ssp. *pekinensis* (Napa cabbage)
Capsicum annuum 'Pizza Pepper' (hot pepper)
Cucurbita maxima (kabocha squash)
Cucumis sativus 'Shintokiwa' (Chinese cucumber)
Mormordica charantia (bitter melon)
Ocimum basilicum 'Siam Queen' (Thai basil)
Solanum melongena (Thai eggplant)
Vigna unguiculata (Asian long bean)

Teen Urban Farmers farm stand

Kitchen garden

- Kitchen garden (2008) includes herbs, vegetables, berries, and espaliered fruit trees.
  - Other kitchen garden features (2009) include entry arbor, teepee trellises, two gates built from reused doors, a locust tree pergola with benches, and wheelchair-accessible raised planters. Two beehives and a movable chicken shed with five chickens were added in 2014. Honey is harvested from the hives, and the chicken eggs are used in programs and sold at the farm stand. Surplus produce is donated to Friendship Donations Network.
  - Teen Urban Farmers farm stand (2013) sells fresh produce to visitors during the summer. Teens learn horticultural, entrepreneurial, and leadership skills as they grow, harvest, prepare, and sell produce.

Straw-bale troll house

- Straw-bale troll house (2008), with its green roof, is an insulated timber frame structure that showcases a natural building style using green materials and construction. It is a popular hiding space for children.
- Bird garden (2009), planted with selected trees, shrubs, and perennials, attracts local wildlife. A child-sized birdhouse is painted with a colorful mural showcasing seventeen bird species that can be spotted from the garden. A kid-sized bird's nest invites kids to flap and sing like a bird. The bird garden is a site for Cornell Lab of Ornithology's Celebrate Urban Birds program, which is conducted at thousands of sites throughout North America. The program's bird guides and tally sheets are used as curriculum materials, says Leigh Mc-Donald-Rizzo, Ithaca Children's Garden education director.

Bulb Labyrinth Memorial Garden

- Bulb Labyrinth Memorial Garden (2012), a sixty-four-by-sixty-four-foot healing and contemplative space planted with thirty thousand bulbs and three hundred perennials, provides visitors with a labyrinth walk while observing and celebrating the cycles of the seasons. The labyrinth was developed in collaboration with the Ithaca Childbearing Loss Support Network as a special place to remember babies and children lost in the community.
- Willow tunnel huts (2013) features stickwork sculptures installed under the guidance of the renowned stick sculptor Patrick Dougherty in cooperation with Cornell University's Messenger Lecture Series. Children interact with environmental art as they play, hide, and explore the sheltered world within.

Rice paddy pond

- Kids' Kitchen (2013), a solar-powered, community-built structure and the garden's first covered space for gathering, was built for activities such as cooking, eating, meeting, and art projects.
- Rice paddy pond (2013–2014), a water habitat with child-scale docks, provides opportunities for aquatic explorations of frogs, tadpoles, and water insects. Iris, taro, lilies, and rice in the pond create a small ecosystem.

Building willow tunnel huts, 2013, stickwork sculptures installed by Cornell University Art of Horticulture students with one hundred community members, under the guidance of renowned artist Patrick Dougherty

- Hands-on-Nature Anarchy Zone (2012) is one of the first adventure playgrounds in the United States opened to the public in the twenty-first century. The Hands-on-Nature Anarchy Zone is a union of nature play and adventure playground modeled after nature-based learning and play settings in Germany, Scandinavia, and the United Kingdom.
- The Cherry Guild (2015) is a garden that mimics natural layers in a forest while producing food and fiber for human use. In the complex and symbiotic planting scheme, the ultimate goal is to create a regenerative, self-sustaining ecosystem with minimal human intervention required beyond the harvesting of fruits, nuts, roots, and berries.
- The Very Hungry Caterpillar Boardwalk (2015–2017), a collaboration with the Family Reading Partnership and the Eric Carle Foundation, is in development to tell Eric Carle's classic story of the Very Hungry Caterpillar through an interactive, kinesthetic experience along the length of the boardwalk, which flanks the east edge of the garden.

Ithaca Children's Garden is maintained by staff and volunteers. Since 1998, Teen Urban Farmers, a youth development and workforce program consisting of teenagers ages fourteen to nineteen, work in the garden for six weeks during the summer. In 2015, this program expanded to include a year-round after-school component that includes teen support for garden maintenance. Ithaca Children's Garden relies heavily on student volunteer groups from Cornell University, Ithaca College, and Tompkins County Community College for its maintenance. Local residents work regularly in the garden throughout the year. Ithaca Children's Garden is a wonderful outdoor laboratory for all who seek learning opportunities in horticulture, ecology, environmental education, and youth development. Children enrolled in the garden's summer camps and visitors also engage in garden maintenance through service learning programs.

CONCLUSION

After more than ten years, Ithaca Children's Garden continues to develop, implement, and evaluate its innovative learning programs with a high degree of community input. The garden's focus on play and permaculture ethics engages and delights children and families. Ithaca Children's Garden's initiatives have evolved and expanded since its beginning to proactively address and respond to community needs. To plan for the growth and build-out of the garden, Whitman Planning and Design prepared a three-phase master plan: phase 1 (taking place in 2014), phase 2 (2015–2017), and phase 3 (2018–2020).

Hands-on-Nature Play Anarchy Zone

Ithaca Children's Garden

105

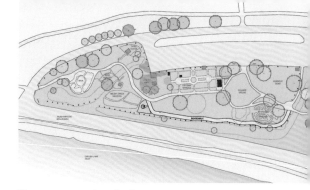

Phase 1: 2013–2014 boardwalk

Ithaca Children's Garden
Route 89 (Taughannock Boulevard) at the southern end of Cass Park, Ithaca, New York
607-319-4203   http://www.ithacachildrensgarden.org

Opening date: 2004
Project size: 3 acres (0.8 hectares) within Cass Park's 84-acre (4-hectare) site

Design and Implementation Team
Project founders: Harriet Becker, Monika Roth, and Mary Alyce Kobler
Teen Urban Farmers founders: Mary Alyce Kobler and Lee Ginenthal
Ithaca Children's Garden:
    Executive director: Erin Marteal
    Education director: Leigh MacDonald-Rizzo
Landscape architects:
    2004 concept plan and 2007 kitchen garden plan: Rick Manning
    2006–present: Daniel Krall
    2014 master plan: Whitman Planning and Design LLC

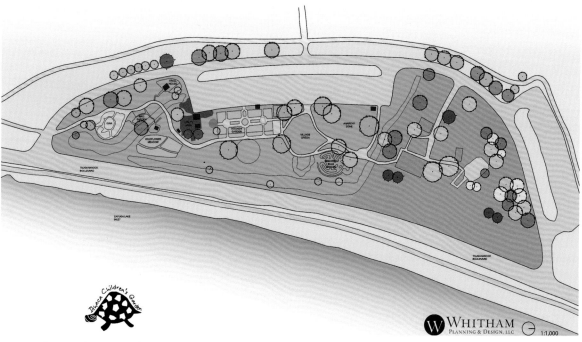

Ithaca Children's Garden 2013 site plan

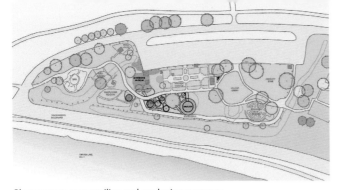
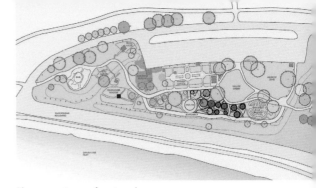

Phase 2: 2015–2017 pavilion and gardening museum

Phase 3: 2018–2020 forest garden

Gardens and features built through the efforts of artists, landscape architects, volunteers, and community support:

Gaia and wetlands: Rick Manning, landscape architect, and the team: Irene Lekstutis, landscape architect; Bo Atkinson (turtle); Victoria Romanoff (moon plates); Triad Foundation; a New York State environmental protection fund grant; Donald Ferlow (wetlands); and Plantsman Nursery

Sod salamander sculpture: Danielle Hodgins, Teen Urban Farmers

Wildflower meadow: Louise Raimondo, Ithaca Garden Club

Kitchen garden: Rick Manning, Dan Krall, Whitmore Fence, a New York State environmental protection fund grant

Straw-bale troll house and green roof: Aaron Dennis and E. J. George of Tugley Wood Timberframing; Lexie Hain and Marguerite Wells of Motherplants Nursery

Recycled bottle greenhouse: 2010 residents of Cornell's Keeton House; Tom Brown and Locust Lumber Co.

Beehives: Marvin Pritts

Cluckingham Palace movable chicken tractor: Alan Vogel, Andy Moore

Bird garden and bird's nest: Teen Urban Farmers, Mike Carpenter

Child-sized birdhouse: Teen Urban Farmers in 2010, painted by artists Camille and Marika Chew in 2011

Bulb Labyrinth Memorial Garden: Nicole Deister, Dan Krall, Dan Klein, Jeanne Grace, Melissa Kitchen, Kate Dimpfl, Lisa Machlin, and Marsha and Wilson Pond, in collaboration with Ithaca Childbearing Loss Network and 320 volunteers

Cherry Guild: Megan Shay and Dan Krall; major stone work by LeWalter Design; funding by Ithaca Garden Club

The Very Hungry Caterpillar Story boardwalk: Construction led by Alan Vogel; earthworks by Elmore Enterprises; concept development with Brigid Hubberman, the Family Reading Partnership, and Eric Carle Foundation

Kids' Kitchen: Alan Vogel, Renovus Solar, GrassRoots volunteers

Rice paddy pond: Dan Krall, Cornell University's rice breeding program

Teen Urban Farmers farm stand: Structure donated by Kristen McClellan of SnappyScreen, Alan Vogel and friends retrofitted the shed into a farm stand; Steve Austin installed the rain catchment system with Teen Urban Farmers

Hands-on-Nature Anarchy Zone: U.S. Fish and Wildlife Service, in partnership with David Stilwell, Rusty Keeler of EarthPlay, and Elizabeth Stilwell, with major support from the Park Foundation

Current Contacts

Ithaca Children's Garden executive director: Erin Marteal
Ithaca Children's Garden education director: Leigh MacDonald-Rizzo

Interviews and Personal Communications

Leigh MacDonald-Rizzo, June 10, 2010; Erin Marteal, January 21, 2016

Hill Country grotto

8

Luci and Ian Family Garden
at Lady Bird Johnson Wildflower Center

AUSTIN, TEXAS

GOAL

The University of Texas at Austin's Lady Bird Johnson Wildflower Center was founded by former first lady Lady Bird Johnson and actress Helen Hayes in 1982 as an organization "to protect and preserve North America's native plants and natural landscapes" (Lady Bird Johnson Wildflower Center, n.d. "About"). The goal of the Luci and Ian Family Garden is to further the Wildflower Center's educational program and its mission to "conserve, restore and create healthy landscapes with native plants" (Lady Bird Johnson Wildflower Center, n.d., "Plant Selection").

CONCEPT

The 4.5-acre (1.8-hectare) Family Garden, named after daughter Luci Baines Johnson and her husband, Ian Turpin, was designed for children, adults, and families. Luci Johnson says, "This is a family commitment. If we don't join in that commitment from our very youngest to our very eldest, then we are missing out on the joy that we can bring to multiple generations" (Central Texas Gardener 2014).

The design process began in 2007 and was completed in 2008. Construction began in 2013, and the garden was built within Sustainable Sites Initiative guidelines for the sustainable design, construction, and maintenance of landscapes. In May 2014, the garden was opened to the public. Landscape architect and artist W. Gary Smith, designer of several prominent children's gardens, worked on the design with Andrea DeLong-Amaya, director of horticulture at the Lady Bird Johnson Wildflower Center. They began the design process by interviewing staff and volunteers who worked in the garden. According to Smith, "The main concept was to engage people with the center's mission through informal play and enjoyment, inspiring individuals' imagination." The garden was designed to be a safe and interactive place where kids are allowed to run around. TBG Partners was the landscape architecture firm of record for design and development.

Illustrative plan by
W. Gary Smith Design

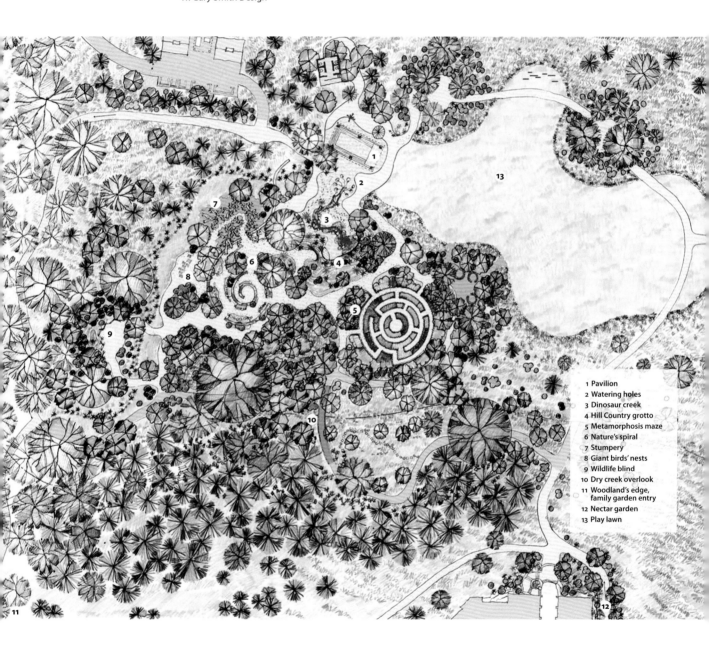

1 Pavilion
2 Watering holes
3 Dinosaur creek
4 Hill Country grotto
5 Metamorphosis maze
6 Nature's spiral
7 Stumpery
8 Giant birds' nests
9 Wildlife blind
10 Dry creek overlook
11 Woodland's edge,
   family garden entry
12 Nectar garden
13 Play lawn

Xeric collection, north garden, showing *Hesperocyperis arizonica* 'Blue Ice' (Arizona cypress), *Salvia greggii* (cherry sage), *Salvia farinacea* 'Henry Duelberg' (mealy blue sage), and *Scutellaria ovata* (heart-leaf skullcap)

DESIGN

The main focus of the garden is immersing children in nature and exposing them to native plants through imagination and play rather than educational exhibits. Smith incorporated creative ideas from his own imagination and knowledge of the regional landscapes mixed with English influence. Smith added upside-down and bundled trees in the stumpery. The Fibonacci sequence, integrated in the nature's spiral, depicts a collection of plants with spiraling flowers, seeds, and leaves. This was a perfect way to bring mathematics into the garden and fulfill educational programming to meet curriculum standards in the Austin school district. The Hill Country grotto stemmed from Smith's love of English follies and his fascination with the Texas Hill Country caves and Hamilton Pool in Dripping Springs, Texas. Historic West Texas pictographs were the inspiration for the graphics in the cave.

Listed below are thirteen unique interactive spaces and their highlights in the Luci and Ian Family Garden that provide a rich environment for children's exploration, learning, and enjoyment.

1 Pavilion: Open-air solar-powered pavilion with high ceiling fans
2 Watering holes: Farm water pump, watering cans, and karst boulders
3 Dinosaur creek: Giant dinosaur footprints set within native limestone paving around a stream
4 Hill Country grotto: Limestone grotto and cave adorned with West Texas pictographs
5 Metamorphosis maze: Hedge maze using a variety of native shrubs
6 Nature's spiral: Spiral with colorful mosaics and spiraling plants
7 Stumpery: Inverted cedar stumps, large tree logs salvaged from the Austin area, tree cookies, and tree bundles
8 Giant birds' nests: Three giant nests woven from grape vines and branches
9 Wildlife blind: Cedar woven fence with peepholes for viewing a wildlife habitat area—a place with water, plants, and space for raising young
10 Dry creek overlook: An ADA-accessible ramp that elevates visitors into the trees to overlook a rocky area below
11 Woodland's edge, family garden entry: Plants suitable for half-day sun and half-day shade
12 Nectar garden, family garden entry: A variety of nectar-rich plantings
13 Play lawn: 0.75-acre (0.3-hectare) lawn area

Top and bottom: Stumpery

Opposite top: Giant birds' nests

Opposite bottom: Escarpment live oak tree

Luci and Ian Family Garden at Lady Bird Johnson Wildflower Center

Hill Country grotto cave

THE MAGIC OF CHILDREN'S GARDENS

Top: Hill Country grotto cave with West Texas pictographs

Bottom: Hill Country grotto

Luci and Ian Family Garden at Lady Bird Johnson Wildflower Center

THE MAGIC OF CHILDREN'S GARDENS

Left: Nature's spiral; *center:* Escarpment live oak tree; *back:* Pavilion; *right:* Hill Country grotto

Interpretive signage is minimized in the garden. Children may have fun without even realizing they are absorbing information and learning. At the watering holes, for example, children fill pitchers from the farm water pump and pour water into the native Texas karst boulders. "They might just have fun pouring water and having it go into the ground and may not know that it's demonstrating groundwater recharge. But they may come back a second or third time because they had fun the first time. Maybe at that time, they will learn about groundwater recharge," says Smith. Children are capable of transformational experiences.

Top: Dinosaur creek
Bottom: Hill Country grotto

Luci and Ian Family Garden at Lady Bird Johnson Wildflower Center

Nature's spiral

Luci Baines Johnson and Ian J. Turpin at the entrance of the Luci and Ian Family Garden

CONCLUSION

The Luci and Ian Family Garden embraces the Lady Bird Johnson Wildflower Center's mission to conserve, restore, and create healthy landscapes through informal play and enjoyment while inspiring the visitor's imagination. As Luci Baines Johnson aptly states, "It won't be one of those destinations where you've been, you've seen, you've conquered, you know it. It will be a place that entices you and invites you to come again, play again, have fun again, learn again . . . but learn because it's sheer delight, not sheer instruction" (Central Texas Gardener 2014).

Play lawn

Selected plants in the garden

3 Dinosaur creek

Amorpha fruticosa
Andropogon glomeratus
Anemopsis californica
Canna glauca
Cephalanthus occidentalis
Conoclinium betonicifolium
Crinum americana
Hibiscus lasiocarpos
Hydrocotyl umbellata
Iris fulva
Iris giganticaerulea
Lobelia cardinalis
Marsilea macropoda
Nymphaea mexicana
Nymphaea odorata
Physostegia intermedia
Potamogeton nodosus
Sabal minor
Saururus cernuus
Thalia dealbata
Thelypteris kunthii
Vallisneria americana

5 Metamorphosis maze

Dermatophyllum secundiflorum
Ilex vomitoria
Ilex vomitoria 'Nana'
Ilex vomitoria 'Will Fleming'
Juniperus virginiana
Leucophyllum frutescens
Malpighia glabra
Morella cerifera

6 Nature's spiral

Astrolepis sinuata
Berlandiera lyrata
Cephalanthus occidentalis
Echinacea purpurea
Equisetum hyemale
Liatris mucronata
Lobelia cardinalis
Malvaviscus arboreus var. *drum-mondii*
Onosmodium bejariense
Pavonia lasiopetala
Phacelia congesta
Phyla nodiflora
Rudbeckia hirta

Rudbeckia maxima
Sphaeralcea incana
Thelypteris kunthii
Vernonia lindheimeri

9 Wildlife blind

Ageratina havanensis
Andropogon glomeratus
Callicarpa americana
Capsicum annuum
Ilex decidua
Ilex vomitoria
Lantana urticoides
Mahonia trifoliolata
Malpighia glabra
Panicum virgatum
Phyla nodiflora
Prunus mexicana
Rivina humilis
Verbesina virginica
Viburnum rufidulum

10 Dry creek overlook

Acer grandidentatum
Aesculus pavia
Ehretia anacua

Fraxinus albicans
Leucaena retusa
Malus ioensis
Quercus laceyi
Styphnolobium affine
Styrax platanifolia
Viburnum rufidulum

12 Nectar garden

Agerantina havanensis
Anisacanthus quadrifidus var. *wrightii*
Berlandiera lyrata
Callirhoe involucrata
Conoclinium greggii
Dalea frutescens
Echinacea purpurea
Helianthus maximiliani
Lantana urticoides
Melampodium leuncathum
Rudbeckia maxima
Salvia farinacea
Salvia greggii 'Furman's Red'
Symphyotrichum oblongifolium
Yucca rupicola
Wedelia texana

Hill Country grotto in foreground
and watering holes in background

Luci and Ian Family Garden at the Lady Bird Johnson Wildflower Center

4801 La Crosse Avenue, Austin, TX 78724

512-232-0100 http://wildflower.org/family_garden

Opening date: May 2014

Project size: 4.5 acres (1.8 hectares) within Lady Bird Johnson Wildflower Center's 289-acre
(117-hectare) site

Planning and Design Team

Lady Bird Johnson Wildflower Center:

Senior director and project manager: Damon Waitt

Director of horticulture: Andrea DeLong-Amaya

University of Texas project management and construction services: Daniel Heath

Landscape architects:

Lead landscape architect and artist: W. Gary Smith Design

Landscape architect of record: TBG Partners (Brian Ott, Charlotte Tonsor, Julie Gossage, Ronnie
Stafford)

General contractor: SpawGlass (Michael Harrington, Chris Schubnel, Joey Clepper)

Current Contact

Lady Bird Johnson Wildflower Center director of horticulture: Andrea DeLong-Amaya

Interviews and Personal Communications

Andrea DeLong-Amaya, July 14, 2015; W. Gary Smith, September 27, 2015

Longwood Gardens' Indoor Children's Garden

KENNETT SQUARE, PENNSYLVANIA

GOAL

The Indoor Children's Garden, opened in 2007, is triple the size of the previous garden (which existed from 1987 to 2003) it replaced. It celebrates the devotion to children expressed by Pierre S. du Pont (1870–1954), industrialist, philanthropist, and creator of Longwood Gardens. The garden has a focus on plants and water features—two of du Pont's garden passions.

Du Pont's wish was to "exploit the sentiments and ideas associated with plants and flowers in a large way" (Longwood Gardens, n.d., "1916–1926"). Thus, the new garden is a space where children can immerse themselves in the sensory experience of plants and gardens every day of the year.

CONCEPT

The planning and design team consisted of the Longwood's design staff (a planning and design specialist, a section gardener, and a visitor education and flower show specialist) and several focus groups. Longwood's design staff met with adults (caregivers and parents) and children grouped by age (three to five, five to ten, and eleven to sixteen) to assemble and analyze issues pertinent to the Indoor Children's Garden design.

The Central Cove

THE INDOOR CHILDREN'S GARDEN

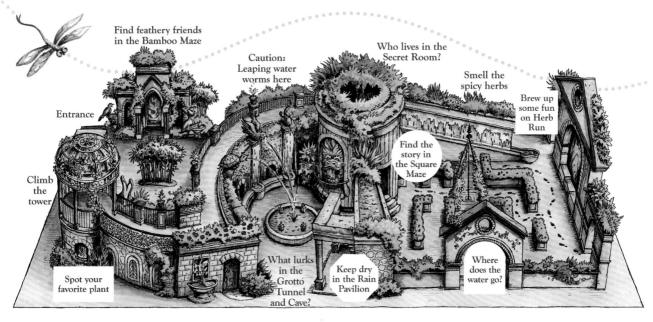

Find feathery friends
in the Bamboo Maze

Caution:
Leaping water
worms here

Who lives in the
Secret Room?

Smell the
spicy herbs

Brew up
some fun
on Herb
Run

Entrance

Find the
story in
the Square
Maze

Climb
the
tower

What lurks
in the
Grotto
Tunnel
and Cave?

Keep dry
in the Rain
Pavilion

Where
does the
water go?

Spot your
favorite plant

Kids' map and guide

Longwood's design staff visited and researched case studies of other public gardens such as the Michigan 4-H Children's Garden, the Everett Children's Adventure Garden in the New York Botanical Garden, and the Children's Garden in the Atlanta Botanical Garden. They also visited and studied other prominent gardens, including Villa Lante and Villa d'Este, both in Italy; Gardens of Versailles, France; and Longwood Gardens itself. "The new children's garden was influenced by the Gardens of Bomarzo—[also called] Park of the Monsters—in Italy," says Paul Redman, executive director of Longwood Gardens. In addition, the design staff also applied the lessons learned from their previous experience and knowledge about children's gardens:

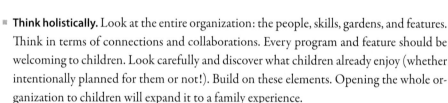

Sketch of fish sculpture by Tres Fromme

- **Think holistically.** Look at the entire organization: the people, skills, gardens, and features. Think in terms of connections and collaborations. Every program and feature should be welcoming to children. Look carefully and discover what children already enjoy (whether intentionally planned for them or not!). Build on these elements. Opening the whole organization to children will expand it to a family experience.
- **Be yourself.** Draw from the organization's specific strengths and identity. Create a unique children's experience that visitors could not imagine finding anywhere else. Link the experience back to the organization's mission. Ask how the goals established can be shared with young visitors. Excite them about the goals and perspectives concerning horticulture and public gardens.
- **Diversify within unity.** Create many types of experiential opportunities for children. Offer various levels of interaction and layers of meaning to enrich the visit. Try to appeal to all learning styles, age groups, abilities, and so on. Some elements should completely seduce and delight every visitor.

Animal sculptures in the Central Cove

Square Maze at the main entrance
during and after construction

THE MAGIC OF CHILDREN'S GARDENS

- **Collaborate.** Use professionals with a wide variety of backgrounds and perspectives, since collaboration generates rich and dynamic experiences. Efforts and resources throughout the organization are more effective when working across departments, job responsibilities, and disciplines. Collaboration invests everyone in the success of the children's experience.
- **Customize resource requirements.** The garden does not need to expend a large amount of money or staff time. Discovering and strengthening children's experiences may not require the huge budget of a major project. Collaboration extends responsibility and costs throughout the organization.

The planning and design team determined important considerations, or the preliminary big issues, of the project. They identified the essential elements necessary for a creative and unique project: mood, stimulation, activity and interaction, types of spaces, water and maze, materials, safety, and other details.

Apse and Water Arbor (in Square Maze)

Sketch and side view of apse and water arbor in Square Maze

Labels within the conceptual garden plan (middle image):
Bamboo Maze
Ramp
Secret Room
Central Cove
Square Maze
Perimeter Run

Top: Children's garden conceptual paving
plan by Tres Fromme, March 21, 2000
Middle: Conceptual garden plan
Bottom: Study model

DESIGN

"The Indoor Children's Garden was designed with a spatial organization comprising four key components: main central space, perimeter walkway, service areas, and crossover circulation areas," says Tres Fromme, landscape designer of the garden. Each area provides specific functions:

- The main central space is occupied by the children's garden. It is primarily a space designed for children to enjoy their activities and to give the impression that adults are excluded.
- The perimeter walkway around the garden is a place for older visitors and adults to enjoy the garden and watch the younger children.
- The service areas throughout the garden provide stopping points for stroller parking, drinking from water fountains, sitting, and so forth.
- The crossover circulation and visual connection at various intersections across the main garden provide spaces for the adults to interact with children and reach them if necessary. The garden's theme areas are all accessible to the physically challenged.

Left: Indoor Children's Garden completed, 2007

Right: Indoor Children's Garden under construction, 2004

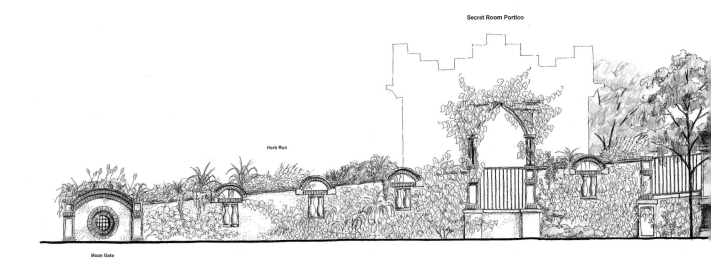

Secret Room Portico

Herb Run

Moon Gate

Conceptual elevations

Tower and Grotto Cave

GrottoTunnel

Focal Fountain

Entry to Grotto Tunnel

Central Cove

THE MAGIC OF CHILDREN'S GARDENS

Ramp

Tower and Grotto Cave

Door to Grotto Tunnel (from Bamboo Maze)   Sitting Benches in Grotto Tunnel

Bamboo Maze

Children's Garden
longwood gardens, Inc.

<u>Conceptual Elevations (PS #1)</u> - REV. 11/99 TF
Tres Fromme, Mary Allinson, Brian Magargee

October 1999   Scale: ½ inch equals 1 foot

Secret Room and Balcony

Triumphal Arch

Square Maze

Sitting Niche   Waterfall and Tunnel (to Square Maze)

Children's Garden
longwood gardens, Inc.

<u>Conceptual Elevations (PS #1)</u>
Tres Fromme, Mary Allinson, Brian Magargee

October 1999   Scale: ½ inch equals 1 foot

Top: The entrance ramp

Bottom left: Secret Room under construction

Bottom middle and right: Happily touching the water leaping from the "glow worm" and water jets while ascending into the secret room

The garden has five distinct but integrated theme areas.

1 The Central Cove features a tree-covered seating area, a central pool with flower-shaped water jets and jewel-like mosaics, and three animal-adorned water pilasters shooting streams of water overhead into the pool.

2 The Secret Room is home to the Drooling Dragon. Children have the chance to move underneath the Rain Pavilion and into the Square Maze of plants accented by story tiles and shooting jets of water.

3 The ramp is accented by an ever-changing Water Curtain and animated by the leaping water "glow worm" that leads children to the tower overlooking the Bamboo Maze.

4 The Grotto Cave Tunnel is located underneath the tower and contains a shallow fog-covered pool activated by water dripping from sculpted snakes coiled overhead.

5 The Bamboo Maze offers a jungle of tree-size bamboos for children to explore. The maze contains the Gothic Folly, a stained-glass window, and five visitor-activated water features accented with ornate bird sculptures.

Numerous intricate water features were designed and detailed to engage children throughout the garden. According to the general contractor, Tim O'Connell, "Every type of construction material imaginable is used to create a display that fascinates all senses." Carefully crafted fantastical animal statues spray water into pools and lurk in the exuberant plantings. Custom-designed mosaics, painted tiles, and murals cover the walls and floors. Ornate door handles are detailed in the form of insects and animals.

CONCLUSION

The Children's Garden at Longwood Gardens intentionally does not emphasize a typical educational approach, instead creating a space that allows simple enjoyment and exploration in a garden setting. Careful planning, ornate details, and fine crafting were key to the realization of an exquisite project that leaves long-lasting and memorable impressions.

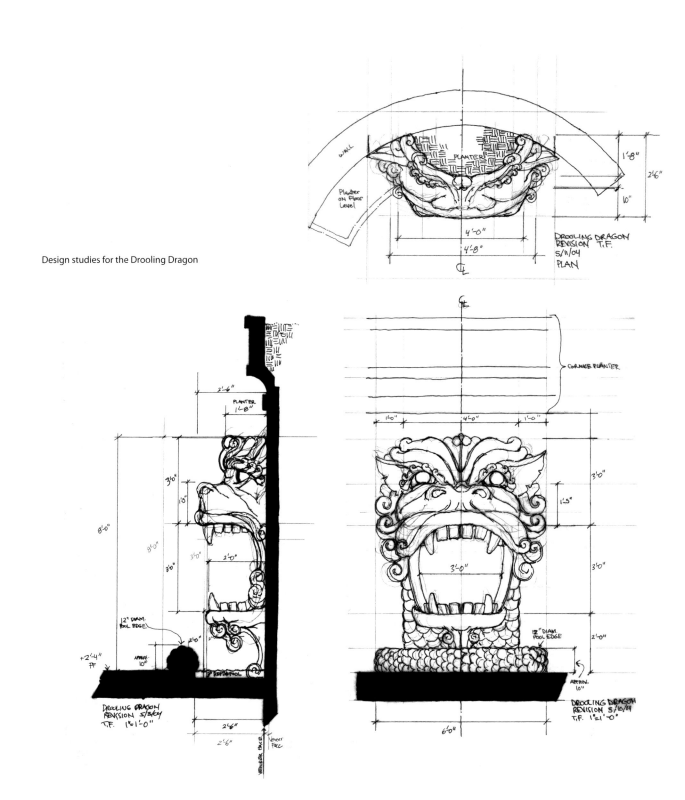

Design studies for the Drooling Dragon

Left: Drooling Dragon set in place by
Tim O'Connell and Sons, general contractor

Right: Drooling Dragon in the Secret Room

Study sketch and model

Details in the garden

Longwood Gardens' Indoor Children's Garden

Details in the garden

Children's garden planting plan by
Mary Allinson and Tres Fromme, July 16, 2001

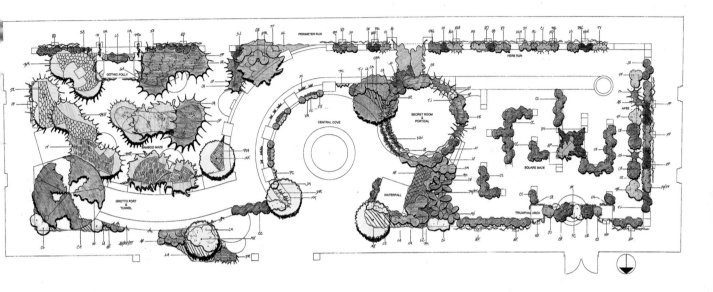

Permanent plant list

Trees
Bambusa eutuldoides 'Viridi-
  vittata'
Bambusa multiplex 'Alphonso-
  Karrii'
Bambusa vulgaris 'Vittata'
Citrus × *microcarpa* 'Variegata'
Magnolia × *soulangeana* 'Alba'
Quercus virginiana 'QVTIA'
  Highrise
Stauntonia hexaphylla
Strelitzia nicolai
Tipuana tipu

Shrubs
Acalypha hispida
Aechmea blanchetiana
Asparagus densiflorus 'Myersii'
Aspidistra elatior
Chirita 'Moonwalker'

Clivia miniata
Cyrtomium falcatum 'Rochfor-
  dianum'
Dianella tasmanica 'Variegata'
Doryanthes palmeri
Dracaena marginata 'Tricolor'
Duranta erecta 'Cuban Gold'
Elaeagnus × *ebbingei*
Ficus elastica 'Ruby'
Macfadyena unguis-cati
Myrtus communis
Neomarica caerulea
Nephrolepis biserrata 'Macho'
Nephrolepis exaltata
Nephrolepis obliterata 'Sunjest'
  Jester's Crown
Origanum majorana 'Max'
Otatea acuminata ssp.
  aztecorum

Philodendron bipinnatifidum
Phlebodium aureum 'Blue Star'
Pileostegia viburnoides
Podocarpus macrophyllus var.
  maki
Polyscias fruticosa 'Snowflake'
Rosmarinus 'Gold Dust'
Spathiphyllum spp.

Vines/groundcovers
Asparagus densiflorus 'Sprengeri'
Bougainvillea 'Raspberry Ice'
Epipremnum aureum
Ficus pumila
Hedera algeriensis 'Gloire de
  Marengo'
Hedera helix 'Chicago'
Hedera helix 'Ivalace'
Jasminum polyanthum
Lygodium japonicum

Monstera deliciosa 'Variegata'
Plectranthus lanuginosus
Tetrastigma voinierianum
Trachelospermum jasminoides

Seasonal plants
Begonia richmondensis
Bellis 'Tasso Strawberries and
  Cream'
Euphorbia pulcherrima
Guzmania spp.
Hippeastrum 'Minerva'
Hydrangea macrophylla
Kalanchoe blossfeldiana
Narcissus 'Tete-a-Tete'
Pelargonium spp.
Petunia hybrid
Selaginella kraussiana
Senecio cineraria 'Cirrus'
Zantedeschia 'Gold Rush'

Grotto Fort

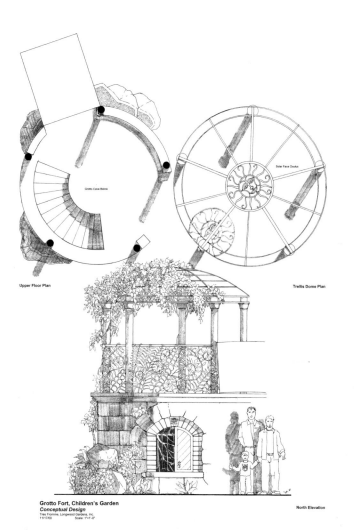

Upper Floor Plan

Grotto Cave Below

Solar Face Oculus

Trellis Dome Plan

Grotto Fort, Children's Garden
Conceptual Design
Tres Fromme, Longwood Gardens, Inc.
11/17/00   Scale: 1"=1'-2"

North Elevation

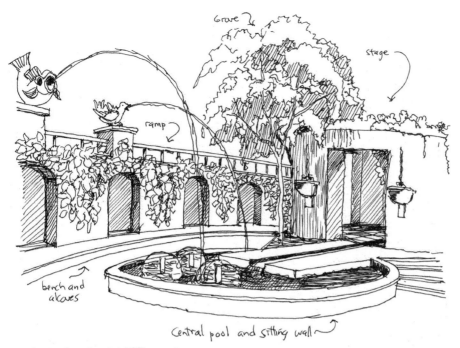

Grove

stage

ramp

bench and alcoves

Central pool and sitting wall

CENTRAL COVE

Children's Garden 10/20/98 T.F.

Central Cove

Top left and right and bottom left: Activated water features accented with ornate bird sculptures in Bamboo Maze

Bottom right: Stained-glass window in Gothic Folly

Opposite: Gothic Folly in Bamboo Maze

Opposite: Inside Grotto Cave
Right: Outside Grotto Cave

Longwood Gardens' Indoor Children's Garden

Opposite left: Sketch of entry to Secret Room from Square Maze

Opposite right: Getting water in the Secret Room to paint on wall

Painting with water in the Secret Room

Longwood Gardens Indoor Children's Garden

1001 Longwood Road, Kennett Square, PA 19348

610-388-1000   http://longwoodgardens.org/gardens/indoor-childrens-garden

Opening date: October 27, 2007

Project size: A glass house of 3,700 square feet (343.7 square meters) within
Longwood Gardens' 1,077-acre (435.8-hectare) site

Design and Construction Team

Longwood Gardens:

Landscape planning and lead designer: Tres Fromme

Section gardener, codeveloper of initial concept design, and codesigner of planting
scheme: Mary Allinson

Executive director: Fred Roberts

General services foreman: Dave Jones

GIS/CAD systems coordinator: Gregg Erhardt

Horticulture department head and project leader: Sharon Loving

Maintenance department head and project manager: Robert Underwood

Planning and design assistant: Nick Nelson

Architect: Leonard Sophrin Architect Inc.

Electrical and mechanical engineer: Hough Associates

Electrical contractor: Tri-M

Structural engineer: Gannet Flemming (Gary Gabarcik)

Design-build and general contractor: Tim O'Connell and Sons Inc.

Water feature consultant: Alan Robinson

Artisan management: Claro Creative Studios

Current Contacts

Director of marketing: Marnie Conley

Communications manager: Patricia Evans

Interviews and Personal Communications

Mary Allinson, August 5, 2014; Marnie Conley, August 5, 2014; Patricia Evans, August 5, 2014; Tres
Fromme, October 13, 2015; Tim O'Connell, October 22, 2015; Abigail Palutis, September 30, 2015;
Paul Redman, March 18, 2015

Rainbow area with butterfly
area in foreground

Michigan 4-H Children's Garden
at Michigan State University

EAST LANSING, MICHIGAN

GOAL

Michigan 4-H Children's Garden is part of the 14-acre (6-hectare) Horticulture Gardens on the Michigan State University campus. The mission of the Michigan 4-H (which stands for health, heart, hands, and head) Children's Garden is to "promote an understanding of plants and why they are important in our daily lives, nurture the wonder in a child's imagination and curiosity, [and] provide a place of enrichment and delight for children of all ages" (Michigan State University, n.d., "Information"). This 0.7-acre (0.3-hectare) garden consists of fifty-six thematic areas. Its motto is "Experience plants!" (Michigan State University, n.d., "Information"). It is a "magical place of learning" (Michigan State University, n.d., "Help").

CONCEPT

The concept for a child-focused garden began in 1987. At that time, few public gardens in the United States had a focus on children. Instead, the emphasis was on providing the children with their own garden plot that they could care for during the summertime. These gardens reached a small group of children but not the many hundreds of children who came with families to gardens where it was not uncommon to see signs stating, "Stay on the path" and "Do not touch."

After a literature search, Jane L. Taylor, a staff member at the 4-H Foundation at Michigan State University, realized there were no case studies for children and garden experiences for children under age nine. Taylor, who initiated the conceptual design and fund-raising for the garden, requested Alice Whiren to pursue a research project. Whiren was a professor in the Family and Child Ecology Department and director of two laboratory preschools. Taylor recalls, "Dr. Whiren's research sought to define where children's first garden impressions were initiated and what they might want to see when visiting a garden." In addition to the preschool-age children, who represented seventeen different racial and ethnic groups, older children in 4-H garden clubs and many 4-H horticulture leaders throughout the state were canvassed for ideas. Whiren's published research guided the selection of thematic areas within the garden.

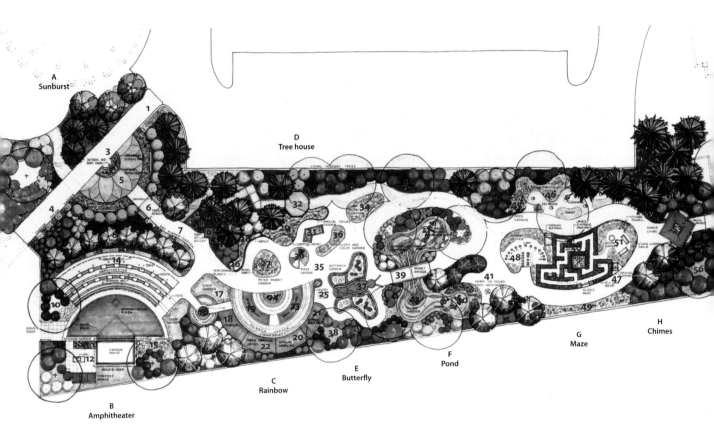

A
Sunburst

1

D
Tree house

3

5

4

6

7

14

10

17

18

20

22

15

12

B
Amphitheater

C
Rainbow

E
Butterfly

35

25

37

39

38

F
Pond

41

G
Maze

H
Chimes

32

34

36

46

48

51

47

49

56

Illustrative plan by
Michigan State University
Division of Campus Park
and Planning

Activity day: Making firefly
collage

Teddy bear topiary
in the sunburst area

The landscape architects for the project were Jeffrey Kacos and Deborah Kinney, both staff at the Division of Campus Park and Planning at the university. Taylor collaborated extraordinarily well with the landscape architects throughout the design process. Changes and modifications to the design could be made daily because the three key staff persons worked together. Taylor was later named curator of the 4-H Children's Garden and adjunct faculty member in the Horticulture Department.

DESIGN

Fifty-six different thematic areas were created within six main gardens. These gardens display plants that children can relate to in their daily lives. The attention to details throughout the garden provides children countless opportunities for exploration and discovery. Themes from children's literature and popular foods were adapted in the gardens.

Plants and special features of the theme gardens

Theme garden	Plants and special features
A Sunburst	
1 Imagination Grows Garden	Motto for 4-H Garden is on a bronze plaque at the main entrance area: "In a child's garden, imagination grows"
2 Story Book Garden	Plants and items related to children's literature
3 Animal Garden	Giant topiary teddy bears; plants with animal names
4 Crayon Color Garden	Plants with names of crayon colors
5 Sunburst Terrace	Vegetables mixed with flowers
6 Imagination Arbor	Colorful arbor with a sign that says, "Welcome to the 4-H Children's Garden"; tribute to Liberty Hyde Bailey through the arbor
7 ABC Kinder-Garten	Annuals and perennials from *A* to *Z* in 26 planting blocks
8 Dwarfed Fruit Trees	Dwarfed fruit trees
9 Train Garden	Garden railway, miniature plants, and rock bridges
B Amphitheater	
10 Enchanted Garden	Plants associated with mythical creatures in literature and many cultures
11 Health for Better Living Garden	Vegetables with the top nine rated by the U.S. Department of Agriculture for good health
12 Creation Station	Hands-on area for garden craft and cooking/eating activities
13 Kitchen Garden	A mix of minivegetables and culinary herbs
14 Amphitheater	A demonstration plaza stage area
15 Cottage Garden	Minivegetables

Rainbow area with butterfly area in foreground

Small World Globe

THE MAGIC OF CHILDREN'S GARDENS

Milk, Meat, and
Wool Garden

Theme garden	Plants and special features
C Rainbow	
16 Cereal Bowl Garden	Plants found in cereal; the millstone represents the Cereal Bowl
17 Meat, Milk, and Wool Garden	Plants that provide the food for farm animals; sheep sculpture for climbing
18 Pioneer Garden	Heirloom vegetables
19 International Garden	This display changes annually
20 African American Garden	Plants introduced by African Americans
21 Hispanic American Garden	Vegetables introduced from Central and South America
22 North American Indian Garden	Plants grown by the Indians before 1492
23 Asian American Garden	Plants introduced from Asia
24 Small World Globe	Globe identifies where the food comes from in the Rainbow gardens
25 Pot o' Gold	A giant pot o' gold of 'Gold Nugget' yellow marigolds
D Tree house	
26 Perfume Garden	Fragrant plants
27 Peter Rabbit Garden	Plants from Beatrix Potter's Peter Rabbit books
28 Little Prairie Garden	Prairie and meadow plants
29 Scent-sational Herb Garden	A potpourri of herbs and Chocolate Garden
30 Pizza Garden	Plants that make up pizza ingredients
31 Special Child's Garden	A raised bed for physically challenged children
32 Tree house	Northern Michigan white cedar tree house
E Butterfly	
33 Pharmacy Garden	Healing plants
34 Science Discovery Garden	New varieties of plants created by MSU researchers
35 4-H Granite Clover	The 4-H symbol and "heart, hands, health, head" are set in the pavement
36 Cloth and Color Garden	Plants for making and dying clothing
37 Butterfly Garden	Plants that attract butterflies
38 Scarecrow Garden	Scarecrows used by gardeners

Monet Bridge

Tree house

THE MAGIC OF CHILDREN'S GARDENS

Peter Rabbit Garden

Cereal Bowl Garden

Theme garden	Plants and special features
F Pond	
39 Monet Bridge	Replica of the bridge in Monet's garden in Giverny, France
40 Bog Garden	Plants that thrive in moist places
41 Merry-Go-Round Fountains	Children turn the swing gate to activate frogs spitting water into the pond
42 Magic Bubble Fountains	Young children touch the fountain near water's edge
43 The Pond and Water Garden	Water lilies and other aquatic plants
44 Performing Plants Garden	Plants that are activated when touched
G Maze	
45 Rock Garden	Rocks of rock types and minerals including Michigan's Petoskey stone
46 Dinosaur Garden	Plants that survived the dinosaur era; the Dino Dig area
47 Maze Overlook	A higher view of the garden from here
48 Sundial Garden	Plants around sundial demonstrate biorhythm; four-o'clocks are planted at the 4 o'clock mark
49 Wild Garden	Michigan native and introduced wildflowers, some commonly planted along roadsides
50 Alice in Wonderland Maze	A keyhole in a door with views to the garden, stone features from the books, and a gazebo/tea house
51 The Secret Garden	A door to the Secret Garden and a statue of Mary Lennox
H Chimes	
52 Garden of Delight	A celebration of herbs through the centuries
53 Dance Chimes	Plants with musical names
54 Jack and the Giant's Garden	Biggest-plants display
55 Observation Tower	A play structure to climb on to see a spectacular view of the garden
56 All-Aboard Train	A play structure to climb on to see adjacent train tracks

Perfume Garden

CONCLUSION

The Horticulture Gardens, including the 4-H Children's Garden, were officially opened and dedicated on August 11, 1993. This children's garden was the first of its kind in the United States and attracted thousands of visitors. The world of public gardens took notice and began to realize the need to reach out to a wider, younger audience and then began to adapt ideas from the 4-H Children's Garden.

Dinosaur Garden

Michigan 4-H Children's Garden at Michigan State University

Plants in the garden

A Sunburst area

1 Imagination Grows Garden

Celosia cristata 'Dwarf Coral Garden Mix' (cockscomb)
Cleome hassleriana 'Violet Queen' (spider flower)
Cosmos bipinnatus 'Sunset' (cosmos)
Festuca glauca (blue fescue grass)
Lantana spp. (lantana)
Stachys byzantina 'Big Ears' (lamb's ear)
Salvia farinacea 'Fairy Queen' (scarlet sage)
Salvia splendens 'Bonfire' (flowering sage)
Tagetes erecta 'Moonsong Deep Orange' (marigold)

2 Storybook Garden

Antirrhinum majus 'Black Prince', 'Cinderella', 'Magic Carpet' (snapdragon)
Calceolaria × *herbeohybrida* 'Cinderella Mix' (pocketbook plant)
Helianthus annuus 'Teddy Bear' (sunflower)
Hemerocallis 'Fairy Tale', 'Winnie-the-Pooh' (daylilies)
Lobularia maritima 'Wonderland Blue' (alyssum)
Rudbeckia hirta 'Chim Chiminee' (black-eyed Susan)
Zinnia elegans 'Enchantress', 'Persian Carpet', 'Thumbelina' (zinnia)

3 Teddy Bears and Animal Garden

Amaranthus gangeticus 'Elephant Head' (amaranth)
Antirrhinum majus 'Brighton Rock', 'Night and Day' (snapdragon)
Cleome hassleriana, 'Rose Queen', 'Violet Queen', 'White Queen' (spider flower)
Coleus cvs. (coleus)
Helianthus annuus 'Teddy Bear' (sunflower)
Lagurus ovatus (bunny tails)
Leonotis leonurus (lion's tail)
Stachys byzantina 'Big Ears' (lamb's ear)

Lagurus ovatus (bunny tails)

4 Crayon Color Garden

Centaurea cyanus 'Blue' (cornflower)
Cucurbita pepo 'Jack Be Little' (pumpkin)
Dianthus caryophyllus 'Carnation Pink' (carnation)
Fragaria vesca 'Pink Panda' (strawberry)
Lavandula angustifolia (lavender)
Solidago rigida 'Peter Pan' (goldenrod)

5 Sunburst Terrace Garden

Cosmos bipinnatus 'Sunset' (cosmos)
Salvia splendens 'Bonfire' (scarlet sage)
Tagetes erecta 'Inca Gold' (marigold)

6 Imagination Arbor

Ipomoea purpurea 'Kniolas Black Knight' (morning glory)
Lablab purpureus (hyacinth bean)

Liberty Hyde Bailey tribute

Cornus sericea 'Baileyi' (redtwig dogwood)
Dianthus plumarius (cottage pink)

7 ABC Kinder-Garten

A: Alyssum (*Alyssum* 'Royal Carpet')
B: Begonia (*Begonia* spp.)
C: Cockscomb (*Celosia cristata* 'Dwarf Coral Garden Mix')
D: Daisy (*Bellis perennis*)
E: Eyeball plant (*Acmella oleraceae*)
F: Four-o'clocks (*Mirabilis jalapa* 'Stars and Stripes')
G: Geranium (*Pelagonium* cvs.)
H: Hollyhock (*Malva sylvestris* 'Zebrina')
I: Iris (*Iris* cvs.)
J: Jacob's ladder (*Polemonium caeruleum*)
K: Kohlrabi (*Brassica oleracea* 'Purple Vienna')
L: Lovage (*Levisticum officinale*)
M: Marigold (*Tagetes patula* 'Bonanza Mix')
N: Nasturtium (*Tropaeolum majus* 'Ladybird Cream')
O: Ornamental grass
P: Petunia (*Petunia* spp.)
Q: Quinoa (*Chenopodium quinoa* 'Brightest Brilliant Rainbow')
R: Rose (*Rosa* cvs.)
S: Sage (*Salvia splendens* 'Bonfire')
T: Thyme (*Thymus* spp.)
U: Umbrella plant (*Schefflera* spp.)
V: Verbena (*Verbena officinalis*)
W: Wormwood (*Artemisia* spp.)
X: Xeranthemum (*Xeranthemum annuum* 'Double Mix')
Y: Yarrow (*Achillea millefolium*)
Z: Zinnia (*Zinnia elegans* 'Benary's Giant')

9 Train Garden

Celosia cristata 'Dwarf Coral Garden Mix' (cockscomb)

Cosmos bipinnatus 'Sunset' (cosmos)
Salvia splendens 'Bonfire' (scarlet sage)
Tagetes patula 'Janie Flame' (marigold)
Tropaeolum majus 'Whirlybird Blend' (nasturtium)

B Amphitheater area

10 Enchanted Garden

Anthemis arvensis (chamomile)
Antirrhinum majus 'Black Prince', Cinderella Mix (snapdragon)
Calceolaria × *herbeohybrida* 'Cinderella Mix' (pocketbook plant)
Cleome hassleriana 'Rose Queen' (spider flower)
Convallaria majalis (lily-of-the-valley)
Corylus avellana 'Contorta' (contorted hazel)
Cucurbita maxima 'Cinderella', 'Rogue Vif D'Etampes' (pumpkin)
Dicentra spectabilis (bleeding heart)
Gypsophila paniculata (baby's breath)
Iberis sempervirens 'Dwarf Fairy Mix' (candy tuft)
Lagurus ovatus (bunny tails)
Linaria maroccana 'Fairy Bouquet' (Moroccan toadflax)
Nicotiana × *sanderae* 'Sensation Daylite Mix' (flowering tobacco)
Nigella damascene (love-in-a-mist)
Proboscidea louisianica (unicorn plant)
Salvia farinacea 'Fairy Queen' (flowering sage)
Scabiosa columbaria 'Black Knight' (sweet scabious)
Zinnia elegans 'Enchantress', 'Thumbelina' (zinnia)

11 Health for Better Living Garden

Abelmoschus esculentus 'Jambalaya' (okra)
Allium fistulosum 'Evergreen Bunching' (onion)
Beta vulgaris 'Bright Lights' (Swiss chard)
Beta vulgaris 'Dark Red Detroit' (beet)
Brassica oleracea 'Early Jersey Wakefield' (cabbage)
Brassica oleracea 'Early White Vienna' (kohlrabi)
Brassica oleracea 'Vates' (collard)
Chenopodium quinoa 'Brightest Brilliant Rainbow' (quinoa)
Daucus carota 'Kinko' (carrot)
Lactuca sativa 'Red Romaine' (red romaine lettuce)
Raphanus sativus 'Cherry Belle' (radish)

12 Creation Station

Actinidia kolomikta (kiwi)
Aesculus parviflora (bottlebrush)
Ampelopsis brevipedunculata (porcelain vine)
Cobaea scandens (cup-and-saucer vine)

Cassia didymobotrya (popcorn flower)

13 Kitchen Garden

Basil Box

Ocimum americanum 'Lime' (lime basil)
Ocimum basilicum 'Cinnamon' (cinnamon basil)
Ocimum basilicum 'Italian Large Leaf' (Italian large-leaf basil)
Ocimum basilicum 'Mexican Spice' (Mexican spice basil)
Ocimum basilicum 'Minette' (dwarf bush basil)
Ocimum basilicum 'Purple Ruffles' (purple basil)
Ocimum basilicum 'Thai' (Thai basil)
Ocimum citriodorum 'Lemon' (lemon basil)

Edible Flower Box

Begonia spp. (begonia)
Borago spp. (borage)
Calendula spp. (pot marigold)
Centaurea cyanus 'Jubilee Gem' (cornflower)
Chrysanthemum elegans 'Sunset' (chrysanthemum)
Helianthus annuus 'Dwarf Sensation' (sunflower)
Tagetes patula 'Janie Flame' (marigold)
Tropaeolum spp. (nasturtium)

Soup Box

Abelmoschus esculentus 'Jambalaya' (okra)
Allium fistulosum 'Evergreen Bunching' (onion)
Beta vulgaris 'Bright Lights' (Swiss chard)
Brassica oleracea 'Lacinato' (dinosaur kale)
Brassica oleracea 'Vates' (collard)
Brassica rapa 'Purple Top White Globe' (turnip)
Daucus carota 'Kinko' (carrot)
Origanum majorana (sweet marjoram)
Petroselinum crispum var. *neapolitanum* (Italian parsley)
Phaseolus vulgaris 'Henderson's Bush' (bean)
Pisum sativum 'Burpeeana Early' (pea)
Solanum lycopersicum 'Tip Top' (tomato)

14 Amphitheater

Lysimachia nummularia 'Aurea' (golden moneywort)
Thymus praecox 'Coccineus' (creeping red flowered thyme)

15 Cottage Garden

Antirrhinum majus 'Night and Day' (snapdragon)
Aquilegia canadensis 'McKana Giants' (columbine)
Centaurea cyanus 'Blue Boy' (bachelor's button)
Chenopodium quinoa 'Brightest Brilliant Rainbow' (quinoa)
Cleome hassleriana 'Violet Queen' (spider flower)
Delphinium cvs. (larkspur)
Hesperis matronalis (dame's rocket)
Heuchera cvs. (coral bells)
Houttuynia cordata 'Chameleon' (chameleon plant)
Impatiens balsamina Bush Flowered Mix (balsam)
Ipomoea purpurea 'Kniolas Black Knight' (morning glory)
Lamium maculatum (deadnettle)
Lathyrus odorata Knee High Fragrant Mix, Royal Mix (sweet pea)
Limonium statice 'Forever Blend', 'Twilight Lavender' (statice)
Lobularia maritima 'Royal Carpet' (alyssum)
Lupinus polyphyllus Minarette Mix (dwarf lupine)
Matthiola incana 'Giant Excelsior Mix' (stock)
Myosotis sylvatica (forget-me-not)
Nicotiana × sanderae 'Sensation Daylite Mix' (flowering tobacco)
Nigella damascene (love-in-a-mist)
Platycodon grandifloras (balloon flower)
Thalictrum cvs. (meadow rue)
Veronica spicata 'Sunny Border Blue' (speedwell)
Zinnia elegans 'Candy Cane' (zinnia)

C Rainbow area

16 Cereal Bowl Garden

Avena sativa (oats)
Beta vulgaris (sugar beet)
Fagopyrum esculentum (buckwheat)
Triticum aestivum 'Winter Red' (wheat)
Zea mays 'Honey and Cream' (corn)

17 Meat, Milk, and Wool Garden

Medicago sativa 'Webfoot' (alfalfa)
Medicago spp. (clover)
Trifolium pratense (red clover)

18 Pioneer Garden

Amaranthus caudatus (love-lies-bleeding)
Beta vulgaris 'Dark Red Detroit' (beet)

Calendula officinalis Pacific Beauty Mix, 'Pink Surprise' (pot marigold)
Cucurbita pepo 'Black Beauty' (zucchini)
Cucurbita moschata 'Early Butternut' (squash)
Cucurbita pepo 'Lady Godivia' (pumpkin)
Lablab purpureus (hyacinth bean)
Phaseolus coccineus 'Painted Lady' (scarlet runner bean)
Solanum lycopersicum 'Golden Gem' (tomato)

19 International Garden (theme changes annually)

Antirrhinum majus 'Black Prince' (snapdragon)
Calendula officianalis 'Indian Prince' (pot marigold)
Cleome hassleriana 'Rose Queen', 'Violet Queen' (spider flower)
Lobelia erinus 'Crystal Palace' (garden lobelia)
Salvia farinacea 'Fairy Queen' (flowering sage)
Limonium aureum 'Royal Purple' (statice)
Tropaeolum minor 'King Theodore' (nasturtium)
Zinnia elegans 'Royal Purple', 'Scarlet King' (zinnia)

20 African American Garden

Abelmoschus esculentus 'Jambalaya' (okra)
Amaranthus cvs. (amaranth)
Arachis hypogara 'Early Spanish' (peanut)
Brassica oleracea 'Vates' (collard)
Citrullus lanatus 'Moon and Stars' (watermelon)
Matricaria chamomilla (German chamomile)
Osteospermum ecklonis, 'Sky and Ice' (African daisy)
Pelargonium cvs. (geranium)
Solanum lycopersicum 'Sun Sugar' (tomato)
Tropaeolum minor 'Out of Africa' (nasturtium)

21 Hispanic American Garden

Capsicum annuum 'California Wonder', 'Early Jalapeno' (pepper)
Chenopodium ambrosiodes (epazote)
Coriandrum sativum 'Slo-Bolt' (cilantro)
Melothria scabra 'Mexican Sour' (gherkin)
Ocimum americanum 'Lime' (lime basil)
Ocimum basilicum 'Cinnamon' (cinnamon basil)
Ocimum basilicum 'Mexican Spice' (Mexican spice basil)

Ocimum citriodorum 'Lemon' (lemon basil))
Persea americana (avocado)
Physalis ixocarpa (pineapple tomatillo)
Tithonia rotundifolia 'Mexican Torch' (Mexican sunflower)
Solanum tuberosum 'All Blue' (potato)
Solanum lycopersicum 'Matt's Wild' (tomato)
Zea mays 'Honey and Cream' (corn)
Zinnia elegans 'Giant Lime' (zinnia)

22 North American Indian Garden

Cucurbita pepo 'Black Beauty' (zucchini)
Cucurbita pepo 'Lady Godiva' (pumpkin)
Helianthus annuus 'Moulin Rouge' (sunflower)
Helianthus tuberosus (Jerusalem artichoke)
Lagenaria siceraria (long handled dipper gourd)
Nicotiana rustica 'Hopi Tobacco', 'Wild Aztec' (flowering tobacco)
Phaseolus coccineus 'Painted Lady' (scarlet runner bean)
Rudbeckia hirta 'Cherokee Sunset' (black-eyed Susan)
Solanum lycopersicum 'Cherokee Purple' (tomato)
Zea mays 'Honey and Cream', 'Hopi Blue Dent' (corn)

23 Asian American Garden

Brassica chinensis (purple bok choy)
Brassica rapa 'Green Rocket' (Chinese cabbage)
Mizuna 'Kyoto' (Asian greens)
Ocimum basilicum 'Thai' (Thai basil)
Oryza sativa (upland rice)
Perilla frutescens (red shiso)
Vigna unguiculata 'Red Noodle' (bean)
Zea mays (baby corn)

24 Small World Globe

Gomphrena globosa, 'Strawberry Fields' (globe amaranth)

25 Pot o' Gold

Tagetes erecta 'Inca Gold', 'Gold Nugget' (marigold)

D Tree house area

26 Perfume Garden

Aloysia citrodor (lemon verbena)
Asarum canadense (ginger)
Cassia didmobotrya (popcorn plant)
Lavendula spp. (lavender)
Limonium sinuatum 'Forever Blend', 'Royal Purple' (statice)
Lobularia maritime 'Royal Carpet' (alyssum)
Lythyrus oderata 'Knee High', Fragrant Mix (sweet pea)
Matthiola incana 'Giant Excelsior Mix' (brompton stock)
Melissa officinalis (lemon balm)
Mentha × piperita (peppermint)
Mentha suaveolens (pineapple mint)
Nicotiana × sanderae 'Sensation Daylite Mix' (flowering tobacco)
Pelargonium cvs. (scented geranium)
Rosmarinus officinalis (rosemary)
Salvia leucantha (Mexican sage)

27 Peter Rabbit Garden

Beta vulgaris 'McGregor's Favorite' (beet)
Borago officinalis (borage)
Brassica oleracea 'Early Jersey Wakefield' (cabbage)
Brassica 'Early White Vienna' (kohlrabi)
Daucus 'Kinko' (carrot)
Gossypium hirsutum (cotton)
Lactuca sativa 'Red Romaine' (red romaine lettuce)
Lagurus ovatus (bunny tail)
Lavendula cvs. (lavender)
Matricaria chamomilla (German chamomile)
Mentha cvs. (mint)
Raphinus 'Long Scarlet' (radish)

Bird's-eye perspective of theme gardens

28 Little Prairie Garden

Asclepias tuberosa (butterfly milk-weed)
Geum triflorum (prairie smoke)
Hieracium venosum (rattlesnake weed)
Monarda fistulosa (bee balm)
Ratibida pinnata (yellow coneflower)
Rudbeckia hirta (black-eyed Susan)
Senecio pauperculus (ragwort)
Solidago canadensis (Canadian goldenrod)
Veronicastrum virginicum (Culver's root)

29 Scent-sational Herb Garden

Allium schoenoprasum (chives)
Allium tuberosum (garlic chives)
Althaea officinalis (marshmallow)
Anethum graveolens (dill)
Anthriscus cerefolium (chervil)
Artemisia dracunculus (tarragon)
Calendula officinalis 'Apricots and Oranges' (pot marigold)
Carum carvi (caraway)
Coriandrum sativum 'Slo-Bolt' (cilantro)
Foeniculum vulgaris (fennel)
Levisticum officinale (lovage)
Mentha cvs. (mint)
Ocimum americanum 'Lime' (lime basil)
Ocimum basilicum 'Cinnamon' (cinnamon basil)
Ocimum basilicum 'Italian Large Leaf' (Italian large-leaf basil)
Ocimum basilicum 'Mexican Spice' (Mexican spice basil)
Ocimum basilicum 'Minette' (dwarf bush basil)
Ocimum basilicum 'Purple Ruffles' (purple basil)
Ocimum basilicum 'Thai' (Thai basil)
Origanum majorana (sweet marjoram)
Petroselinum crispum var. *neapolitanum* (Italian parsley)
Salvia cvs. (sage)
Satureja Montana (winter savory)
Symphytum sofficinale (comfrey)
Thymus × citriodorus 'Aureus' (golden thyme)
Thymus cvs. (thyme)

Chocolate Garden

Aquilegia 'Chocolate Soldier' (columbine)
Berlandiera lyatra (chocolate daisy)
Centaurea moschata 'Dairy Maid' (sweet sultan)
Helianthus annuus 'Choco Sun' (sunflower)
Ipomea nil 'Chocolate' (chocolate morning glory)

Helianthus annuus 'Moulin Rouge' (sunflower)

Pelargonium quercifolium (chocolate geranium)
Sedum cvs. 'Chocolate Drop' (stonecrop)

30 Pizza Garden

Allium fistulosum 'Evergreen Bunching' (onion)
Allium sativum (garlic)
Allium tuberosum (garlic chives)
Ananas comosus (pineapple)
Capsicum annuum 'Early Jalapeno' (pepper)
Ocimum basilicum 'Italian Large Leaf' (Italian large-leaf basil)
Origanum vulgare (Greek oregano)
Solanum lycopersicum 'Tip Top' (tomato)
Triticum aestivum 'Hard Red' (wheat)
Tropaeolum majus 'Milkmaid' (nasturtium)

31 Special Child's Garden

Antirrhinum majus 'Night and Day' (snapdragon)
Beta vulgaris 'Bright Lights' (Swiss chard)
Brassica rapa 'Purple Top White Globe' (turnip)
Calendula officinalis 'Apricots and Oranges' (pot marigold)
Celosia cristata Coral Garden Mix (cockscomb)
Helianthus annuus 'Teddy Bear' (sunflower)
Lagurus ovatus (bunny tails)
Mimosa pudica (sensitive plant)
Raphanus sativus (daikon radish)
Solanum aethiopicum (pumpkin-on-a-stick)
Tagetes erecta 'Moonsong Deep Orange' (marigold)

32 Tree house

Mentha × piperita f. *citrata* 'Chocolate' (chocolate mint)

E Butterfly area

33 Pharmacy Garden

Acmella oleacea (eyeball plant)
Aloe vera (aloe vera)
Calendula officianalis Pacific Beauty Mix, 'Pink Surprise' (pot marigold)
Echinacea purpurea 'Primadonna Deep Rose' (purple coneflower)
Eschscholzia californica (California poppy)
Eucalyptus spp. (eucalyptus)
Hypericum perforatum (St. Johnswort)
Matricaria chamomilla (German chamomile)
Mentha pulegium (pennyroyal)
Plectranthus purpuratus (Vicks plant)
Reseda odorata 'True Machet' (mignonette)
Rumex crispus (curled dock)
Taxus canadensis (yew)

34 Science Discovery Garden

Beta vulgaris 'Dark Red', 'Light Red', 'Yellow' (Swiss chard)
Fragaria ananassa 'Allstar' (strawberry)
Phaseolus vulgaris 'Capri Cran', 'Henderson's Bush', 'Jaguar Black', 'Matterhorn', 'Sedona Pink' (bean)
Solanum tuberosum 'Michigan Purple' (potato)
Zea mays 'Colored', 'Science', 'Silver Queen' (corn)
Zinnia elegans 'Spartan Rainbow' (zinnia)

36 Color and Cloth Garden

Alcea rosea 'Nigra' (hollyhock)
Allium fistulosum 'Evergreen Bunching' (onion)
Amaranthus cruentus 'Hopi Red Dye' (amaranth)
Anthemis tinctoria (golden marguerite)
Boehmeria nivea (ramie)
Dipsacus sativus (fuller's teasel)
Galium verum (yellow bedstraw)
Gossypium hirsutum (cotton)
Helianthus annus 'Hopi Black Dye' (sunflower)
Isatis tinctoria (woad)
Linum usitatissimum (flax)
Luffa aegyptica (luffa sponge gourd)
Lycopus europaeus (gypsywort)
Rubia tinctorum (madder)

37 Butterfly Garden

Anethum graveolens 'Vulgare' (dill)
Asclepias incarnata 'Cinderella' (milkweed)
Asclepias curassavica 'Red Butterfly' (milkweed)
Cleome hassleriana 'Rose Queen', 'Violet Queen', 'White Queen' (spider flower)

Scarecrow Garden

Echinacea purpurea 'Magnus' (purple coneflower)
Foeniculum vulgare 'Florence' (fennel)
Heliopsis cvs. (sunflower)
Heliotrope cvs. (heliotrope)
Hemerocallis cvs. (daylily)
Lantana cvs. (lantana)
Lavendula angustifolia 'Hidcote' (lavender)
Pentas cvs. (penta)
Sedum spectabile 'Autumn Joy' (showy stonecrop)
Verbena bonariensis (vervain)
Zinnia elegans 'Benary's Giant' (zinnia)

38 Scarecrow Garden

Coreopsis cvs. (tickseed)
Eschscholzia californica (California poppy)
Helianthus annuus 'Teddy Bear' (sunflower)
Juncus effuses 'Twister' (common rush)
Lagenaria siceraria (apple gourd)
Leonotis leonurus (lion's tail)
Papaver orientale 'Oriental Pizzicato' (poppy)
Rudbeckia occidentalis 'Green Wizard' (western coneflower)

F Pond area

39 Monet Bridge

Centaurea cyanus 'Blue Boy' (bachelor's button)
Helianthus annuus 'Monet's Palette' (sunflower)
Lagurus ovatus (bunny tails)
Lobularia maritima 'Wonderland Blue' (alyssum)
Perovskia atriplicifolia (Russian sage)
Tagetes erecta 'Moonsong Deep Orange' (marigold)
Tropaeolum majus 'Whirlybird Blend' (nasturtium)
Zinnia elegans 'Candy Cane', 'Royal Purple' (zinnia)

40 Bog Garden

Begonia cvs. (begonia)
Chelone glabra (turtle head)
Coleus cvs. (coleus)
Convallaria majalis (lily-of-the-valley)
Hosta cvs. (hosta)
Salix alba 'Snake' (willow)
Tiarella cordifolia 'Candy Striper' (foamflower)

43 Pond and Water Garden

Cyperus spp. (sedge)
Nymphaea cvs. (water lily)

44 Performing Plants Garden

Cardiospermum halicacabum (love-in-a-puff)
Dictamnus albus (gas plant)
Gomphocarpus physocarpus (fur balls)
Impatiens balsamina Bush Flowered Mix (balsam)
Mimosa pudica (sensitive plant)
Mirabilis jalapa 'Broken Colors' (four-o'clock)
Phaseolus vulgaris 'Yin Yang', 'Snow Cap' (bean)
Platycodon grandiflorus (balloon flower)
Silphium lacinatum (compass plant)
Silphium perfoliatum (cup plant)
Sorghum bicolor (broom corn)
Vigna unguiculata 'Pretzel Bean' (cowpea)
Vigna unguiculata ssp. *sesquipedalis* (yardlong bean)
Zea mays var. *everta* 'Strawberry' (popcorn)

G Maze area

45 Rock Garden

Opuntia spp. (prickly pear cactus)
Sedum cvs. (stonecrop)
Sempervivum tectorum (hen and chicks)
Verbascum bombyciferum 'Artic Summer', 'Polar Summer' (mullein)
Yucca latifolia (yucca)

Bellis perennis (daisy)

46 Dinosaur Garden

Amaranthus gangeticus 'Elephant Head' (amaranth)
Brassica oleracea (dinosaur kale)
Equisetum arvense (common horsetail)
Equisetum hyemale (rough horsetail)
Euphorbia spp. (spurge)
Ginkgo biloba (ginkgo)
Lagenaria siceraria 'Caveman's Club', 'Dinosaur' (gourd)
Portulaca grandiflora 'Double Mix' (rose moss)
Tracheophyta spp. (fern)

48 Sundial Garden

Antirrhinum majus 'Night and Day' (snapdragon)
Coreopsis grandiflora 'Early Sunrise' (tickseed)
Cosmos bipinnatus 'Daydream', 'Sunset' (cosmos)
Chrysanthemum carinatum 'Sunset' (chrysanthemum)
Gallaridia × *grandiflora* 'Arizona Sun' (blanket flower)
Helianthus annuus 'Giganteus' (sunflower)
Ipomoea purpurea Celestial Mix (morning glory)
Limonium aureum 'Twilight Lavender' (statice)
Matthiola longipetala 'Starlight Sensation' (night-scented stock)
Mirabilis jalapa 'Tea Time' (four-o'clock)

Tropaeolum majus (nasturtium)

Oenothera glazioviana, 'Tina James' Magic' (evening primrose)
Sedum spectabile 'Autumn Joy' (showy stonecrop)
Tagetes erecta 'Moonlight', 'Moonsong Deep Orange' (marigold)
Tropaeolum majus (nasturtium)

49 Wild Garden

Arisaema atrorubens (jack-in-the-pulpit)
Daucus carota (Queen Anne's lace)
Erythronium americanum (adder's tongue)
Eupatorium perfoliatum (boneset)
Eupatorium purpureum (Joe-Pye weed)
Hibiscus palustris (rose mallow)
Lupinus perennis (lupine)
Sanguisorba canadensis (Canadian burnet)
Symphyotrichum novae-angliae (New England aster)
Trillium grandiflorum (trillium)

Antirrhinum majus (snapdragon)

51 The Secret Garden

Amaranthus caudatus (love-lies-bleeding)
Anemone spp. (wind flower)
Antirrhinum majus 'Brighton Rock' (snapdragon)
Aquilegia spp. (columbine)
Cleome hassleriana 'Rose Queen', 'Violet Queen', 'White Queen' (spider flower)
Cosmos bipinnatus 'Sunset' (cosmos)
Heuchera spp. (coral bells)
Impatiens spp. (true impatiens)
Ipomoea purpurea 'Kniolas Black Knight' (morning glory)
Limonium aureum 'Forever Blend', 'Twilight Lavender' (statice)
Myosotis sylvatica (forget-me-not)
Polygonum aubertii (silver lace vine)
Reseda odorata 'True Machet' (mignonette)
Rosa spp. (miniature rose)
Salvia farinacea 'Fairy Queen' (flowering sage)
Salvia splendens 'Bonfire' (flowering sage)
Zinnia elegans 'Whirligig' (zinnia)

52 Garden of Delight

Calendula officinalis 'Pacific Beauty Mix' (pot marigold)
Melissa officinalis (lemon balm)
Ocimum basilicum 'Italian Large Leaf' (Italian large-leaf basil)
Origanum majorana (sweet marjoram)
Origanum vulgare (oregano)
Pelargonium cvs. (scented geranium)

H Chimes area

53 Dance Chimes

Arundo donax (giant reed)
Calendula officinalis 'Radio' (pot marigold)
Cosmos bipinnatus Sonata Dwarf Mix (cosmos)
Cucurbita pepo (spinning or dancing gourd)
Helianthus annuus 'Dwarf Music Box' (sunflower)
Tagetes patula Disco Mix (marigold)

54 Jack and the Giant's Garden

Colocasia esculenta (elephant ears)
Musa spp. (banana tree)
Phaseolus coccineus 'Scarlet Runner' (bean)

Sunflower House

Helianthus annuus 'Cherry Rose', 'Jolly Joker', 'Kong', 'Monet's Palette', 'Moulin Rouge', 'Teddy Bear' (sunflower)

56 All-Aboard-Train, by Bouge Street entrance

Hostas cvs. (hosta)
Ipomoea cvs. (morning glory)
Perennials (selected varieties)
Annuals (selected varieties in window box)

Sunflower Maze

The Secret Garden

Michigan 4-H Children's Garden

Michigan State University Horticulture Gardens

1066 Bogue Street, East Lansing, MI 48824

517-355-5191 ext. 1-349   http://4hgarden.cowplex.com

Opening date: August 11, 1993

Project size: 0.7 acre (0.3 hectare) within 14-acre (6-hectare) Michigan State University Horticulture Gardens

Design and Construction Team

Michigan State University:

    Child Development Laboratory school director: Alice Whiren

    Landscape architects from Division of Campus Park and Planning: Jeff Kacos, Deb Kinney

    Michigan 4-H Children's Garden curator and horticulturist: Jane L. Taylor

Superintendent of site construction: Dennis Hansen of Campus Park and Planning

Manufacturer of play equipment: Kompan

Current Contacts

Curator: Norm Lownds

Education coordinator: Jessica Wright

Interviews and Personal Communications

Norm Lownds, October 7, 2015; Jane Taylor, September 21, 2015; Jessica Wright, September 24, 2015

Aerial view of the Morton Arboretum
Children's Garden

Morton Arboretum Children's Garden

LISLE, ILLINOIS

GOAL

The 4-acre (1.6-hectare) Children's Garden was built within the 1,700-acre (688-hectare) Morton Arboretum, a primarily natural landscape and collections-based institution engaged in global research and conservation efforts. The goal of the Children's Garden is to teach children about plants and nature through play. The design of the garden integrates built elements, exhibits, and interpretive signs. These features are intended to facilitate a special learning experience primarily through self-guided interpretation. Information is also included throughout the garden for the benefit of adult visitors.

CONCEPT

Morton Arboretum Children's Garden features ten plant-themed outdoor garden rooms that make up two main garden areas—the Backyard Discovery gardens for younger children and toddlers and the Adventure Woods for children ages six to ten—linked by a central plaza where program activities are held. "The idea is that children and suburban families are divorced from nature, but they are not afraid of their own backyard. So we incorporated elements that children would see at their own house. The front section, more heavily designed, was created for children to be comfortable. As the children mature, they can go into the woods, and from there, they can head out into nature," explains Herb Schaal, landscape architect of the garden.

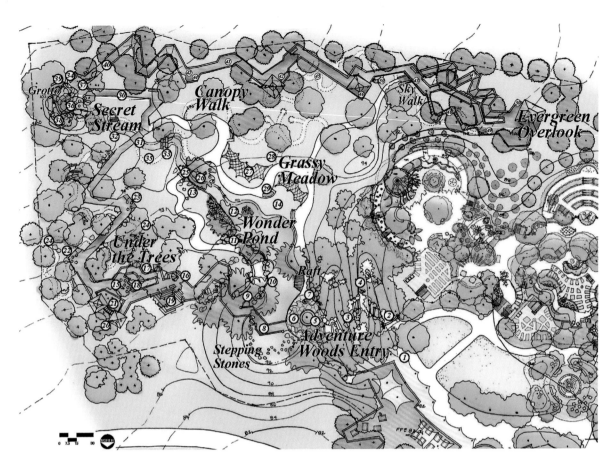

Adventure Woods plan

Adventure Woods

Entry
1 Orientation kiosk
2 Rustic gateway
3 Stone steps
4 ADA ramp
5 Seat wall

Wonder Pond
6 Orientation plaza
7 Orientation panel
8 Boardwalk
9 Ramp down to underwater viewing
10 Touch port
11 Underwater viewing
12 Beaver lodge/dam
13 Beaver stumps
14 Grassy meadow

Under the Trees
15 Periscope
16 Tot tower
17 Treetop towers
18 Amphitheater
19 Tree canopy interpretation
20 Forest houses
21 Rope bridges
22 Sighting scopes/seating
23 Activity station
24 Rabbit trails

Grassy Meadow
25 Bridge
26 Secret station
27 Net crawl
28 Path to Burrow Bubbles
29 Parent seating

Secret Stream
30 Boardwalk
31 Bridge
32 Riparian plants
33 Log crossing
34 Seating
35 Grassy rabbit trail
36 Grotto/stream source
37 Fossils
38 Steps to top
39 Ramp to top
40 Ramp to Canopy Walk

Canopy Walk
41 Canopy Walk
42 Booster stumps
43 Interpretive panels
44 Cantilevered niche
45 Rabbit trails

Evergreen Overlook
46 Activity station shelter
47 Ramp down
48 Sky walk
49 Scopes
50 Stairs down

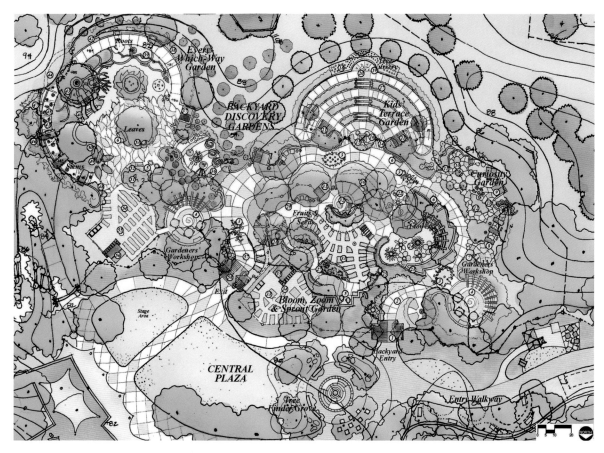

Backyard Discovery gardens plan

Backyard Discovery gardens

Entry/path

1 Trellis house
2 Backyard gardens
.3 Plant hoppers

Facilitated spaces

4 Gardener's workshop
5 Activity stations
6 Activity carts

Curiosity Garden

7 Shadow wall
8 View tunnel
9 Playhouse
10 Touch tank
11 Touch pond
12 Sensory gardens
13 Rubbing station

Kids' Terrace Garden

14 Garden tool gate
15 Windmill

16 Drinking fountain
17 Garden plots
18 Tree nursery
19 Birthday trees
20 Sundial
21 Tool storage

Bloom, Zoom, and Sprout Garden

22 Entry area

Flowers area

23 Flower gardens
24 Pollen movers activity
25 Flower ID station
26 Flower rubbing station

Fruits and Seeds area

27 Fruits and seeds gardens
28 Fruits and seeds ID station
29 Seed dispersal activity

30 Fruit and seed rubbing station
31 Shelter
32 Sprouting seeds activity

Growing gardens

33 Garden plots
34 Water spout
35 Garden shed

Every-Which-Way Garden

36 Entry area
37 Shelter

Roots area

38 Root gardens
39 Water play
40 Root climber and slides
41 Ramp
42 Root rubbing station
43 Deck
44 Root house

Stems area

45 Tree slices
46 Stem gardens
47 Stem rubbing station
48 Stem ID station

Leaves area

49 Leaf climber
50 Log drums
51 Leaf garden
52 Leaf rubbing station
53 Leaf ID station

Growing gardens

54 Garden plots
55 Water spout
56 Garden shed

Backyard exit

57 Backyard gardens
58 Trellis house

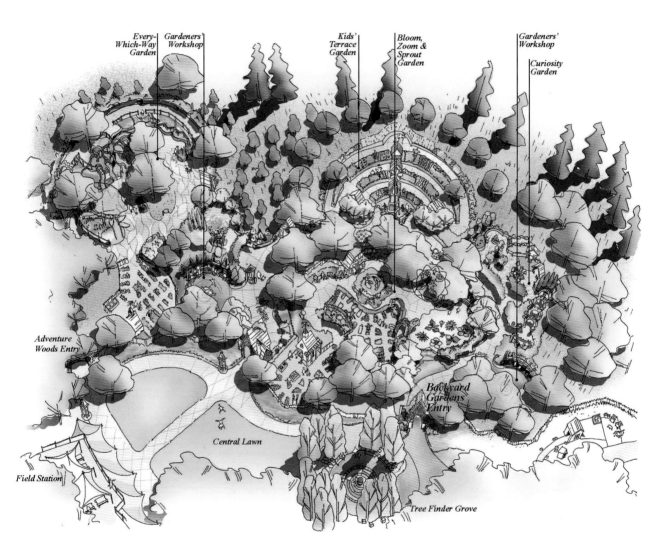

Every-
Which-Way
Garden

Gardeners'
Workshop

Kids'
Terrace
Garden

Bloom,
Zoom &
Sprout
Garden

Gardeners'
Workshop

Curiosity
Garden

Adventure
Woods Entry

Backyard
Gardens
Entry

Central Lawn

Field Station

Tree Finder Grove

Bird's-eye view of Backyard Discovery gardens

The intense process for creating the Children's Garden took two years to plan and three years for construction. The design team visited public gardens across the United States for a year, talking with experts to learn about best practices, which influenced their design. Inspired by great gardens such as the Everett Children's Adventure Garden at New York Botanical Garden and the Children's Garden at Brooklyn Botanic Garden, Morton Arboretum incorporated playful engagement with real plants and program spaces.

Since 4 acres (1.6 hectares) is a large garden for children, each themed area is a small pocket that creates a secure and safe setting. Children move from one outdoor room to the next. Each themed garden is designed with play structures, art forms, or signs that match the theme of that garden. According to Hannah Rennard, manager of curriculum and instruction, the purpose of the garden is to "introduce and teach children about trees and plants through interactive play and in more subtle ways."

Acorn climbing sculpture in Fruits and Seeds Gardens

Perhaps the most distinguishing feature of this garden is the interspersed creative play structures and art forms in the holistic landscape. "The arboretum built a variety of these elements into the design to attract families with children. Through play, our goal is to teach children about plants and nature," says Susan Jacobson, landscape architect at the Morton Arboretum. This garden is a lively place. It is animated and festive, with children participating in planting workshops. Children can run, jump, and climb their way through the garden. They immerse their little fingers and toes in the fountain, streams and ponds, and listen intently to the interpretive and interactive sound boxes. The idea is for children to absorb everything around them, learn about plants and nature, have fun, and develop a memorable and indelible experience.

Study model

Raised bed with tiles
Plant hopper
Garden fountain
Bird bath
Try-This Garden
Lath entry structure
Window box
Whimsical garden art
Gazing balls
Arch pergolas

Top and bottom: Main entrance at the
Morton Arboretum Children's Garden

Doghouse in Fruits
and Seeds Garden

DESIGN

The main entrance into the garden is through a gate and lath structure, which has an integral attendant counter and rain shelter.

Backyard Discovery gardens is an area for toddlers that presents familiar things they might recognize from their own backyards. These gardens encourage deeper exploration by children.

Backyard Discovery gardens

- **Curiosity Garden:** See a garden in new ways by using senses to explore plants. Children discover spitting frogs and a vine-covered trellis.
- **Bloom, Zoom, and Sprout Garden:** Learn how plants grow. Interpretive signs describe the role of seeds and their characteristics through imprints in the pavement. Larger-than-life musical flowers show the important parts of the flower.
- **Every-Which-Way Garden:** Learn that all plants have three basic parts (roots, stems, and leaves). They need sunlight, water, and air, and they change over time. Custom-fabricated giant tree roots allow children to play hide and seek in lifelike roots.
- **Windmill Garden:** Learn about food production and crop rotation.

Roots area in Every-Which-Way Garden

THE MAGIC OF CHILDREN'S GARDENS

Adventure Woods is the final destination of the garden and is designed for children ages six to ten. Adventure Woods presents the world beyond the backyard. The trees and plants in the Children's Garden reflect those of the arboretum at large and the rest of the natural world. Children find places to crawl, climb, and splash through the natural world. After entering Adventure Woods through the wooden arched entryway, children can continue along the path and explore the gardens.

Adventure Woods

- **Wonder Pond, Grotto, and Secret Stream:** Experience plants that grow in ponds and streams and the wildlife that is attracted to these environments while playing in the water.
- **Under the Trees:** Learn about trees and treetops while playing on elevated play structures.
- **Grassy Meadow:** Learn about indigenous grasses.
- **Evergreen Overlook:** Experience a mature conifer tree cover while winding up an ADA-accessible boardwalk to a viewing deck, shade structure, and play structure.

Study model

Grove   Field station   Maypole   Adventure Woods entry   Information kiosk   Colorful border

Growing area

Central plaza and tented veranda

THE MAGIC OF CHILDREN'S GARDENS

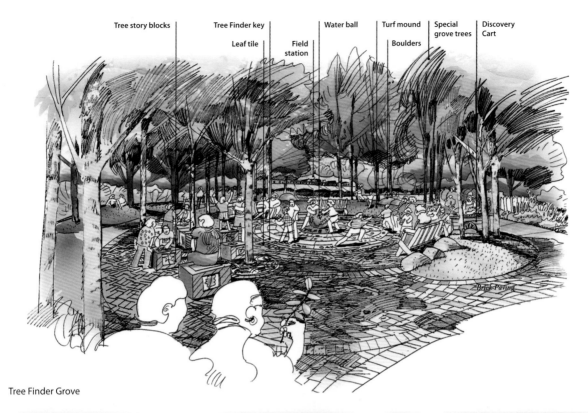

Tree story blocks   Tree Finder key   Water ball   Turf mound   Special   Discovery
                                                                    grove trees Cart

Leaf tile   Field   Boulders
             station

Brick Paving

Tree Finder Grove

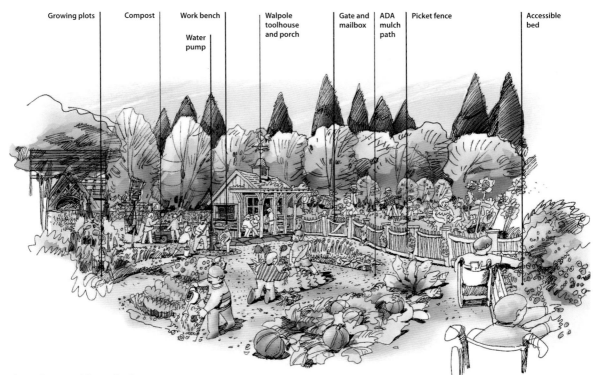

Growing plots   Compost   Work bench   Walpole toolhouse and porch   Gate and mailbox   ADA mulch path   Picket fence   Accessible bed

Water pump

Bloom, Zoom, and Sprout Garden

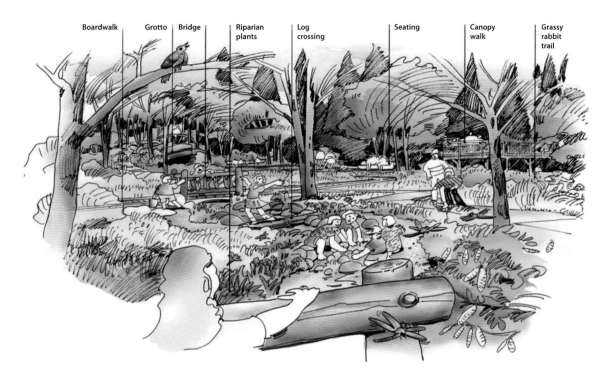

Boardwalk Grotto Bridge Riparian plants Log crossing Seating Canopy walk Grassy rabbit trail

Secret Stream

Top: Windmill in Kids' Terrace Garden
Bottom: Touch pond in Curiosity Garden
Opposite bottom: Flowers garden area

THE MAGIC OF CHILDREN'S GARDENS

CONCLUSION

The 1,700-acre (688-hectare) Morton Arboretum—home to a vast collection of natural landscapes covered with woodlands, wetlands, and prairies along with some cultivated garden areas—provides children with playful engagement with real plants, plant exhibits, and program spaces. It is a perfect place for families to unplug from their electronic devices and reconnect with each other and with nature.

The Morton Arboretum has a long and impressive tradition of offering educational classes for school groups and children in summer camp as well as weekend and evening programs with environmental education concepts. This garden has successfully offered these programs since 2005.

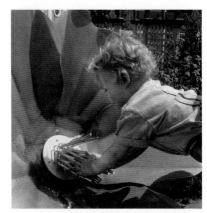

Adventure Woods entry

Entry walkway

Plants in the garden

Shade trees

Acer saccharinum 'Skinneri'
Acer saccharum 'Green Mountain'
Acer saccharum 'Seneca Chief'
Acer saccharum 'Temples Upright'
Acer × freemanii 'Jeffers Red'
Acer × freemanii 'Marmo'
Aesculus × carnea 'Fort McNair'
Betula alleghaniensis
Betula nigra 'Cully' Heritage
Carya cordiformis
Carya ovata
Catalpa speciosa
Cercidiphylum japonicum
Cladrastris lutea
Diospyros virginiana
Fagus sylvatica 'Spaethiana'
Fraxinus americana 'Autumn
    Applause'
Fraxinus pensylvanica 'Sherwood
    Glen'
Ginkgo biloba 'Autumn Gold'
Gleditsia triacanthos f. inermis
    'Shademaster'
Gymnocladus dioicus 'Espresso'
Juglans nigra
Larix decidua
Larix decidua 'Varied Directions'
Liquidambar styraciflua 'Moraine'
Phellodendron amurense 'Macho'
Platanus × acerifolia 'Bloodgood'
Populus tremuloides
Quercus alba
Quercus bicolor
Quercus ellipsoidalis
Quercus imbricaria
Quercus macrocarpa
Quercus rubra
Salix alba 'Tristis'

Sassafras albidum
Tilia tomentosa 'Sterling'
Ulmus 'Morton'
Ulmus carpinifolia × parvifolia

Evergreen trees

Abies concolor
Abies homolepis
Cupressus nootkatensis 'Green
    Arrow'
Cupressus nootkatensis 'Pendula'
Picea abies 'Aurea'
Picea glauca var. densata
Picea omorika
Picea pungens var. glauca 'Pendula'
Picea pungens 'Hoopsii'
Picea pungens 'Iseli Foxtail'
Pinus cembra
Pinus cembra 'Columnaris'
Pinus flexilis 'Vanderwolf's Pyramid'
Pseudotsuga menziesii
Taxodium distichum
Thuja occidentalis 'Lutea'
Thuja plicata
Tsuga canadensis

Intermediate trees

Acer griseum × nikoense
Acer pseudosieboldianum
Acer triflorum
Alnus glutinosa
Amelanchier × grandiflora 'Autumn
    Brilliance'
Amelanchier × grandiflora 'Princess
    Diana'
Carpinus caroliniana
Cercis canadensis
Cornus mas 'Golden Glory'

Fargesia nitida 'Wakehurst'
Ginkgo biloba 'Pendula'
Halesia carolina
Hamamelis virginiana
Magnolia 'Ivory Chalice'
Magnolia × loebneri 'Leonard
    Messel'
Magnolia stellata 'Gold Star'
Malus 'Orange Crush'
Malus 'Satin Cloud'
Malus 'Louisa'
Malus 'Sugar Tyme'
Malus 'Strawberry Parfait'
Malus × domestica 'McIntosh'
Malus × zumi 'Calocarpa'
Prunus maackii
Prunus 'Montmorency'
Prunus 'North Star'
Prunus 'Reliance'
Prunus sargentii
Ptelea trifoliata
Pyrus calleryana 'Chanticleer'
Syringa pekinensis 'Morton'
Syringa reticulata
Syringa reticulata 'Ivory Silk'

Deciduous shrubs

Aesculus parviflora
Aesculus pavia
Aronia arbutifolia 'Brilliantissima'
Aronia arbutifolia 'Morton'
Berberis thunbergii 'Helmond Pillar'
Berberis thunbergii var. atropurpurea
    'Intermedia'
Buddleja davidii 'Pink Delight'
Buddleja davidii 'Ellen's Blue'
Callicarpa dichotoma 'Issai'
Clethra alnifolia 'Rosea'
Clethra alnifolia 'September Beauty'

Cornus alba 'Argenteo-marginata'
Cornus alba 'Bailhalo'
Cornus alba 'Bud's Yellow'
Cornus racemosa
Cornus sericea 'Baileyi'
Cornus sericea 'Isanti'
Cornus sericea 'Winter Flame'
Cornus stolonifera 'Allemans'
Corylus americana
Corylus avellana 'Contorta'
Cotinus coggygria 'Young Lady'
Cotoneaster apiculatus
Daphne × burkwoodii 'Carol Mackie'
Deutzia × lemoinei
Fothergilla gardenii 'Beaver Creek'
Hamamelis vernalis 'Autumn
    Embers'
Hydrangea anomala var. 'Petiolaris'
Hydrangea arborescens 'Annabelle'
Hydrangea arborescens 'White
    Dome'
Hydrangea paniculata 'Limelight'
Hydrangea quercifolia 'Alice'
Hydrangea quercifolia 'Snow Queen'
Hypericum kalmianum
Itea virginica 'Morton'
Kalmia 'Bullseye'
Kerria japonica 'Golden Guinea'
Kerria japonica 'Honshu'
Lindera benzoin
Philadelphus × virginalis 'Miniature
    Snowflake'
Physocarpus opulifolius 'Diablo'
Rhamnus frangula 'Fine Line'
Rhodotypos scandens
Rhus aromatica 'Gro-Low'
Rhus aromatica 'Green Globe'
Rhus glabra
Rhus typhina
Ribes alpinium 'Spreg'

Wonder Pond

Fruits and Seeds Gardens

Rosa 'Nearly Wild'
Rosa 'Alexander MacKenzie'
Rosa 'Meipitac' Carefree Wonder
Rosa 'Champlain'
Rosa 'NOA250092' Flower Carpet
  Pink
Rosa 'Radrazz' Knock Out
Rosa 'Noaschnee' Flower Carpet
Rosa 'Schneekoppe' Snow Pave-
  ment
Rosa rugosa 'Frau Dagmar Hastrup'
Salix gracilistyla 'Melanostachys'
Sambucus nigra 'Gerda'
Spiraea × cineria 'Grefsheim'
Symphoricarpos × doerenbossii
  'Amethyst'
Symphoricarpos × doerenbossii
  'White Hedge'
Syringa patula 'Miss Kim'
Syringa 'Baildust'
Viburnum carlesii
Viburnum dentatum 'Blue Muffin'
Viburnum dentatum 'Morton'
Viburnum dentatum 'Red Regal'
Viburnum dentatum 'Synnestvedt'
Viburnum dilatatum 'Erie'
Viburnum plicatum var. *tomento-
  sum* 'Fireworks'
Viburnum trilobum 'Compactum'
Viburnum trilobum 'J. N. Select'
Viburnum trilobum 'Johnston'
Viburnum × juddii
Weigela florida 'Elvera'
Weigela florida 'Java Red'
Weigela florida 'Midnight Wine'
Weigela florida 'Pink Delight'
Weigela florida 'Red Prince'

Evergreen shrubs

Juniperus chinensis (Chinese juniper
  pom pom form)
Juniperus horizontalis 'Blue Chip'
Juniperus horizontalis 'Mother Lode'
Juniperus sabina 'Broadmoor'
Picea glauca 'Conica'
Taxus × media 'Bergi'
Thuja occidentalis 'Nigra'
Thuja occidentalis 'Smaragd'

Semievergreen shrubs

Buxus 'Green Mountain'
Ilex verticillata 'Afterglow'
Ilex verticillata 'Jim Dandy'
Mahonia aquifolium
Yucca filamentosa 'Bright Edge'

Groundcovers

Asarum canadense
Brunnera macrophylla 'Dawson's
  White'
*Epimedium versicolor × 'Sulphu-
  reum'
Hedera helix 'Thorndale'
Liriope spicata
Pachysandra terminalis 'Green
  Carpet'
Polytrichum commune
Sedum dasyphyllum var. *glandu-
  liferum*
Sedum spurium 'Dragon's Blood'
Thuidium delicatulum
Vinca minor 'Blue and Gold'
Vinca minor 'Illumination'
Vinca minor 'Ralph Shugert'
Vinca minor 'Emily Joy'

Perennials

Achillea millefolium 'Citronella'
Achillea millefolium 'Paprika'
Adiantum pedatum
Adiantum venustum
Alchemilla mollis 'Auslese'
Amsonia hubrichtii
Artemesia ludoviciana 'Valerie
  Finnis'
Artemesia 'Powis Castle'
Asclepias sullivantii
Aster dumosus 'Professor Kippen-
  burg'
Aster novi-belgii 'Purple Dome'
Aster shortii
Astilbe chinensis 'Superba'
Astilbe × arendsii 'Bressingham
  Beauty'
Astilbe × arendsii 'Fanal'
Astilbe × arendsii 'White Gloria'
Baptisia australis
Bergenia 'Bressingham Ruby'
Boltonia asteroides 'Snowbank'
Brunnera macrophylla
Calamagrostis acutiflora 'Karl
  Foerster'
Campanula glomerata 'Joan Elliot'
Campanula glomerata 'Superba'
Campanula punctata 'Cherry Bells'
Campanula 'Samantha'
Campsis radicans 'Flava'
Carex elata 'Bowles Golden'
Carex morrowii 'Ice Dance'
Chasmathium latifolium
Clematis 'Multiblue'
Clematis 'Nelly Moser'
Clematis 'Niobe'
Clematis 'Snow Queen'
Clematis 'Sugar Candy'

Clematis 'Jackmannii'
Clematis terniflora
Coreopsis grandiflora 'Sunray'
Coreopsis verticillata 'Moonbeam'
Coreopsis verticillata 'Zagreb'
Deschampsia cespitosa 'Schottland'
Dianthus 'Firewitch'
Dianthus gratianopolitanus 'Bath's
  Pink'
Dianthus 'Mountain Mist'
Dicentra 'Luxuriant'
Echinacea purpurea 'Bravado'
Echinacea purpurea 'White Swan'
Echinops bannaticus 'Blue Glow'
Euphorbia polychroma
Festuca glauca 'Elijah Blue'
Fragaria virginiana
Fragaria × ananassa 'Brighton'
Gaillardia 'Fanfare'
Gaillardia × grandiflora 'Kobold'
Galium boreale
Geranium 'Ann Folkard'
Geranium macrorrhizum 'Bevans
  Variety'
Geranium macrorrhizum 'Ingwer-
  sen's Variety'
Geranium × magnificum
Helianthus helianthoides 'Summer
  Sun'
Hemerocallis 'Angel's Realm'
Hemerocallis 'Cherry Cheeks'
Hemerocallis 'Chicago Peach'
Hemerocallis 'Happy Returns'
Hemerocallis 'Mary Todd'
Heuchera 'Amethyst Mist'
Heuchera 'Cathedral Windows'
Heuchera 'Obsidian'
Heuchera 'Plum Pudding'
Heuchera 'Strawberry Candy'
Heuchera villosa 'Purpurea'

Rope bridge in Under the Trees

Seating along Under the Trees

Hibiscus moscheutos 'Southern Belle'
Hibiscus 'Super Rose'
Hosta 'Abiqua Drinking Gourd'
Hosta 'Blue Angel'
Hosta 'Blue Mammoth'
Hosta 'Choo Choo Train'
Hosta 'Frosted Jade'
Hosta 'Great Expectations'
Hosta 'Hadspen Blue'
Hosta 'June'
Hosta 'Medusa'
Hosta 'Patriot'
Hosta 'Paul's Glory'
Hosta 'Striptease'
Hosta 'Whirlwind'
Iberis sempervirens 'Alexander's White'
Iris 'Christmas Time'
Iris pallida 'Variegata'
Iris siberica 'Blue King'
Iris siberica 'Butter and Sugar'
Iris siberica 'Caesar's Brother'
Iris siberica 'Perry Blue'
Hibiscus moscheutos 'Southern Belle'
Hibiscus 'Super Rose'
Lamium maculatum 'Orchid Frost'
Lavandula angustifolia 'Munstead'
Leucanthemum × *superbum* 'Snowcap'
Liatris spicata 'Kobold'
Ligularia dentata 'Desdemona'
Ligularia stenocephala 'The Rocket'
Lilium 'Casa Blanca'
Lilium 'Stargazer'
Lobelia cardinalis
Lonicera × *brownii* 'Dropmore Scarlet'

Lunaria annua
Malva alcea 'Fastigiata'
Malva sylvestris
Miscanthus sinensis 'Morning Light'
Miscanthus sinensis 'Nippon'
Miscanthus sinensis 'Strictus'
Monarda didyma 'Aquarius'
Monarda 'Gardenview Scarlet'
Molinea arundinacea 'Sky Racer'
Nepeta × *faassenii* 'Walker's Low'
Osmunda cinnamomea
Osmunda regalis
Panicum virgatum 'Northwind'
Panicum virgatum 'Rotstrahlbusch'
Panicum virgatum 'Shenandoah'
Parthenocisus tricuspidata
Pennisetum alopecuroides
Pennisetum alopecuroides 'Hamelin'
Pennisetum alopecuroides 'Japonicum'
Pennisetum alopecuroides 'Viridescens'
Perovskia atriplicifolia 'Little Spire'
Perovskia atriplicifolia 'Longin'
Perovskia atriplicifolia 'Filigran'
Phlox carolina 'Miss Lingard'
Phlox paniculata 'Becky Towe'
Phlox paniculata 'Bright Eyes'
Phlox paniculata 'David'
Phlox paniculata 'Miss Jessica'
Physostegia virginiana 'Variegata'
Physostegia virginiana 'Vivid'
Platycodon grandiflorus 'Mariesii Splash'
Polygonatum hirtum
Pulmonaria saccaharata 'Raspberry Splash'
Rubus 'Autumn Bliss'

Rudbeckia fulgida var. *fulgida* 'Goldsturm'
Salvia nemorosa 'Caradonna'
Salvia nemorosa 'Mainacht'
Salvia verticillata 'Purple Rain'
Salvia × *superba* 'East Friesland'
Scabiosa columbaria 'Fama'
Schizachyrium scoparium 'The Blues'
Sedum spectabile 'Brilliant'
Sedum spectabile 'Neon'
Solidago rugosa 'Fireworks'
Sporobolus heterolepis
Stachys byzantina 'Big Ears'
Stachys byzantina 'Helen Von Stein'
Tiarella 'Jeepers Creepers'
Veronica spicata 'Royal Candles'
Wisteria frutescens 'Amethyst Falls'
Wisteria macrostachya 'Aunt Dee'

Bulbs

Allium aflatunense 'Purple Sensation'
Allium thunbergii 'Ozawa'
Crocus sieberi
Narcissus 'Carlton'
Narcissus 'Ice Follies'
Tulipa 'Queen of Sheba'

Aquatic plants

Tropical lilies/lotus

Nelumbo nucifera 'Alba Grandiflora'
Nelumbo nucifera 'Joyful Eyes'
Nelumbo nucifera 'Maggie Belle Slocum'
Nelumbo nucifera 'Perry's Super Star'

Hardy lilies

Nymphaea 'Blue Beauty'
Nymphaea 'Ellisiana'
Nymphaea 'Glorie de Temple-sur-lot'
Nymphaea 'Gonnere'
Nymphaea 'Mayla'
Nymphaea 'Moorei'
Nymphaea 'Perry's Baby Red'
Nymphaea 'Red Spider'
Nymphaea 'Virginalis'
Nymphaea × *marliacea* 'Chromotella'

Marginal plants

Acorus calamus 'Variegatus'
Colocasia esculenta 'Metallica'
Cyperus alternifolius
Echinodorus osiris 'Rubra'
Equisetum hyemale 'Robustum'
Gymnocoronis spilanthoides
Iris pseudoacorus
Juncus inflexis 'Afro'
Peltandra virginica
Pontederia cordata 'Crown Point'
Ranunculus longirostris
Sagittaria latifolia 'Arrowhead'

Oxygenators/floating plants

Mimulus guttatus
Myriophyllum 'Brasliensis'
Neptunia aquatica
Oenanthe javanica 'Flamingo'
Ranunculus acris

Secret Stream

Morton Arboretum Children's Garden

Forest Bird Feeders   Booster Stumps   Activity Station Shelter   Grotto   Interpretive Panels   Cantilevered Niche   Rabbit Trail

Standing Rail

CANOPY WALK

Top: Evergreen Walk and Lookout design sketches by Herb Schaal from early workshop

Bottom: Built Evergreen Walk and Lookout

Opposite left: Three-dimensional model by Hitchcock Design Group

Opposite center and right: Early design sketches by Herb Schaal

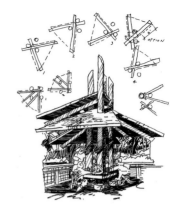

Morton Arboretum Children's Garden

4100 Illinois Route 53, Lisle, IL 60532

630-968-0074   http://www.mortonarb.org/visit-explore/activities-and-exhibits/childrens-garden

Opening date: 2005

Project size: 4 acres (1.6 hectares) within the Morton Arboretum's 1,700-acre (688-hectare) site

Design and Construction Team

Morton Arboretum:

   Director of project and president and chief executive officer: Gerard Donnelly

   Children's Garden manager during design and construction: Katherine Johnson

   Staff landscape architect during design and construction: Scott Mehaffey

Landscape architect:

   Conceptual and schematic design: EDAW/AECOM (Herb Schaal, principal landscape architect; Denise George, associate landscape architect and project manager; Mark Kosmos, associate landscape architect)

   Landscape architect of record: Hitchcock Design Group (Andy Howard and Eric Hornig, landscape architects for design, development, and construction documents)

Child learning and interpretive consultant: Becky Lindsay, former director of exhibits and programs at the Dupage Children's Museum

Illustrator: Joe McGrane

General contractor: Featherstone Inc. (Tom Featherstone and Jim Boyd, construction managers)

Manufacturer of rope suspension bridges and net climbing structures: Richter Spielgerate

Manufacturer of flip slide for embankment root slide: Gametime

Manufacturer of glass-fiber-reinforced-concrete tree root and acorn climber sculpture: Cemrock

Current Contacts

Landscape architect: Susan L. B. Jacobson

Children's Garden manager: Lesley Kolaya

Interviews and Personal Communications

Andy Howard, May 20, 2014; Susan Jacobson, May 14, 2014; Hannah Rennard, April 15, 2014; Herb Schaal, February 15, 2015

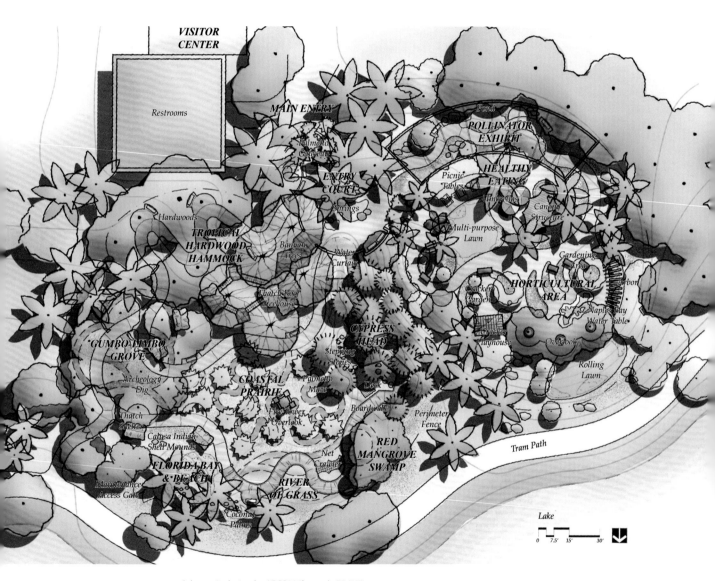

VISITOR CENTER

Restrooms

MAIN ENTRY

Palmetto Gateway

ENTRY COURT

Springs

Hardwoods

TROPICAL HARDWOOD HAMMOCK

Banyan Trees

Water Curtain

Thatch Roof Treehouse

GUMBO-LIMBO GROVE

Archeology Dig

Thatch Shelter

Calusa Indian Shell Mounds

FLORIDA BAY & BEACH

Maintenance Access Gate

COASTAL PRAIRIE

Palmetto Maze

Fire Tower Overlook

Coconut Palms

RIVER OF GRASS

Net Crawler

Stepping Stones

CYPRESS HEAD

Deck

Boardwalk

RED MANGROVE SWAMP

Perimeter Fence

POLLINATOR EXHIBIT

Pond

HEALTHY EATING

Picnic Tables

Umbrellas

Multi-purpose Lawn

Canopy Structure

Gardening Area

Cracker Garden

HORTICULTURAL AREA

Arbor

Naples Bay Water Table

Cracker Playhouse

Overlook

Rolling Lawn

Tram Path

Lake

0   7.5'   15'   30'

Schematic design by AECOM (formerly EDAW)

Vicky C. and David Byron Smith Children's Garden at Naples Botanical Garden

NAPLES, FLORIDA

GOAL

"A Walk through Florida: From Tree to Sea" is the theme of the Vicky C. and David Byron Smith Children's Garden. The goal is to allow children to play in the environment and to learn about the Florida context and ecosystem. Designed to be an experiential interactive learning garden, it is for children ages three to eight and has natural areas accommodating children up to age thirteen. The 1-acre (0.4-hectare) garden lies within the 170-acre (68.8-hectare) Naples Botanical Garden, which boasts "Gardens with Latitude," featuring "plants and cultures of the tropics and subtropics between the latitudes of 26 degrees North and 26 degrees South including Brazil, the Caribbean, Southeast Asia and Florida" (American Public Gardens Association, n.d.). Naples Botanical Garden includes six cultivated gardens, 2.5 miles (4 kilometers) of walking trails, and 90 acres (36.4 hectares) of restored native preserve.

CONCEPT

Naples Botanical Garden was conceived in 2006 under the leadership of Brian Holley, executive director of Naples Botanical Garden. The goal was to create a garden with a sense of place, emphasizing the native ecosystem and plants of southwest Florida. The Smith Children's Garden was the first of four gardens that opened at Naples Botanical Garden in 2009. The Children's Garden is composed of two distinct sections, both reached from the entry Play Fountain Plaza. The first area emphasizes horticulture and the cultural history of south Florida. The second area spreads out over a lower elevation and shows south Florida's unique native plant communities. Both areas are ADA accessible. Since the site was flat, to create greater topographic interest, the design built up the terrain, which also alleviates inundation and salt accumulation in the soils. "The site elevation of the Smith Children's Garden was about two to three feet above sea level when we started. Now, the lower elevation is about six feet, and the upper elevation is about fourteen feet," says Holley.

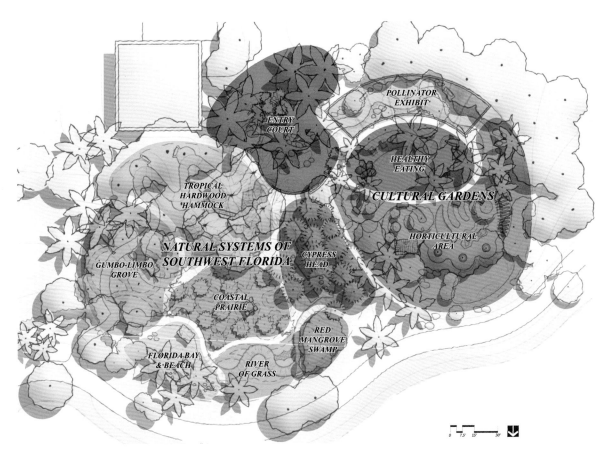

Garden organization

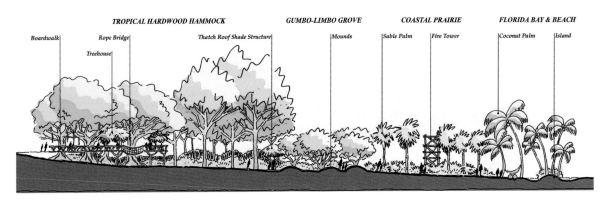
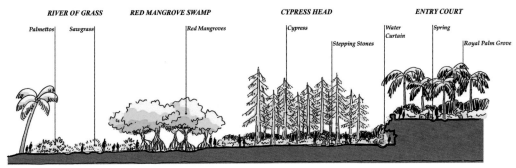

Garden sections

THE MAGIC OF CHILDREN'S GARDENS

To design the Children's Garden, Holley engaged the help of the landscape architect Herb Schaal, who had already designed many children's gardens by this time. Schaal collaborated with a local landscape architecture firm, Goetz and Stropes, that did the construction drawings and management. From February to June of 2006, Schaal was involved in fact finding and workshops as well as developing design ideas, schematic plans, and cost estimates. To solicit input from the main audience of the garden, eight workshops were held at regional schools with children ages three through thirteen. They were asked to draw a picture of their dream garden. These drawings were analyzed and, according to their frequency, children's creative ideas, such as butterflies or mazes, were incorporated in the garden design. Ultimately, the design, composed of two distinct sections, included

Water curtain in the Cypress Head area

waterfalls, tree houses, unusual plants, many palm trees, a hidden garden with fanciful plantings in found objects, and seven child-size re-creations of native habitats. During the construction process, every facet of the garden was carefully detailed. Ellin Goetz, collaborating landscape architect, says, "It was a tremendous process selecting and directing all details large and small—moving that giant ficus tree into the site prior to the tree house getting built around it, working with the contractors to get the textures and colors just right on the concrete rock spring grotto as well as the pavement!" When the project was completed, the most popular spaces were the butterfly house, play fountain, tree house, and fire tower.

Spray fountain

Saw Palmetto Gate
in 2009 and 2015

DESIGN

Visitors enter the Smith Children's Garden just past the ticket booth, through the shaded Saw Palmetto Gate. They immediately spill into the Play Fountain Plaza. Visitors are greeted with the words inscribed in the pavement around the fountain: "The Fountain of Youth lies not in the water but in allowing children to awaken our playful spirit and sense of wonder, Herb Schaal." This fountain is reminiscent of the Fountain of Youth reputed to be in Florida that Spanish explorer Juan Ponce de León searched for in 1513. Visible from the play fountain are nearly all the gardens in the upper elevation. To get to the lower elevation, visitors meander from the Play Fountain Plaza through the Tropical Hardwood Hammock, at an elevation six feet above sea level.

The perimeter of the garden is discretely fenced. Children are free to "walk through Florida, from tree to sea," to stop, explore, and play in all parts of the upper and lower garden.

Upper garden
- **Saw Palmetto Gate:** Tunnel through the entry court.
- **Play fountain:** Splash around the water fountain and jets.
- **Pfeffer-Beach Butterfly House:** Learn about native species of butterflies.
- **Tree house:** Climb the two-story tree house complete with climbing platforms and rope bridges; experience the amazing views of habitats from above; and learn about the tropical plants such as the strangler fig, banana, bromeliads, and air plants.
- **Vicki Oppenheimer Healthy Eating Garden:** Learn about a variety of organically grown vegetables that change with the seasons.
- **Nancy and Jonathan Hamill Florida Cracker House Garden:** Experience a taste of the vernacular architecture of early pioneers. Garden in this area and fill watering cans with hand pumps.
- **Hidden Garden:** Locate hidden items in this scavenger's garden. Find plants growing and sprouting in objects that collect rainwater (like a kettle, pottery, purses, shoes, lamps, sinks, and a clogged toilet).
- **Judy Herb's Herb Garden:** Experience wonderful fragrances such as mint as well as the more exotic galangal.

Cracker House

THE MAGIC OF CHILDREN'S GARDENS

Lower garden

- **Repp Family Hardwood Hammock (tropical hardwood hammock):** Traverse through native Florida plants, through the Gumbo Limbo grove and shell mounds, to the beach area surrounded by sea oats and ample beach toys for castle-building needs. Pass by the beach and experience a meadow reminiscent of the Everglades, where dragonflies hover over pickerelweed and a net crawl allows kids to peer into the grasses below. A bouncing raft and stepping-stones allow close-up views.
- **Flegel Boardwalk:** Learn about the importance of mangroves and explore the Waud Cypress Head and Waterfall by following the stepping-stones over and through the water.
- **Fire tower:** Climb the tower in the middle of the prairie habitat and experience a panoramic view of grasslands where fire is an important part of the ecosystem.

CONCLUSION

"A Walk through Florida: From Tree to Sea" is a small 1-acre (0.4-hectare) garden that immerses children and families in an experiential interactive learning environment. This garden has a special sense of place characterized by the native ecosystem and plants of southwest Florida. With two distinct garden sections, one at the upper and the other at the lower elevation, visitors experience tropical landscape with palm and banyan trees and diverse plant communities at elevations from six to fourteen feet.

Getting water at the hand pump

Arbor   Naples Bay Water Table   Cracker Playhouse   Citrus Tree   Small Arbor

Hand Pump

Healthy Eating Garden in the horticultural area

Top: Multipurpose lawn
and amphitheater area

Bottom: Amphitheater

Vicky C. and David Byron Smith Children's Garden at Naples Botanical Garden

| Banyan Tree | Cypress Head | Grass Maze | Fire Tower | Sable Palms | Palmettos | Coconut Palms |

Fire tower overlook in Coastal Prairie

THE MAGIC OF CHILDREN'S GARDENS

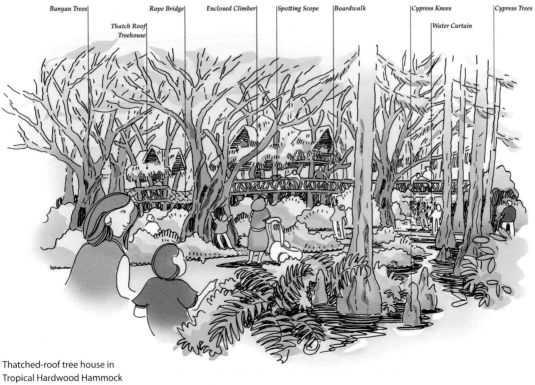

Banyan Trees   Rope Bridge   Enclosed Climber   Spotting Scope   Boardwalk   Cypress Knees   Cypress Trees

Thatch Roof
Treehouse

Water Curtain

Thatched-roof tree house in
Tropical Hardwood Hammock

Vicky C. and David Byron Smith Children's Garden at Naples Botanical Garden

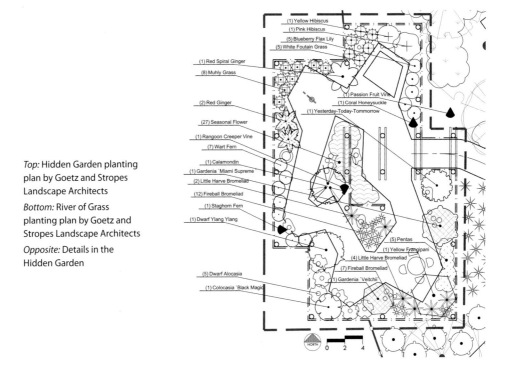

Top: Hidden Garden planting plan by Goetz and Stropes Landscape Architects

Bottom: River of Grass planting plan by Goetz and Stropes Landscape Architects

Opposite: Details in the Hidden Garden

(1) Yellow Hibiscus
(1) Pink Hibiscus
(5) Blueberry Flax Lily
(5) White Foutain Grass
(1) Red Spiral Ginger
(8) Muhly Grass
(1) Passion Fruit Vine
(1) Coral Honeysuckle
(2) Red Ginger
(1) Yesterday-Today-Tommorow
(27) Seasonal Flower
(1) Rangoon Creeper Vine
(7) Wart Fern
(1) Calamondin
(1) Gardenia `Miami Supreme`
(2) Little Harve Bromeliad
(12) Fireball Bromeliad
(1) Staghorn Fern
(1) Dwarf Ylang Ylang
(5) Pentas
(1) Yellow Frangipani
(4) Little Harve Bromeliad
(7) Fireball Bromeliad
(1) Gardenia `Veitchii`
(5) Dwarf Alocasia
(1) Colocasia `Black Magic`

NORTH   0 2 4

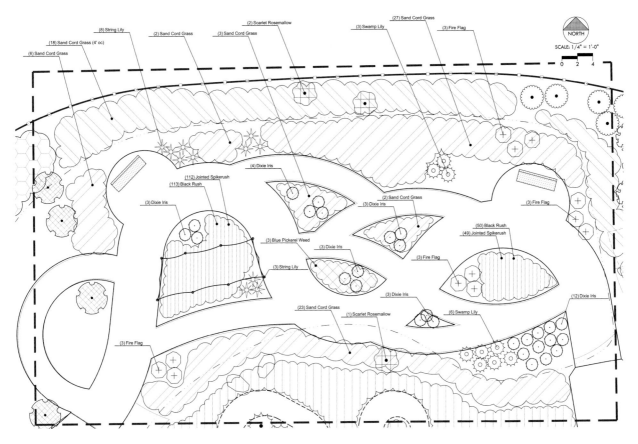

(18) Sand Cord Grass (4' oc)
(8) String Lily
(2) Sand Cord Grass
(3) Sand Cord Grass
(2) Scarlet Rosemallow
(3) Swamp Lily
(27) Sand Cord Grass
(3) Fire Flag
(6) Sand Cord Grass
NORTH
SCALE: 1/4" = 1'-0"
0 2 4
(112) Jointed Spikerush
(113) Black Rush
(4) Dixie Iris
(2) Sand Cord Grass
(3) Dixie Iris
(3) Dixie Iris
(3) Dixie Iris
(50) Black Rush
(49) Jointed Spikerush
(3) Fire Flag
(3) Blue Pickerel Weed
(3) Dixie Iris
(3) Fire Flag
(3) String Lily
(3) Dixie Iris
(12) Dixie Iris
(3) Dixie Iris
(23) Sand Cord Grass
(1) Scarlet Rosemallow
(6) Swamp Lily
(3) Fire Flag

Plants in the garden

Trees

Acer rubrum
Adansonia digitata
Annona glabra
Bursera simaruba
Carica papaya var. *kamiya*
Chorisia speciosa
Chrysophyllum oliviforme
Citrofortunella vulgaris
Citrus aurantifolia
Citrus aurantium
Citrus medica × *limon*
Citrus maxima
Citrus × *tangelo* 'Minneola'
Clusia rosea
Coccoloba diversifolia
Coccoloba uvifera
Conocarpus erectus
Couroupita guianensis
Crescentia cujete
Delonix regia
Eriobotrya japonica
Ficus aurea
Ficus nitida
Fortunella crassifolia
Guaiacum sanctum
Kigelia pinnata
Lysiloma latisiliqua
Magnolia virginiana
Musa acuminata
Musa acuminata 'Dwarf Cavendish'
Musa acuminata 'Ice Cream'
Musa acuminata 'Nana'
Musa acuminata 'Zebrina'
Peltophorum dubium
Pseudobombax ellipticum
Psidium littorale
Quercus virginiana
Rhizophora mangle
Senna didymobotrya
Simarouba glauca
Swietenia mahogani
Tabebuia caraiba
Tamarindus indica
Taxodium distichum

Palms

Coccothrinax argentata
Coccothrinax crinita
Cocos nucifera 'Green Malayan'
Cocos nucifera 'Maypan'
Hyophorbe lagenicaulis
Hyophorbe verschaffeltii
Nolina recurvata
Pseudophoenix sargentii
Roystonea regia
Sabal palmetto
Serenoa repens
Thrinax morrissii
Thrinax radiata
Veitchia winin
Wodyetia bifurcata

Shrubs

Acacia choriophylla
Arundo donax 'Versicolor'
Asclepias tuberosa
Caesalpinia pauciflora
Callicarpa americana
Capparis cynophallophora
Chrysobalanus icaco
Citharexylum spinosum
Conradina canescens
Eugenia axillaris
Galphimia gracilis
Hamelia nodosa
Hamelia patens
Ilex cassine
Ilex vomitoria
Ilex vomitoria 'Stokes Dwarf'
Myrcianthes fragrans
Morella cerifera
Psychotria nervosa
Rapanea punctata
Sabal minor
Scaevola plumieri
Serenoa repens
Serenoa repens 'Cinerea'
Sophora tomentosa var. *truncata*
Stachytarpheta jamaicensis
Stachytarpheta urticifolia
Zamia floridana

Grasses

Paspalum vaginatum
Stenotaphrum secundatum 'Seville'

Groundcovers

Andropogon virginicus var. *glaucus*
Argusia gnaphalodes
Blechnum serrulatum
Borrichia arborescens
Dianella tasmanica
Dietes iridioides
Eragrostis elliottii
Helianthus debilis
Ipomoea pes-caprae
Licania michauxii
Microsorum scolopendrium
Mimosa strigillosa
Muhlenbergia capillaris
Nephrolepis biserrata
Nephrolepis exaltata
Osmunda cinnamomea
Osmunda regalis var. *spectabilis*
Pennisetum setaceum
Peperomia obtusifolia
Pteris bahamensis
Ruellia caroliniensis
Salvia coccinea

Spartina bakeri
Suriana maritima
Tripsacum dactyloides
Tripsacum dactyloides × *floridana*
Tripsacum × *floridana*
Uniola paniculata
Yucca filamentosa

Marginal/aquatic plants

Acrostichum aureum
Acrostichum danaeaefolium
Iris hexagona

Materials

Sand
Eucalyptus mulch
Pine needle mulch
Shell crushed
Planting soil
Eucalyptus mulch (in Hidden Garden)

River of Grass

Crinum americanum
Eleocharis interstincta
Iris hexagona
Hibiscus coccineus
Hymenocallis latifolia
Juncus roemerianus
Pontederia cordata 'Blue'
Spartina bakeri
Thalia geniculata

Hidden Garden

Aechmea chantinii
Alocasia odora 'California'
Alpinia purpurata
Brunfelsia pauciflora
Citrofortunella vulgaris
Cananga odorata var. *fruticosa*
Colocasia esculenta 'Black Magic'
Costus barbatus
Dianella tasmanica
Gardenia augusta 'Miami Supreme'
Gardenia augusta 'Veitchii'
Hibiscus rosa-sinensis
Hibiscus rosa-sinensis 'Seminole'
Lonicera sempervirens
Microsorum scolopendrium
Muhlenbergia capillaris
Trachelospermum asiaticum 'Tricolor'
Passiflora edulis
Pennisetum setaceum
Pentas lanceolata
Platycerium bifurcatum
Plumeria spp.
Quisqualis indica

Edible Garden

Aloe vera
Alpinia zerumbet 'Variegata'
Ananas comosus
Bambusa multiplex
Cananga odorata var. *fruticosa*
Carambola spp.
Carissa grandiflora
Chrysophyllum cainito
Clerodendrum thomsoniae
Gardenia augusta 'Belmont'
Gardenia augusta 'Miami Supreme'
Gardenia augusta 'Mystery'
Gardenia augusta 'Radicans'
Gardenia augusta 'Veitchii'
Gardenia augusta 'Vietnam Snowflake'
Gardenia taitensis 'Tahitian'
Hamelia nodosa
Kalanchoe thyrsiflora
Kalanchoe gastonis-bonnieri
Mangifera indica 'Glenn'
Monstera deliciosa
Murraya paniculata 'Lakeview'
Myrciaria cauliflora
Passiflora caerulea
Pentas lanceolata
Petrea volubilis
Philodendron 'Burle Marx'
Philodendron xanadu
Pimenta dioica
Plumeria obtusa 'Dwarf Singapore Pink'
Pouteria sapota
Quisqualis indica
Saccharum officinarum
Strelitzia reginae
Strongylodon macrobotrys
Synsepalum dulcificum
Theobroma cacao
Trachelospermum asiaticum 'Tricolor'
Tulbaghia violacea
Vaccinium myrsinites
Vitis vinifera 'Flame Seedless'

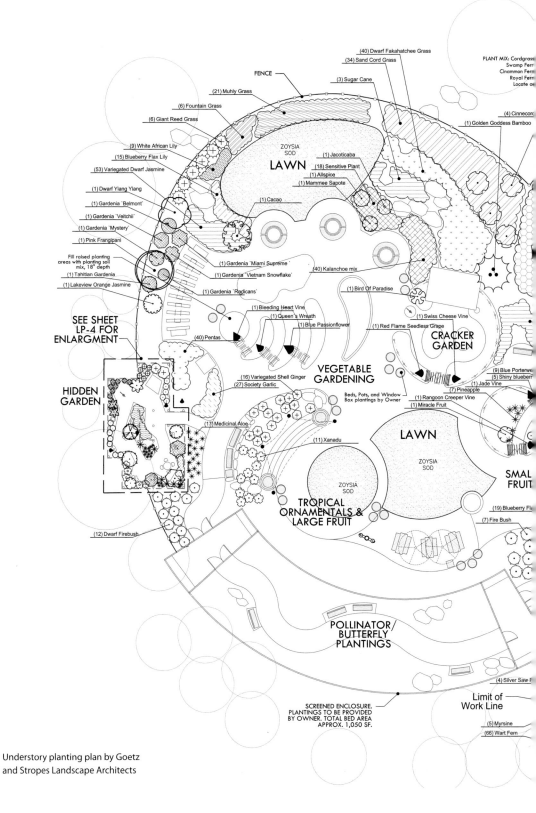

FENCE

(40) Dwarf Fakahatchee Grass
(34) Sand Cord Grass
(3) Sugar Cane

PLANT MIX: Cordgrass
Swamp Fern
Cinammon Fern
Royal Fern
Locate on

(21) Muhly Grass
(6) Fountain Grass
(6) Giant Reed Grass

(4) Cinnecord
(1) Golden Goddess Bamboo

ZOYSIA SOD

LAWN

(9) White African Lily
(15) Blueberry Flax Lily
(53) Variegated Dwarf Jasmine
(1) Dwarf Ylang Ylang
(1) Gardenia 'Belmont'
(1) Gardenia 'Veitchii'
(1) Gardenia 'Mystery'
(1) Pink Frangipani

(1) Jacoticaba
(18) Sensitive Plant
(1) Allspice
(1) Mammee Sapote

(1) Cacao

Fill raised planting
areas with planting soil
mix, 18" depth
(1) Tahitian Gardenia
(1) Lakeview Orange Jasmine

(1) Gardenia 'Miami Supreme'
(1) Gardenia 'Vietnam Snowflake'
(40) Kalanchoe mix

(1) Gardenia 'Radicans'

(1) Bird Of Paradise

(1) Bleeding Heart Vine
(1) Queen's Wreath
(1) Blue Passionflower

(1) Swiss Cheese Vine
(1) Red Flame Seedless Grape

SEE SHEET
LP-4 FOR
ENLARGMENT

(40) Pentas

CRACKER
GARDEN

(9) Blue Porterwe
(5) Shiny blueberr
(1) Jade Vine

HIDDEN
GARDEN

(16) Variegated Shell Ginger
(27) Society Garlic

VEGETABLE
GARDENING

Beds, Pots, and Window
Box plantings by Owner

(7) Pineapple
(1) Rangoon Creeper Vine
(1) Miracle Fruit

(17) Medicinal Aloe

LAWN

ZOYSIA
SOD

SMAL
FRUIT

(11) Xanadu

(19) Blueberry Fl
(7) Fire Bush

TROPICAL
ORNAMENTALS &
LARGE FRUIT

ZOYSIA
SOD

(12) Dwarf Firebush

POLLINATOR/
BUTTERFLY
PLANTINGS

(4) Silver Saw

Limit of
Work Line

SCREENED ENCLOSURE.
PLANTINGS TO BE PROVIDED
BY OWNER. TOTAL BED AREA
APPROX. 1,050 SF.

(5) Myrsine
(66) Wart Fern

Understory planting plan by Goetz
and Stropes Landscape Architects

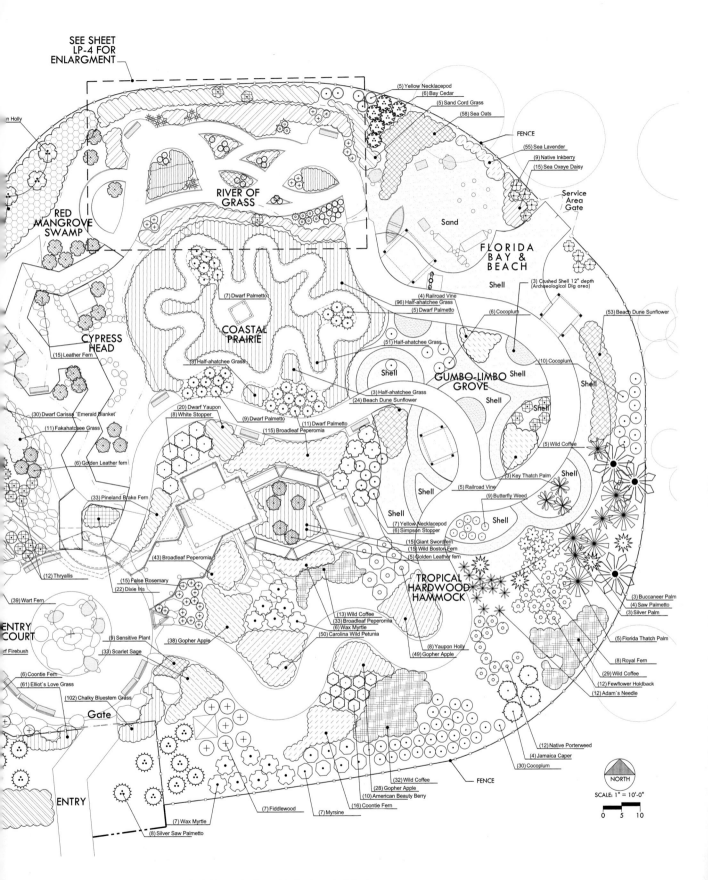

SEE SHEET
LP-4 FOR
ENLARGMENT

(5) Yellow Necklacepod
(6) Bay Cedar
(5) Sand Cord Grass
(58) Sea Oats

FENCE

(55) Sea Lavender
(9) Native Inkberry
(15) Sea Oxeye Daisy

n Holly

RIVER OF
GRASS

Sand

Service
Area
Gate

RED
MANGROVE
SWAMP

FLORIDA
BAY &
BEACH

Shell

(3) Crushed Shell 12" depth
(Archaeological Dig area)

(4) Railroad Vine
(96) Half-ahatchee Grass
(5) Dwarf Palmetto

(6) Cocoplum

(53) Beach Dune Sunflower

(7) Dwarf Palmetto

COASTAL
PRAIRIE

(51) Half-ahatchee Grass

(10) Cocoplum

CYPRESS
HEAD

(15) Leather Fern

Shell

Shell

GUMBO-LIMBO
GROVE

Shell

Shell

(3) Half-ahatchee Grass

(3) Half-ahatchee Grass
(24) Beach Dune Sunflower

(30) Dwarf Carissa 'Emerald Blanket'

(20) Dwarf Yaupon
(8) White Stopper

(9) Dwarf Palmetto

(11) Dwarf Palmetto

(11) Fakahatchee Grass

(115) Broadleaf Peperomia

(5) Wild Coffee

(6) Golden Leather fern

Shell

(3) Key Thatch Palm

Shell

(33) Pineland Brake Fern

Shell

(5) Railroad Vine
(9) Butterfly Weed

(12) Thryallis

(43) Broadleaf Peperomia

Shell

(7) Yellow Necklacepod
(6) Simpson Stopper

(15) Giant Swordfern
(15) Wild Boston Fern
(5) Golden Leather fern

(15) False Rosemary
(22) Dixie Iris

(39) Wart Fern

TROPICAL
HARDWOOD
HAMMOCK

(3) Buccaneer Palm
(4) Saw Palmetto
(3) Silver Palm

ENTRY
COURT

(9) Sensitive Plant

rf Firebush

(33) Scarlet Sage

(38) Gopher Apple

(13) Wild Coffee
(33) Broadleaf Peperomia
(6) Wax Myrtle
(50) Carolina Wild Petunia

(8) Yaupon Holly
(49) Gopher Apple

(5) Florida Thatch Palm

(8) Royal Fern

(6) Coontie Fern

(29) Wild Coffee

(61) Elliot's Love Grass

(12) Fewflower Holdback

(102) Chalky Bluestem Grass

(12) Adam's Needle

Gate

(12) Native Porterweed
(4) Jamaica Caper
(30) Cocoplum

ENTRY

(32) Wild Coffee

FENCE

(28) Gopher Apple
(10) American Beauty Berry
(16) Coontie Fern

NORTH

(7) Wax Myrtle

(7) Fiddlewood

(7) Myrsine

SCALE: 1" = 10'-0"

(8) Silver Saw Palmetto

0   5   10

Vicky C. and David Byron Smith Children's Garden at Naples Botanical Garden

203

Bench Bladderwort Boardwalk Stepping Stones Raft
Swings Cypress Knees

Aquatic plant life in Cypress Head Garden

THE MAGIC OF CHILDREN'S GARDENS

Palmettos Sawgrass Sinuous Boardwalk Coconut Palms Stream Sable Palms Net Crawl Bench

Rope bridge in River of Grass Garden

Vicky C. and David Byron Smith Children's Garden at Naples Botanical Garden

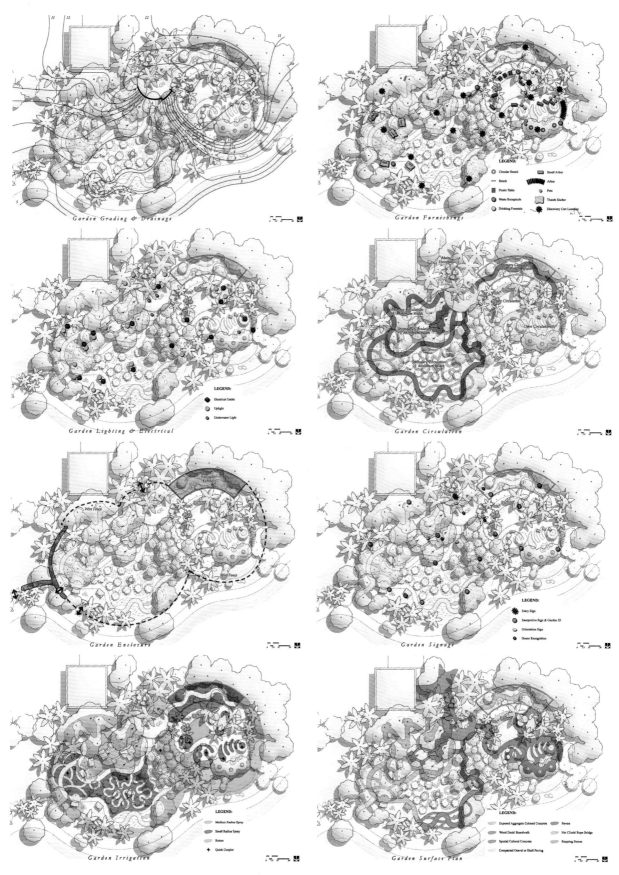

Garden Grading & Drainage

Garden Furnishings

LEGEND:
- Circular Bench
- Bench
- Picnic Table
- Waste Receptacle
- Drinking Fountain
- Small Arbor
- Arbor
- Pots
- Thatch Shelter
- Discovery Cart Location

Garden Lighting & Electrical

LEGEND:
- Electrical Outlet
- Uplight
- Underwater Light

Garden Circulation

Garden Enclosure

Garden Signage

LEGEND:
- Entry Sign
- Interpretive Sign & Garden ID
- Orientation Sign
- Donor Recognition

Garden Irrigation

LEGEND:
- Medium Radius Spray
- Small Radius Spray
- Rotors
- Quick Coupler

Garden Surface Plan

LEGEND:
- Exposed Aggregate Colored Concrete
- Wood Deck/ Boardwalk
- Special Colored Concrete
- Compacted Gravel or Shell Paving
- Pavers
- Net Climb/ Rope Bridge
- Stepping Stones

Vicky C. and David Byron Smith Children's Garden at Naples Botanical Garden

4820 Bayshore Drive, Naples, FL 34112

239-643-7275   http://www.naplesgarden.org/garden/childrens-garden

Opening date: November 9, 2009

Project size: 1 acre (0.4 hectare) within Naples Botanical Garden's 170-acre (68.8-hectare) site

Design and Construction Team
Naples Botanical Garden:

    Executive director: Brian Holley

    Deputy director: Chad Washburn

Landscape architects:

    Schematic design: EDAW/AECOM; Herb Schaal, principal landscape architect; Craig Russell, associate landscape architect and project manager; Mark Kosmos and Megan Moore, associate landscape architects)

    Landscape architect of record: Goetz and Stropes Landscape Architects (Ellin Goetz, principal landscape architect)

Architect: David Corban

Civil engineer: WilsonMiller Inc. (Jared Brown)

Garden structures construction: TMD Construction

Landscape construction: ValleyCrest

Project manager: Rhodes Dahl (John Carson)

Current Contacts
Executive director: Brian Holley

Deputy director: Chad Washburn

Interviews and Personal Communications
Ellin Goetz, September 16, 2015; Brian Holley, June 25, 2010; Herb Schaal, February 17, 2015; Chad Washburn, July 5, 2010

Opposite: Details of the design process

Top: Thatch shelter in Florida Bay and Beach

13

Everett Children's Adventure Garden at New York Botanical Garden

BRONX, NEW YORK

GOAL

The Everett Children's Adventure Garden in the New York Botanical Garden (established in 1891) is designed to be a unique public garden where children learn about plant science in a hands-on and engaging way. Interactive exhibits convey different plant science concepts and processes through signage, exhibits, programs, and explainers.

The project goals are the following:

- To enhance the quality and vitality of basic science education for elementary school-age children, their teachers, and their families
- To restore immediate experiences with plants and nature to children in a safe, discovery-oriented environment
- To enhance the Botanical Garden's appeal to families and expand weekend and afternoon visitation to children and caregivers

Con Edison Pond Gallery

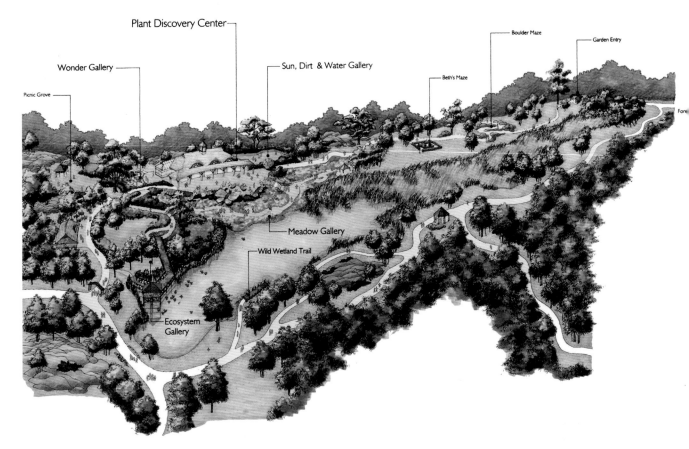

Picnic Grove

Wonder Gallery

Plant Discovery Center

Sun, Dirt & Water Gallery

Boulder Maze

Garden Entry

Beth's Maze

Fore

Meadow Gallery

Wild Wetland Trail

Ecosystem Gallery

Everett Children's Adventure Garden at New York Botanical Garden

CONCEPT

During the initial project, the key New York Botanical Garden staff involved were Catherine Eberbach, manager of the Children's Adventure Program; Glenn Phillips, manager of school programs; Donald Lisowy, manager of teacher enhancement; Barbara Thiers, administrative curator of the Cryptogamic Herbarium; and Charles Peter, associate curator.

The team, known as the Discovery Group, sought the opinions of children and adults. According to Eberbach, "In 1993, the Discovery Group conducted front-end evaluations of twelve focus groups of elementary school children, teachers, and parents to assemble information about attitudes toward science and the outdoors and, specifically, about participants' knowledge of plant biology as well as their reactions to possible garden activities" (Eberbach 2001, 73). Results of the findings were used to make decisions about the garden design that would "reinforce the connection between the design of the exhibits and programs and visitor understanding, experience, and interest" (72).

Formative evaluations for ten exhibits were conducted during the design stage. The exhibits that were selected used real plants, posed operational challenges, informed the design of other exhibit components, or were cognitively challenging.

In 1998, Randi Korn and Associates surveyed visitors to the New York Botanical Garden and conducted postvisit telephone interviews. The design concept development spanned 1992–1998, and the Everett Children's Adventure Garden opened to the public in 1998.

Main entrance

211

Top: Caterpillar topiary adjacent to Steere Discovery Center during different seasons

Bottom: Conceptual sketches of the caterpillar topiary

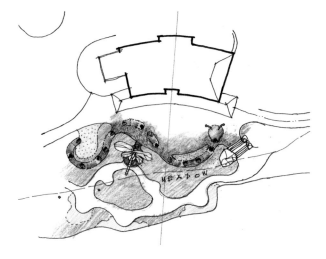

CATERPILLAR TOPIARY
NO SCALE
MKW & A

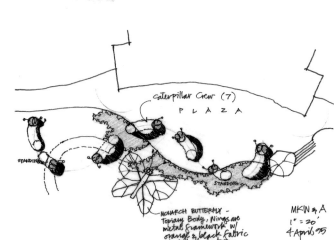

MONARCH BUTTERFLY -
Topiary Body, Wings and
metal framework w/
orange & black fabric
stretched between.

caterpillar crew (7)
PLAZA
STANDING
STANDING

MKW & A
1" = 20'
4 April 95

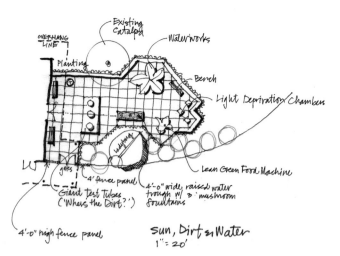

Conceptual plan of Sun, Dirt, and Water Gallery and topiary frog in this garden

DESIGN

The Everett Children's Adventure Garden is a 12-acre (4.9-hectare) outdoor and indoor facility designed for children ages five to twelve to learn about plant science. The programmatic goal is to teach children that (1) plants carry out the life process, (2) plants have life requirements, and (3) plants and their environments are always changing.

"Changing landscapes, themed galleries, and interactive exhibits provide a living and dynamic stage for hands-on learning about plant science," explains Natalie Andersen, vice president for education at New York Botanical Garden. The garden was designed for visitors to explore through self- or staff-guided tours. Visitors have the opportunity to experience more than forty hands-on nature discovery exhibits and activities through interaction with mazes, topiary caterpillars, a giant flower model, plazas, a waterfall, a natural wetland, gardens, a herbarium, and much more. The path through the garden leads to such sites as the Boulder Maze for climbing, a touch tank for examining plants that live in water, and an indoor laboratory for doing experiments and looking through microscopes.

"All programs are created in accordance with New York City Scope and Sequence, the New York State Science Core Curriculum, and the Next Generation Science Standards," says James Boyer, vice president for children's education. The programs respond to Next Generation Science Standards for developing (1) an understanding of the characteristics and life cycles of organisms, (2) an understanding of diversity and adaptation of organisms, (3) an understanding of science and technology, and (4) the ability to do scientific inquiry.

Interpretive sign asks,
"Why do birds build nests?"

Butterfly sculpture

Steere Discovery Center

Touch tank

Boulder Maze

Giant tree cookie

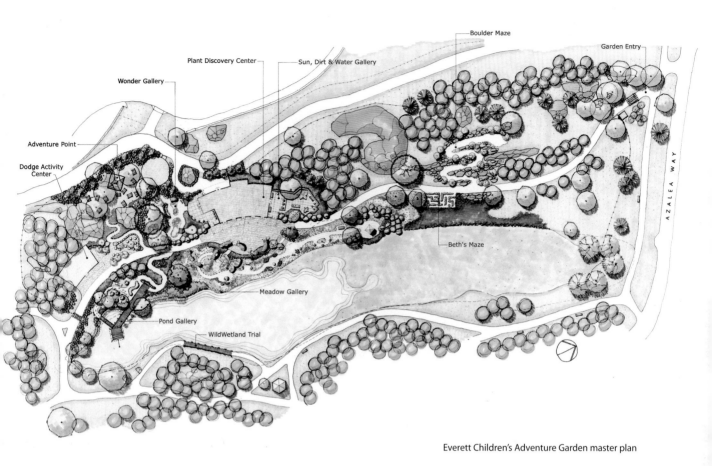

Wonder Gallery

Plant Discovery Center

Sun, Dirt & Water Gallery

Boulder Maze

Garden Entry

Adventure Point

Dodge Activity Center

Beth's Maze

A Z A L E A   W A Y

Meadow Gallery

Pond Gallery

WildWetland Trial

Everett Children's Adventure Garden master plan

Bird's nest

Beth's Maze

Interpretive sign suggests, "Whenever you use the nose, take a good sniff."

Everett Children's Adventure Garden at New York Botanical Garden

215

Heckscher Foundation Wonder Gallery:
Learning plant parts

The Everett Children's Adventure Garden is organized into four outdoor and two indoor learning galleries. Each gallery correlates with a different theme about plant diversity, the life cycles of flowering plants, animal-plant relationships, and photosynthesis. Interactive signs and exhibits within each gallery convey aspects of the theme. Learning takes place during all seasons at the William and Lynda Steere Discovery Center, which houses the Texaco Kids Lab, the Bendheim Kids Herbarium, and the Bendheim Teacher Center.

Top: Plant towers

Bottom: Conceptual sketch of Wonder Gallery

Four outdoor galleries

1 **Heckscher Foundation for Children's Wonder Gallery:** Students learn about the parts of a plant—roots, stems, leaves, and flowers. They compare and contrast different plant parts; invent their very own plants; and make observations about the diversity of plant fragrances, colors, shapes, and sizes.

2 **Arthur Hays and Iphigene Ochs Sulzberger Meadow Gallery:** Students learn about the life cycle of flowering plants. They interact with garden features such as a giant butterfly, learn that flowers attract pollinators, and observe pollination in action.

3 **Vincent Astor Foundation Sun, Dirt, and Water Gallery:** Students learn about photosynthesis. They investigate how the sun helps plants live and grow and why plants are so important.

4 **Con Edison Pond Gallery:** Students explore an ecosystem and discover plant and animal interactions. They investigate what lives near a wetland habitat as they build a bird's nest; collect pond samples; search for cattails, duckweed, frogs and turtles; and play the Food Web Game.

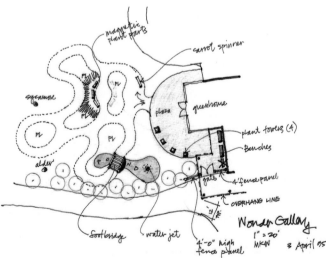

Two indoor galleries

1 **Texaco Kids Lab:** Kids participate in plant experiments, making careful observations and discovering that all science starts by asking questions. They use hand lenses, microscopes, mortars and pestles, and other tools.

2 **Bendheim Kids Herbarium:** Kids are exposed to a library of preserved plants. They examine plant parts by using microscopes and hand lenses, explore discovery boxes, create leaf rubbings, and learn how to prepare a plant specimen for preservation.

UPDATES

The Adventure Garden is constantly evolving. In 2001, the first evaluation of the Everett Children's Adventure Garden was conducted. This was planned in the original design to update and refine existing exhibits. Randi Korn and Associates conducted this evaluation, and enhancements were completed in summer 2005.

Later, in 2012, according to Boyer, "the garden received an Institute for Museum and Library Services grant to conduct visitor surveys, evaluate the Adventure Garden's exhibitry, travel to children's gardens throughout the United States, and pilot test new exhibitry ideas. This grant allowed the garden to [again] hire Randi Korn and Associates to conduct the survey and evaluation components." In 2015, the garden began the redesign of the Adventure Garden to update the educational galleries and plantings and began infrastructure repairs to this seventeen-year-old facility.

Opposite: Steere Discovery Center viewed from across Con Edison Pond Gallery

Top and bottom: Activities in the Con Edison Pond Gallery

Exploring how plants grow
in the water at the touch tank

CONCLUSION

The Everett Children's Adventure Garden, one of the first science-themed gardens for children, has over a dozen galleries, both outdoor and indoor, that allow children to explore nature firsthand and learn the skills and concepts necessary for understanding the natural sciences. The Adventure Garden has educated and entertained over three million visitors since 1998. Annually, the Adventure Garden educates over two hundred thousand visitors through (1) school workshops aligned to New York City Science Scope and Sequence standards, (2) family programs such as summer camps, and (3) drop-in family programs focused on science and nature investigations for children ages three through ten. In 2015, the garden embarked on a redesign project to update and expand the educational concepts and plantings in the Adventure Garden and also make needed repairs to existing paths, fences, and buildings.

Explainer showing a boy aquatic plant roots at the touch tank

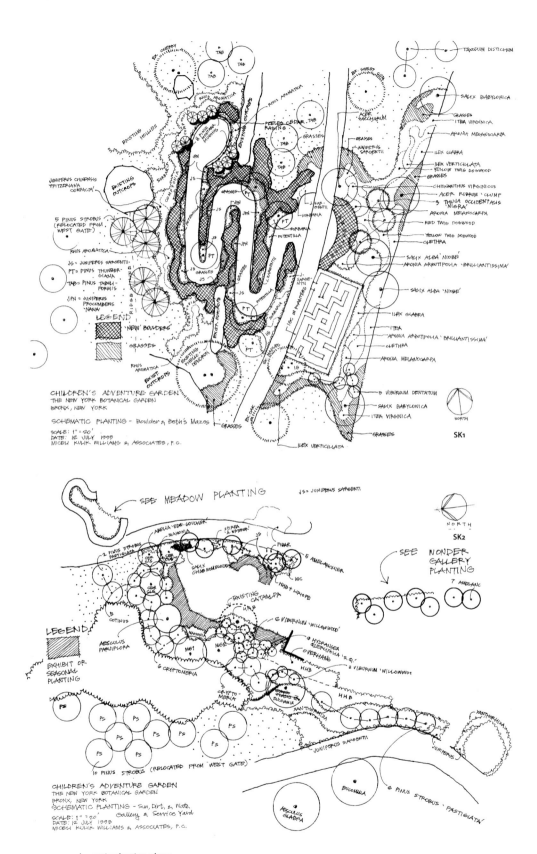

1995 schematic planting plans

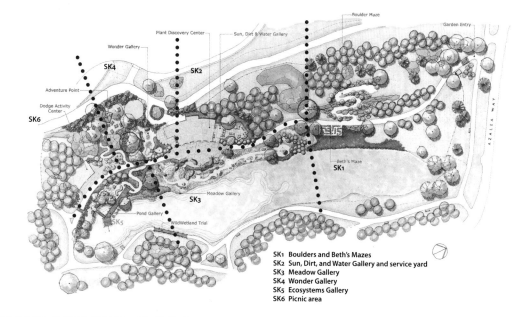

Planting areas

SK1 Boulders and Beth's Mazes
SK2 Sun, Dirt, and Water Gallery and service yard
SK3 Meadow Gallery
SK4 Wonder Gallery
SK5 Ecosystems Gallery
SK6 Picnic area

Plants in the garden

Canopy trees

Acer rubrum
Acer saccharum
Aesculus glabra
Betula nigra 'Cully' Heritage'
Catalpa bignonioides
Celtis occidentalis 'Prairie Pride'
Eucommia ulmoides
Kalopanax pictus
Metasequoia glyptostroboides
Salix alba 'Niobe'
Salix babylonica
Taxodium distichum

Evergreen trees

Abies concolor
Chamaecyparis obtusa 'Gracilis'
Chamaecyparis thyoides
Cryptomeria japonica 'Yoshino'
Ilex × attenuata 'Fosteri'
Ilex pedunculosa
Pinus strobus
Pinus strobus 'Fastigiata'
Pinus tabuliformis
Pinus thunbergii
Sciadopitys verticillata
Thuja occidentalis 'Nigra'

Small trees

Aesculus parviflora
Amelanchier canadensis
Amelanchier canadensis 'White Pillar'
Amelanchier × grandiflora 'Robin Hill Pink'
Cercis canadensis
Cercis canadensis f. *alba*
Chionanthus virginicus
Cornus florida

Franklinia alatamaha
Malus floribunda
Malus 'Prairifire'
Malus 'Snowcloud'
Magnolia virginiana
Oxydendrum arboreum

Large shrubs

Abelia 'Edward Goucher'
Aronia arbutifolia 'Brilliantissima'
Aronia melanocarpa
Buddleja 'White Profusion'
Calycanthus floridus
Cephalanthus occidentalis
Chimonanthus praecox
Clerodendron trichotumum
Clethra alnifolia
Clethra alnifolia 'Rosea'
Cornus alba 'Sibirica'
Cornus sericea 'Flaviramea'
Cornus racemosa
Corylopsis pauciflora
Corylus avellana 'Contorta'
Cotinus coggygria 'Royal Purple'
Cytisus scoparius
Euonymus alata 'Compacta'
Fothergilla gardenii
Hamamelis vernalis
Hamamelis virginiana
Hydrangea quercifolia 'Snow Queen'
Ilex glabra
Ilex glabra 'Compacta'
Ilex verticillata
Ilex verticillata 'Harvest Red'
Ilex verticillata 'Winter Red'
Kerria japonica
Lindera benzoin
Lonicera fragrantissima

Magnolia stellata 'Rubra'
Mahonia bealei
Morella pensylvanica
Pinus mugo
Rhododendron carolinianum
Rhododendron maximum 'Roseum'
Rhododendron periclymenoides
Rhododendron viscosum
Rhus aromatica
Rhus glabra
Rhus typhina
Rosa rugosa
Rosa rugosa 'Alba'
Rubus cockburniana
Salix caprea
Salix melanostachys
Salix purpurea
Sambucus canadensis
Sassafras albidum
Sorbaria sorbifolia
Taxus media 'Hatfieldii'
Vaccinium corymbosum
Virburnum dentatum
Viburnum dilatatum
Viburnum lentago
Viburnum × rhytidophylloides 'Willowwood'
Viburnum setigerum

Shrub mass

Azalea 'Delaware Valley White'
Berberis × gladwynesis 'William Penn'
Berberis thunbergii 'Atropurpurea Nana'
Buddleja davidii 'Nanho Purple'
Buxus microphylla 'Winter Gem'
Callicarpa dichotoma

Caryopteris × clandonensis 'Longwood Blue'
Cassia marilandica
Chamaecyparis obtusa 'Leprechaun'
Comptonia peregrina
Hypericum × 'Hidcote'
Ilex crenata 'Helleri'
Itea virginica 'Henry's Garnet'
Jasminum nudiflorum
Juniperus chinensis 'Pfitzeriana Compacta'
Leucothoe axillaris
Nandina domestica 'Harbor Dwarf'
Pinus mugo 'Gnome'
Pinus strobus 'Sea Urchin'
Potentilla fruticosa 'Abbotswood'
Potentilla fruticosa 'Goldfinger'
Potentilla nepalensis 'Miss Willmott'
Rhododendron 'Dora Amateis'
Rhus aromatica 'Gro-Low'
Rosa 'The Fairy'
Skimmia japonica
Spiraea japonica 'Anthony Waterer'
Spiraea japonica 'Alpina'
Stephanandra incisa 'Crispa'
Symphoricarpos × chenaultii 'Hancockii'
Taxus baccata 'Repandens'
Vaccinium angustifolium
Xanthorhiza simplicissima

Groundcovers

Euonymus fortunei 'Ivory Jade'
Hedera helix 'Baltica'
Juniperus chinensis var. *sargentii*
Juniperus procumbens 'Nana'
Parthenocissus quinquefolia
Parthenocissus tricuspidata 'Veitchii'

Pond Gallery

Perennials

Achillea millefolium 'Hoffnung'
Ajuga pyramidalis 'Silver Carpet'
Ajuga reptans 'Burgundy Glow'
Alchemilla mollis
Allium schoenoprasum 'Schnitt-
    lauch'
Allium senescens
Amsonia tabernaemontana
Anemone tomentosa 'Robustissima'
Aquilegia canadensis
Arabis caucasica 'Flore Pleno'
Arisaema triphyllum
Armeria juniperifolia
Aruncus dioicus
Asclepias incarnata
Asclepias tuberosa
Astilbe chinensis 'Pumila'
Astilbe taquetii 'Purpurlanze'
Baptisia australis
Belamcanda chinensis
Boltonia asteroides 'Snowbank'
Caltha palustris
Cerastium tomentosum
Ceratostigma plumbaginoides
Chelone lyonii
Coreopsis × 'Moonbeam'
Crambe cordifolia
Delosperma cooperi
Dennstaedtia punctilobula
Dicentra spectabilis
Digitalis ambigua
Echinacea purpurea
Echinacea purpurea 'Springbrook's
    Crimson Star'
Echinops bannaticus 'Veitch's Blue'
Epimedium × grandiflorum 'Rose
    Queen'
Epimedium × youngianum 'Niveum'
Epimedium × youngianum 'Roseum'
Eryngium planum 'Blue Cap'
Eryngium planum 'Blue Diamond'
Eutrochium maculatum
Filipendula purpurea
Geranium nodosum
Geranium psilostemon

Geranium sanguineum
Helenium autumnale 'Brilliant'
Helianthus maximillianii
Helleborus orientalis
Hemerocallis 'Penny's Worth'
Hemerocallis 'Summer Wine'
Heuchera micrantha 'Palace Purple'
Hibiscus 'George Regal'
Hibiscus moscheutos 'Lord Balti-
    more'
Hosta plantaginea 'Royal Standard'
Hosta sieboldiana 'Elegans'
Hosta sieboldiana 'Frances Williams'
Iris foetidissima
Iris germanica 'Warrior King'
Lavandula 'Munstead'
Levisticum officinale
Liatris spicata 'Kobold'
Lobelia cardinalis
Lysimachia clethroides
Malva alcea 'Fastigiata'
Matteuccia struthiopteris
Mertensia virginica
Monarda didyma 'Gardenview
    Scarlet'
Monarda 'Raspberry Wine'
Myosotis scorpioides
Opuntia humifusa
Osmunda cinnamomea
Papaver orientale 'Sundance'
Perovskia atriplicifolia
Phlox subulata 'Chuckles'
Physostegia virginiana 'Vivid'
Platycodon grandiflora 'Mariesii
    Blue'
Polygonatum odoratum 'Variega-
    tum'
Polystichum acrostichoides
Pulmonaria saccharata 'Spilled Milk'
Pulsatilla vulgaris 'Rubra'
Rodgersia aesculifolia
Rudbeckia fulgida 'Goldsturm'
Salvia officinalis 'Tri-color'
Santolina chamaecyparissus
Sedum 'Autumn Joy'
Sedum kamtschaticum 'Variegatum'
Sedum sieboldii

Sedum spurium 'Dragon's Blood'
Sedum spurium 'Tricolor'
Sedum 'Ruby Glow'
Sedum 'Vera Jameson'
Sempervivum 'Cobweb'
Sempervivum 'Purple Passion'
Sempervivum tectorum
Stachys byzantina 'Lambrook Silver'
Stachys byzantina 'Silver Carpet'
Thymus × citriodorus
Thymus praecox ssp. arcticus 'Minor'
Tiarella cordifolia
Tricyrtis hirta
Verbascum bombyciferum

Grasses and grasslike plants

Arundo donax
Briza media
Carex muskingumensis
Carex pendula
Chasmanthium latifolium
Eriophorum latifolium
Fargesia nitida
Festuca ovina var. glauca
Glyceria pallida
Hakonechloa macra 'Aureola'
Leersia oryzoides
Liriope muscari 'Variegata'
Miscanthus sinensis 'Gracillimus
    Nana'
Molinia arundinacea 'Staefa'
Panicum virgatum 'Haense Herms'
Pennisetum alopecuroides
Pennisetum alopecuroides 'Hamelin'
Pennisetum alopecuroides 'Little
    Bunny'
Phalaris arundinacea 'Picta'
Sporobolus heterolepis

Vines

Actinidia kolomikta
Aristolochia macrophylla
Hydrangea anomala spp. petiolaris
Lonicera periclymenum 'Graham
    Thomas'

Bulbs

Allium giganteum
Camassia cusickii
Camassia leichtlinii 'Coerula'
Colchicum 'Autumn Queen'
Colchicum autumnale plenum
Colchicum 'Waterlily'
Crocus sieberi 'Tricolor'
Lilium canadense
Lilium 'Rosepoint Lace'
Lilium 'Tiger Babies'
Muscari armeniacum
Muscari armeniacum 'Blue Spike'
Narcissus bulbocodium var.
    conspicuous
Narcissus 'Ice Follies'
Narcissus 'Segovia'
Narcissus 'Sir Winston Churchill'
Narcissus 'Tete-a-Tete'
Narcissus 'Thalia'
Narcissus × gracilis
Narcissus × odorus
Narcissus poeticus 'Actaea'
Scilla siberica 'Spring Beauty'
Tulipa clusiana
Tulipa 'Little Beauty'
Tulipa tarda

Aquatic plants

Azolla caroliniana
Equisetum hyemale var. robustum
Iris pseudacorus
Iris pseudacorus 'Variegata'
Iris versicolor
Nelumbo nucifera 'Momo Botan'
Nymphaea odorata 'Attraction'
Nymphaea odorata 'Marliac White'
Nymphaea odorata 'Rose Arey'
Nymphaea × pygmaea 'Helvola'
Polygonum punctatum
Pontederia cordata
Sagittaria latifolia
Salvinia rotundifolia
Sparganium americanum
Symplocarpus foetidus
Typha angustifolia
Zizania aquatica

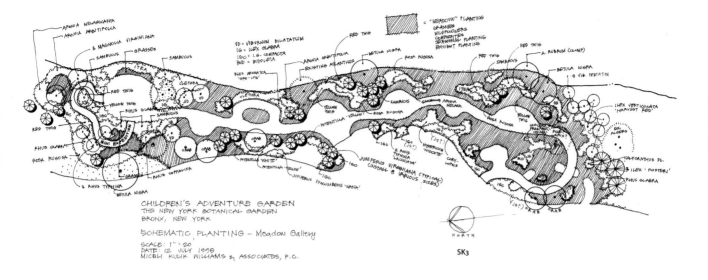

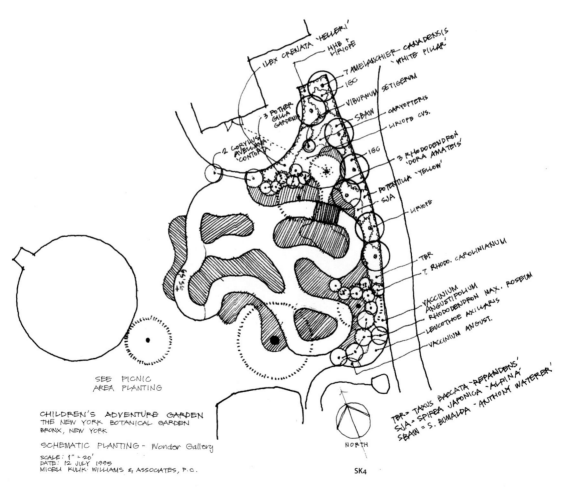

1995 schematic planting plans

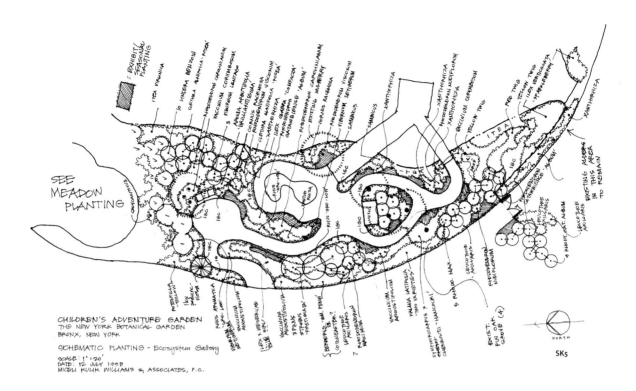

CHILDREN'S ADVENTURE GARDEN
THE NEW YORK BOTANICAL GARDEN
BRONX, NEW YORK

SCHEMATIC PLANTING - Ecosystem Gallery
SCALE: 1"=20'
DATE: 12 JULY 1995
MICELI KULIK WILLIAMS & ASSOCIATES, P.C.

SK5

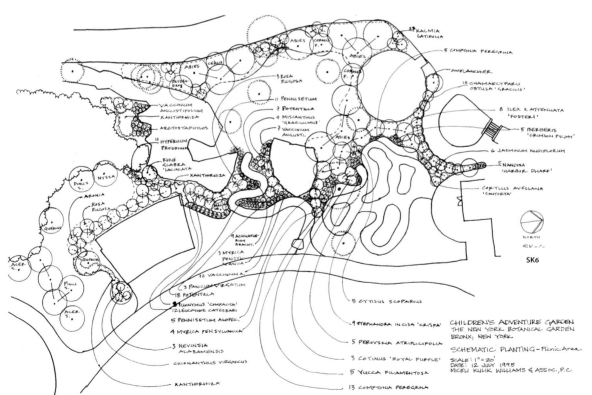

CHILDREN'S ADVENTURE GARDEN
THE NEW YORK BOTANICAL GARDEN
BRONX, NEW YORK

SCHEMATIC PLANTING - Picnic Area
SCALE: 1"=20'
DATE: 12 JULY 1995
MICELI KULIK WILLIAMS & ASSOC., P.C.

SK6

1995 schematic planting plans

Performing a field study

Everett Children's Adventure Garden
New York Botanical Garden
2900 Southern Boulevard, Bronx, NY 10458
718-817-8700   http://www.nybg.org/gardens/adventure-garden/index.php

Opening date: May 1998
Project size: 12 acres (4.9 hectares) within New York Botanical Garden's 250-acre (101.2-hectare) site

1992–1998 Design and Construction Team
New York Botanical Garden:
 Initial concept designer: Coe Lee Robinson Roesch (Jon Coe)
 Children's Adventure Program manager: Catherine Eberbach
 School programs manager: Glenn Phillips
 Teacher enhancement manager: Donald Lisowy
 Cryptogamic Herbarium, administrative curator: Barbara Thiers
 Associate curator: Charles Peter
Landscape architect: MKW and Associates LLC (John Williams, principal in charge; Allen E. Juba,
  project director and designer)
Architect: Dattner Architects (Beth Greenberg, project director)
Civil engineer: Wohl and O'Mara LLP
Consulting engineer: Jack Green Associates
Exhibit designer: Van Sickle and Rolleri Ltd. (Andrea Rolleri)
Landscape contractor: Bulfamante and Sons

2001–2008 Enhancement Project Team
Vice president for education: Natalie Andersen
Children's education programming director: Debra Epstein
Agency design team: Carbone Smolan

2015 Redesign Team
Vice president for children's education: James Boyer
Everett Children's Adventure Garden director: Pattie Hulse
Exhibit designer: Metcalfe Architecture and Design LLC
Landscape architect: Towers/Golde LLC
Architect: Berg and Forster Architects PLLC
Mechanical, electrical, and plumbing engineer: JMV Consulting Engineering PC

Current Contacts
Vice president for children's education: James Boyer
Everett Children's Adventure Garden director: Pattie Hulse

Interviews and Personal Communications
Natalie Andersen, 2005; James Boyer, August 4, 2014; Allen Juba, September 17, 2015

Central Valley: Prairie, Dry Creek, and
Gathering Lawn in the foreground; three
Native American huts in the midground; Glass
House and Harvest Gardens in the background

Childhood's Gate Children's Garden in the Arboretum at Pennsylvania State University

UNIVERSITY PARK, PENNSYLVANIA

GOAL

The goal of Childhood's Gate Children's Garden is to connect children to the living world and instill an appreciation of nature and stewardship in them. The design focuses on creating a garden with a theme that celebrates the indigenous central Pennsylvania environment. In concert with this theme, "Childhood's Gate" refers to a line in Penn State's alma mater: "When we stood at childhood's gate, / Shapeless in the hands of fate, / Thou didst mold us, dear old State, / Dear old State, dear old State." Located within the Arboretum's H. O. Smith Botanic Gardens, this garden connects the academic and research programs of Penn State. The garden is open for the enjoyment of visitors during all seasons of the year.

CONCEPT

The children's garden theme centers on the geomorphology and native flora, fauna, and culture of the region. It was the outcome of a team effort involving Penn State childhood development experts, the design firms EDAW/AECOM and Didier Design Studio, and the Arboretum leadership and staff. The garden is targeted to children ages three through twelve and designed to convey an interesting story to them about what is in their own backyard while deepening connections between generations. "The garden provides a peaceful setting. As families experience the natural setting, parents and grandparents may find time to share stories with their young loved ones," remarks Emmanuel Didier. The idea of bringing children to a children's garden at the Arboretum at Penn State came about in 2009 when Linda Duerr, children's educational programs coordinator, approached Kim Steiner, director of the Arboretum, about it. Didier, a Colorado-based landscape architect who had previously designed children's gardens such as the Ann Goldstein's Children's Rainforest Garden in Sarasota, Florida, was chosen as the lead designer.

The design process began in October 2011 and took seven months. Refinements followed over the course of the following year. Construction commenced in April 2013, plants were added in May and June 2014, and the garden was opened in July 2014.

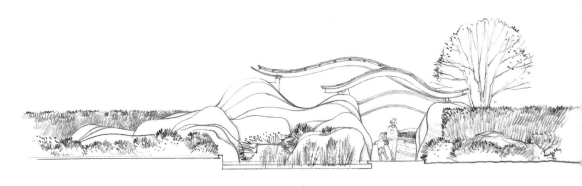

Design sketches and built entrance of Childhood's Gate by Didier Design Studio

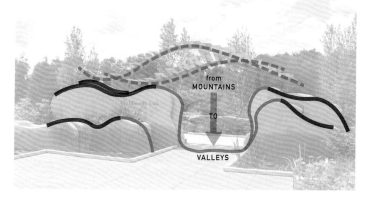

Resine panels celebrate the patterns within the local, agrarian landscape

DESIGN

To design the garden, Didier relied on his knowledge of child psychology, experience from his own childhood, and input from his children. Didier says, "I haven't forgotten what excited me and what it's like to climb up a place and see it from above or go under it. A child sees the world more in three dimensions than adults [do]."

The garden is small, slightly less than an acre. To make the garden appear larger, "the space was designed into a series of rooms that are created by topography, going from ridges to valleys to ridges and so on," explains Didier. The garden is composed of three areas: Rocky Ridges at the entry, Central Valley, and Fossil Gap. Artifacts related to the region's geologic history are integrated within each area.

Rocky Ridges

The entrance to the garden is elegantly defined by stone walls arranged in vertical planes, with "Childhood's Gate" inscribed on the outer wall. A canopy of undulating colored glass panels and lily pools flank both sides of the entry walkway. The entrance design takes its cues from the region's mountain ridges, valleys, and streams. Inside the entrance is Rocky Ridges, a space that showcases a miniature landscape constructed of large boulders and cut stone collected locally. In this space, a spring-like water feature and plants native to ridges within the physiographic Ridge and Valley Province provide the initial atmosphere of the garden approach.

Central Valley

From Rocky Ridges, visitors proceed into the low, rolling, open, and sunny Central Valley. This area features the agrarian culture, past and present, that characterizes the limestone valleys within the Ridge and Valley Province. The story of the Native Americans is told through the display of three willow-woven hut shelters and plantings including the "three sisters" (inter-plantings of maize, beans, and squash). The Prairie Patch, accompanied by a life-size bronze sculpture of a reclining bison, is a reminder that "Penn's Woods" was never completely forested. Anchoring the southern end is the Amphitheater for outdoor events. Highlighting the skyline on the north end is the twenty-foot-tall garden cloche–shaped Glass House with the raised-bed Harvest Gardens nearby. The Gathering Lawn is for group activities. A sod-roofed Garden Shed; the Farm Pump, an interactive water element; small bronze sculptures of local wildlife; and space for creative activities are other features in this area. Permanent plantings in the Central Valley feature species native to the limestone valleys.

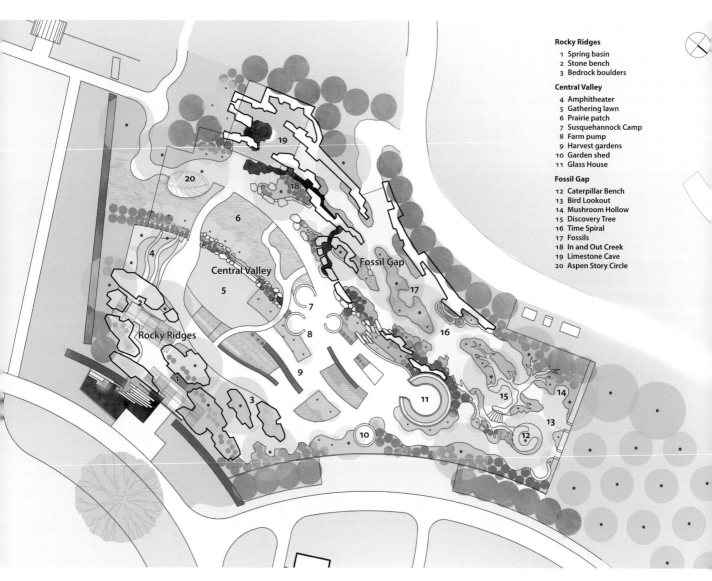

Rocky Ridges

1 Spring basin
2 Stone bench
3 Bedrock boulders

Central Valley

4 Amphitheater
5 Gathering lawn
6 Prairie patch
7 Susquehannock Camp
8 Farm pump
9 Harvest gardens
10 Garden shed
11 Glass House

Fossil Gap

12 Caterpillar Bench
13 Bird Lookout
14 Mushroom Hollow
15 Discovery Tree
16 Time Spiral
17 Fossils
18 In and Out Creek
19 Limestone Cave
20 Aspen Story Circle

Illustrative plan by Didier Design Studio

Bird's-eye view of garden

Childhood's Gate Children's Garden in the Arboretum at Pennsylvania State University

THE MAGIC OF CHILDREN'S GARDENS

Opposite: Glass House and Harvest Gardens

Top left: Glass House and Harvest Gardens

Top right: Amphitheater

Bottom: A teachable moment between instructor and child

Fossil Gap

From the Central Valley, along the circulating In and Out Creek, visitors enter the subterranean Limestone Cave with stalactites and stalagmites, a colony of bronze bats, and a secret passageway. The roof of the cave is an elevated sinkhole. Within the cave, a hidden pump provides a constant supply of dripping water through an oculus in the roof, which also creates light and dark contrasts in the cave as the sun moves.

Beyond the cave and within walls of native stone and shotcrete is a space evocative of the wild and forested ridges and narrow valleys and gaps that stretch south of Nittany Valley. Here the themes are wilderness, native plants and animals, and geologic prehistory. The Time Spiral identifies key plants and animals that existed in the region during the course of evolution, and fossil sculptures depict giant versions of three local creatures from millions of years ago. Mushroom Hollow re-creates the contemporary woodland environment in local mountains. The large shotcrete Discovery Tree stump and a young tree growing within it celebrate life, birth, and cycles of life. The Caterpillar Bench is a giant sculpture of the spicebush swallowtail caterpillar, often found in living form on nearby shrubs. Shotcrete toadstool seats depict a common native mushroom species, and the Bird Lookout offers a view to off-site birdfeeders. Sculptures and seating are nestled underneath selected trees that represent Pennsylvania's native forests. Play opportunities within the Discovery Tree include a chime, peek holes, a fairy garden, and sound tubes.

CONCLUSION

Childhood's Gate Children's Garden is truly a unique and elegantly designed place for discovery and learning about the animals and geomorphology of central Pennsylvania. Visitors experience the garden on a vast and compressed scale through open and constricted detail spaces. Every feature in the garden is carefully studied and meticulously designed to present the garden theme in the most effective and appealing way. The garden fosters an appreciation of nature and the indigenous landscape in children. It bridges play, art, and science.

Top left and right: Study model of wall and satellite image of Pennsylvania geomorphology

Center: Black ridge wall design

Bottom left and right: In and Out Creek and blackboard on west face of main wall

Precedent Image of Penn. Cave With Boulders

Precedent Image of Shotcrete

Precedent Image of Penn. Geology

Precedent Image of Penn. Geology

Precedent Image of Tear Drop Park

Precedent Image of Quarry Boulder

Shotcrete

Stone Type B

Stone Type B

Stone Type B/ Boulder

Grotto: Front, east elevation

Top left and right: Pennsylvania geomorphology and detail of stone layers used for construction

Center: Stone precedent studies and Limestone Cave front elevation

Bottom: Limestone Cave

Childhood's Gate Children's Garden in the Arboretum at Pennsylvania State University

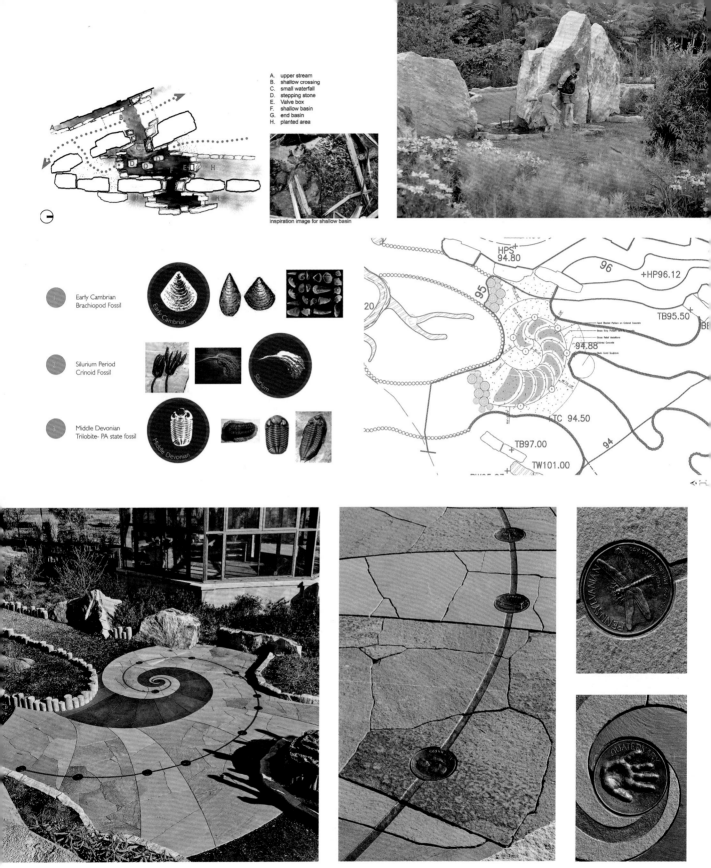

A. upper stream
B. shallow crossing
C. small waterfall
D. stepping stone
E. Valve box
F. shallow basin
G. end basin
H. planted area

inspiration image for shallow basin

1 Early Cambrian
   Brachiopod Fossil

2 Silurium Period
   Crinoid Fossil

3 Middle Devonian
   Trilobite- PA state fossil

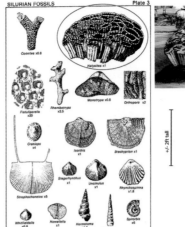

SILURIAN FOSSILS   Plate 3

Halysite fossil sculptural ornament should have smooth edges, and present some shallow cavities on the top.

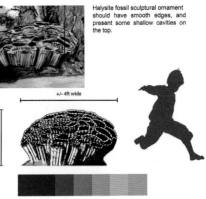

+/- 4ft wide

+/- 2ft tall

Halysite fossil sculptural ornament

Opposite top: Lower stream (In and Out Creek) design intent and boys playing in creek

Opposite middle: Fossil floor medallions

Opposite bottom: Time Spiral and details

Top left: Study model of shell seat

Top right to bottom: Fossil graphics and design by Didier Design Studio

DEVONIAN FOSSILS   Plate 8

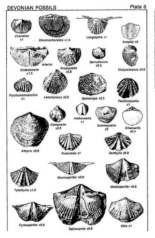

sitting bench fossil shell

SILURIAN AND DEVONIAN FOSSILS   Plate 5

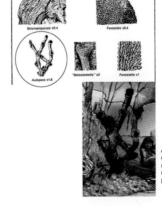

+/- 4ft tall

Aulopora fossil sculptural ornament should have smooth edges, and present some shallow cavities at the nodes as shown on the graphics. The overall structure should be made stable with a footing or base, and be safe for child potential climbing.

Aulopora fossil sculptural ornament

Childhood's Gate Children's Garden in the Arboretum at Pennsylvania State University

Discovery Tree

Selected plants in the garden

Trees

Abies balsamea
Acer negundo
Acer pensylvanicum
Acer rubrum 'Brandywine'
Acer saccharum 'Bailsta' Fall Fiesta
Acer saccharum 'Green Mountain'
Acer saccharum 'Legacy'
Amelanchier laevis
Asimina triloba
Betula alleghaniensis
Betula lenta
Betula papyrifera 'Renci' Renaissance Reflection
Carpinus caroliniana
Carya ovata
Cercis canadensis
Cornus alternifolia
Cornus florida 'Appalachian Spring'
Fagus grandifolia
Juniperus virginiana 'Burkii'
Liriodendron tulipifera
Malus × *domestica* 'Banning Gala'
Malus × *domestica* 'Florina'
Malus × *domestica* 'Co-op 38'
Malus spp.
Nyssa sylvatica
Ostrya virginiana
Pinus rigida
Pinus strobus 'Fastigiata'
Pinus virginiana
Populus tremuloides
Quercus coccinea
Quercus montana
Quercus muehlenbergii
Quercus rubra
Sassafras albidum
Sorbus americana
Tilia americana 'McKSentry' American Sentry
Tsuga canadensis

Shrubs

Aesculus parviflora
Alnus incana
Amelanchier stolonifera
Aronia melanocarpa 'Morton' Iroquois Beauty
Ceanothus americanus
Cephalanthus occidentalis
Comptonia peregrina
Cornus sericea 'Cardinal'
Cornus sericea 'Flaviramea'
Gaultheria procumbens
Hamamelis vernalis
Hamamelis virginiana
Hydrangea arborescens
Hydrangea quercifolia
Ilex verticillata 'Winter Red'
Ilex 'Apollo'
Itea virginica 'Merlot'
Kalmia latifolia
Lindera benzoin
Physocarpus opulifolius
Quercus ilicifolia
Rhododendron maximum
Rhododendron spp.
Rhus aromatica 'Gro-Low'
Rhus copallina
Rhus typhina
Ribes hirtellum 'Pixwell'
Ribes nigrum 'Consort'
Ribes rubrum 'Red Lake'
Rosa virginiana
Rubus odoratus
Salix sericea
Sambucus nigra 'Adams'
Sambucus nigra 'York'
Sambucus nigra
Spiraea alba
Vaccinium angustifolium
Vaccinium corymbosum 'Jersey'
Vaccinium corymbosum 'Patriot'
Viburnum dentatum

Viburnum dentatum 'Christom' Blue Muffin
Viburnum nudum
Viburnum nudum 'Bulk' Brandywine
Viburnum 'Pragense'

Vines

Aristolochia macrophylla
Bignonia capreolata 'Tangerine Beauty'
Campsis radicans 'Flava'
Celastrus scandens 'Bailumn' First Editions Autumn Revolution
Clematis virginiana
Parthenocissus quinquefolia
Vitis labrusca 'Catawba'
Vitis labrusca 'Concord'
Vitis 'Himrod'

Perennials

Actaea racemosa
Allium cernuum
Allium tricoccum
Amsonia hubrichtii
Amsonia 'Blue Ice'
Anemone canadensis
Aquilegia canadensis
Aralia racemosa
Asarum canadense
Asclepias tuberosa
Baptisia australis
Campanula americana
Carex pensylvanica
Carex platyphylla
Chasmanthium latifolium
Chrysogonum virginianum
Dennstaedtia punctilobula
Deschampsia cespitosa
Dicentra eximia
Echinacea pallida
Echinacea 'Matthew Saul' Big Sky Series Harvest Moon

Eryngium yuccifolium
Eurybia divaricate
Geranium maculatum
Geranium maculatum 'Espresso'
Helianthus × *multiflorus* 'Sunshine Daydream' Garden Candy
Heuchera longiflora
Heuchera villosa 'Autumn Bride'
Iris versicolor
Liatris spicata
Lobelia cardinalis
Matteuccia struthiopteris
Meehania cordata
Nassella tenuissima
Onoclea sensibilis
Osmunda cinnamomea
Pachysandra procumbens
Panicum virgatum 'Northwind'
Penstemon digitalis
Phlox paniculata 'David'
Polygonatum biflorum
Polygonatum odoratum 'Variegatum'
Polystichum acrostichoides
Pycnanthemum muticum
Rudbeckia subtomentosa 'Henry Eilers'
Schizachyrium scoparium 'The Blues'
Sesleria autumnalis
Silphium laciniatum
Solidago rugosa 'Fireworks'
Solidago sphacelata 'Golden Fleece'
Sporobolus heterolepis
Symphyotrichum ericoides
Symphyotrichum laeve
Symphyotrichum oblongifolium
Thermopsis villosa
Viola labradorica
Viola walteri 'Silver Gem'

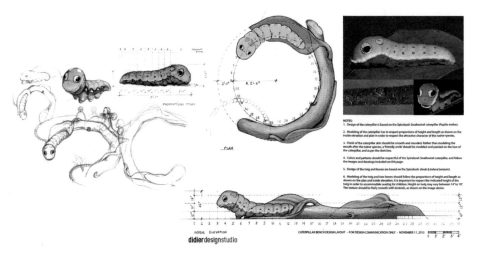

Caterpillar Bench study and detail; design is based on a caterpillar resting on the leaf of a bent twig, creating a reading circle

Childhood's Gate Children's Garden in the Arboretum at Pennsylvania State University

Corner of Park Avenue and Bigler Road, University Park, PA 16802

814-865-9118   https://arboretum.psu.edu/gardens/gardens-groves

Opening date: July 7, 2014

Project size: 0.91 acre (0.36 hectare) within the Arboretum at Penn State's 370-acre (149.7-hectare, including the 35-acre H. O. Smith Botanic Gardens, of which 6 acres are developed and the rest is planned) site

Design and Construction Team

Arboretum at Penn State:

   Arboretum director: Kim Steiner

   Children's educational programs coordinator: Linda Duerr

   Horticulture director and curator: Shari Edelson

   Development director: Patrick Williams

   Event and marketing coordinator: Kate Reeder

   Penn State faculty and facilities: Judy Larkin, project manager; Gordon Turow, director of Campus Planning and Design; David Zehngut, university architect; Derek Kalp, landscape architect; faculty: Eliza Pennypacker, Landscape Architecture Department; Joyce Robinson, Art History Department; Scott Wing, Architecture Department; Peter Wilf, David Gold, and Mark Patzkowsky, Geosciences Department

Landscape architect:

   Landscape architect of record and construction supervisor: EDAW/AECOM (Mike Arnold, project manager)

   Principal landscape architect and creative designer: Didier Design Studio (Emmanuel Didier)

Artist for bronze bison sculpture: J. Clayton Bright

Artist for Time Spiral: Philip Hawk

Electrical and mechanical engineer: AECOM

General contractor: Leonard S. Fiore Inc.

Glass House: Emmanuel Didier (designer); Glass House USA Inc. (fabricator)

Mason: Bair's Stone Masonry

Shotcrete consultant: Dodson Studios Inc. (April Dodson)

Structural engineer: AECOM (Stephanie Kim)

Current Contacts

Arboretum director: Kim Steiner

Interviews and Personal Communications

Emmanuel Didier, November 16, 2015; Judy Larkin, January 5, 2106; Kim Steiner, January 5, 2106

The Children's Garden at River Farm is set within
the formal gardens surrounding the property's
early twentieth-century estate house

Children's Garden at River Farm

ALEXANDRIA, VIRGINIA

GOAL

The Children's Garden at River Farm began as small-scale themed display gardens that were created and featured as part of the kickoff of the American Horticultural Society's National Children and Youth Garden Symposium during the summer of 1993. The goal of the Children's Garden project was to inspire parents, educators, garden designers, and others to become advocates for children's gardens, ultimately leading to the creation of natural play and hands-on study areas in backyards and school grounds. This initiative was fitting to the mission of the society: "To open the eyes of all Americans to the vital connection between people and plants, to inspire all Americans to become responsible caretakers of the Earth, to celebrate America's diversity through the art and science of horticulture" (American Horticultural Society, n.d., "Our Mission"). The circumstances surrounding the creation of the garden—including an aggressive installation time line and limited resources—made it necessary that a creative approach be an integral part of the designers' thinking. The project was built and supported by volunteers and in-kind gifts because of limited resources. This children's garden was novel for its time, a pioneer in its field. It has since served as a model and inspiration for children's gardens across the country.

CONCEPT

The original Children's Garden, created by a diverse group of volunteers including school groups and professional landscape designers, consisted of a dozen small, themed gardens built on 2 acres (0.8 hectare). The gardens were 125 to 300 square feet (11.6 to 27.8 square meters) each—small enough to easily be incorporated into most home backyards or school sites. The initiative was led by Maureen Heffernan, American Horticultural Society education coordinator, and Connie Pearson of Pearson Design Associates. The gardens were designed to stimulate children's interest in plants and nature while also inviting imaginative play and exploration. Heffernan says, "These gardens encourage children to play, dream, explore, discover, and fully use all of their senses . . . and to please touch, taste, smell, feel, and listen" (American Horticultural Society 1993a, 11). Pearson actively encouraged landscape professionals to participate in the Children's Garden project to create "a natural forum for professionals to show wonderful opportunities to these family markets" (11).

Top: Maze Garden planted with zinnias in front
of a scene from *Little House on the Prairie*

Bottom: Sunflower House by Penelope Hobhouse
and Associates

An Imagination Garden

Bat Cave

Alphabet Garden

DESIGN

The twelve small, adjacent garden plots of 1993 were contained within a rectangular space and connected with mulched paths. Each garden was designed independently and was intended to offer a stand-alone experience while contributing to the overall experience. Four of the gardens were created by school groups, and the remainder were the work of garden designers and local nurseries. These original twelve gardens were the foundation for later gardens with different themes. The details in each garden provided children with opportunities for learning and exploration while developing a lifelong appreciation for plants and the natural environment:

- **Alphabet Garden:** An "alphabet book" mixes the familiar with the new. Its brightly painted wooden letters correspond to plants, animals, and other garden objects in this garden and stimulate learning for younger children.
- **A Child's Garden:** A color wheel, an heirloom vegetable garden, a fun "zoo" of plants with animal-inspired names, and a water garden are surrounded by a diverse collection of tropical plants to inspire love of gardening.
- **A Ditch Garden:** A ditch represents the natural stream in our artificial landscapes and provides opportunity for observation of natural phenomena.
- **A Prairie Garden:** Filled with native plants, the garden connects children to plants through the endearing book *Little House on the Prairie*.
- **An Imagination Garden:** Plants in this garden attract a wealth of wildlife and encourage exploration.
- **Colonial Wind, Weather, and Sundial Garden:** Instruments in the garden invite interaction, observation, and weather forecasting. The garden's winding path welcomes exploration and offers an inviting place to sit and stay awhile.

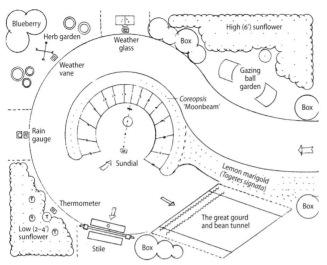

Colonial Wind, Weather and Sundial Garden

Labels within image 1:
Blueberry
Herb garden
Weather glass
Weather vane
Box
High (6') sunflower
Gazing ball garden
Box
Rain gauge
Coreopsis 'Moonbeam'
Sundial
Box
Lemon marigold (*Tagetes signata*)
Thermometer
Low (2–4') sunflower
Stile
Box
The great gourd and bean tunnel

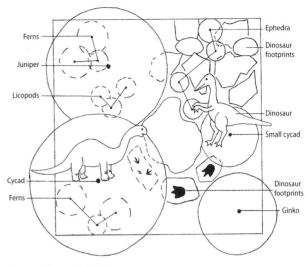

Dinosaur Footprint Garden

Labels within image 2:
Ferns
Juniper
Licopods
Cycad
Ferns
Ephedra
Dinosaur footprints
Dinosaur
Small cycad
Dinosaur footprints
Ginko

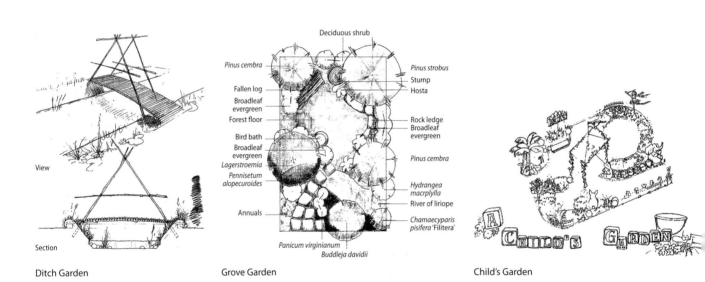

Labels within image 3 (left — Ditch Garden):
View
Section
Ditch Garden

Labels (center — Grove Garden):
Deciduous shrub
Pinus cembra
Fallen log
Broadleaf evergreen
Forest floor
Bird bath
Broadleaf evergreen
Lagerstroemia
Pennisetum alopecuroides
Annuals
Panicum virginianum
Buddleja davidii
Pinus strobus
Stump
Hosta
Rock ledge
Broadleaf evergreen
Pinus cembra
Hydrangea macrplylla
River of liriope
Chamaecyparis pisifera 'Filitera'
Grove Garden

Labels (right — Child's Garden):
A CHILD'S GARDEN
Child's Garden

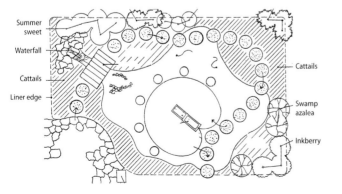

Discovery Pond Garden

Labels within image 4:
Summer sweet
Waterfall
Cattails
Liner edge
Cattails
Swamp azalea
Inkberry

Imagination Garden

Labels within Imagination Garden:
Hemerocallis 'Bountiful Valley'
Sedum 'Autumn Joy'
Aster 'Moench'
Brick pavers and sod
Morus alba 'Chaparral'
Seasonal annuals
Buddleia 'Nanho Purple'
Sand box bench, 6" x 6" g.c. timber, 12" tall
Weathered-edge fieldstone, granite, and sands cobbles, selected for color range
Cymbopogon citratus
Seasonal annuals
Helianthus 'Mammoth'
Spirea 'Anthony Waterer'
Edging of cobbles, tree sections
Ruta graveolens
Apatosaurus (formerly Brontosaurus)
Rheum palmatum
Pennisetum alopecuroides

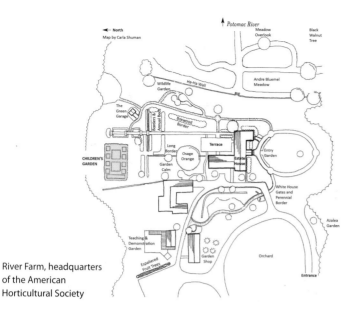

River Farm, headquarters of the American Horticultural Society

The American Horticultural Society is one of the oldest national gardening organizations in the United States. Since 1973, its headquarters has been based at River Farm, which was originally part of George Washington's farmland. Overlooking the Potomac River, River Farm has formal and naturalistic gardens including a four-acre meadow, a vegetable demonstration garden, and a dozen themed children's gardens.

- **Dinosaur Footprint Garden:** Nonflowering gymnosperms and stones imprinted with replicas of fossil dinosaur footprints in the garden introduce land-plant evolution.
- **Discovery Pond Garden:** A thriving pond environment is the centerpiece and introduces children to marshland, cattails, and other native plants.
- **The Grove Garden:** A green grove provides an intimate place for personal experiences with nature.
- **Native Plant Butterfly Garden:** Attracting and providing a habitat for myriad butterflies, the garden provides an environment for learning about habitats.
- **Persian Carpet Garden:** A special floral showcase inspired by Persian carpet designs displays a wide variety of plants with many different flower and foliage colors, forms, and textures and provides pure delight.
- **Sunflower House:** A Wendy house surrounded by sunflowers connects children to plants through the story of Peter Pan.

Originally planned as display gardens of limited duration, the longevity and practicality of the first set of themed gardens varied tremendously. While the framework of the initial garden layout is still evident, most of the original gardens have been replaced or modified over the course of more than twenty years. High-maintenance plantings and exhibit elements have been replaced with lower-maintenance gardens; tired plantings have been reinvigorated; and new themes have been introduced with the eager help of garden clubs, community service organizations, and local youth groups. Additionally, the society's National Children and Youth Garden Symposium, which has enjoyed continued success since its debut in 1993, has taken the message of the importance of youth gardening to different cities across the country each summer. In a nod to its River Farm roots, the symposium returns to its Virginia home base every few years, spurring further renovations and updates to the garden. The themed gardens in 2015 were the Bamboo Hut, the Fairy Tale Garden, the Butterfly Garden, Beau Beau's Garden, the Garden Chalkboard, the Boat Garden, the Little House on the Prairie Garden, Teepee Trellis, Touch 'n' Sniff, the Bat Cave, the Maze Garden, Hide 'n' Seek, the Hummingbird Garden, Rest Stop, and Rock 'n' Roll.

Bamboo Hut

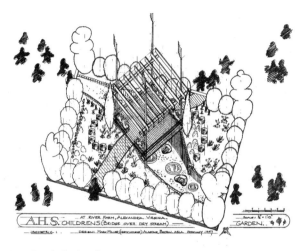

Beau Beau's Garden plan

Beau Beau's Garden

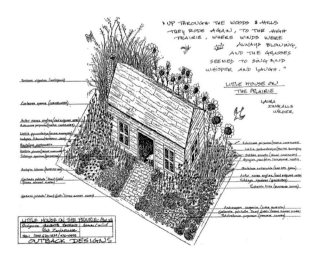

Little House on the Prairie plan

Little House on the Prairie

Fairy Tale Garden

Butterfly Garden

Garden Chalkboard

Boat Garden

Teepee Trellis

Touch 'n' Sniff

Children's Garden at River Farm

CONCLUSION

Founded in 1922, the American Horticultural Society has a long history of supporting gardening and outdoor learning for children and their families, as well as children and youth gardening initiatives. The Children's Garden at River Farm was, and continues to be, a true grassroots effort made possible by volunteers and donations. It is a tribute to the energy and enthusiasm that prevailed in 1993 when the project was first envisioned. The site has evolved into a living laboratory that is constantly changing and has served as an outdoor classroom for scores of horticulturists in training through the society's internship and volunteer programs.

Selected plants in the garden

Trees
Acer palmatum
Cedrus atlantica (Glauca Group)
Fagus sylvatica (Atropurpurea Group)
Lagerstroemia indica
Morus alba 'Pendula'
Picea abies
Rhus typhina

Shrubs
Buddleja alternifolia
Buxus sempervirens
Clethra alnifolia
Euonymus japonica
Hydrangea arborescens
Physocarpus opulifolius
Lonicera nitida
Nandina domestica

Rhus aromatica 'Gro-Low'
Spiraea spp.

Perennials
Acanthus mollis
Allium spp.
Amsonia hubrichtii
Baptisia australis
Chelone glabra
Coreopsis verticillata
Helianthus angustifolius
Heuchera villosa
Hibiscus moscheutos
Hosta spp.
Lychnis coronaria
Monarda didyma
Musa acuminata
Nepeta × *faassenii*
Polygonatum odoratum

Rudbeckia hirta
Salvia officinalis
Sedum 'Autumn Joy'
Sedum kamtschaticum
Solidago rugosa
Stachys byzantina

Grasses
Chasmanthium latifolium
Panicum virgatum

Groundcovers
Liriope muscari
Ophiopogon japonicus

Vines
Bignonia capreolata
Campsis radicans
Lonicera sempervirens

Opposite left to right: The Maze Garden planted with dwarf sunflowers. Adjacent rose arbor contributes to the atmosphere in this garden. Nearby horticultural display beds and garden benches welcome visitors and illustrate the broad appeal of the River Farm gardens.

Right: A child learning to plant in the garden

The Children's Garden at River Farm, American Horticultural Society's Headquarters

7931 East Boulevard Drive, Alexandria, VA 22308

703-768-5700   http://www.ahs.org/about-river-farm/virtual-tour/childrens-garden

Opening date: Father's Day weekend June 19 and 20, 1993

Project size: 2 acres (0.8 hectares) within River Farm's 25-acre (10.1-hectare) site

Design and Construction Team

1993 Children's Garden Project Sponsor: W. Atlee Burpee and Co.

Project coordinators:

    American Horticultural Society education and symposium coordinator: Maureen Heffernan

    Co-coordinator: Connie Pearson of Pearson Design Associates

Individual Display Gardens

Alphabet Garden: Leena Bhimani, Burke, Virginia; Virginia and Kathy Wheeler, Fairfax Station, Virginia

A Child's Garden: Jeff Minnich of Campbell and Ferrara Nursery, Alexandria, Virginia

A Ditch Garden: Alastair Bolton of Lynn Edward Studio, Alexandria, Virginia

A Prairie Garden: Jeanette Redmond of Outback Design, Oakton, Virginia; Toni Zachariasse, Reston, Virginia

An Imagination Garden: John Snitzer and Kerrie Kyde of Snitzer Landscaping, Dickerson, Maryland

Colonial Wind, Weather, and Sundial Garden: Thomas Arnold, Alexandria, Virginia

Dinosaur Footprint Garden: Peter Franz of School Without Walls, Washington, DC

Discovery Pond Garden: H. Kibbe Turner; students, teachers, and parent volunteers from Carl Sandburg Intermediate School, Alexandria, Virginia

The Grove Garden: Emily Davidson, Andrea Lybecker, and Emilie McBride, all with DLM Design, Chevy Chase, Maryland

Native Plant Butterfly Garden: Students, teachers, and parent volunteers from Hollin Meadows Elementary School, Alexandria, Virginia

Persian Carpet Garden: Students, teachers, and parent volunteers from Waynewood Elementary School, Alexandria, Virginia

Sunflower House: Penelope Hobhouse and Simon Johnson, both with Penelope Hobhouse and Associates, Somerset, England

Current Contacts

Executive director: Tom Underwood

Director of communications and editor of *American Gardener*: David J. Ellis

Manager and horticulturist: Sylvia Schmeichel

Interviews and Personal Communications

David J. Ellis, September 30, 2015; Tom Underwood, October 23, 2015

Study model

16

Ann Goldstein Children's Rainforest Garden at Marie Selby Botanical Gardens

SARASOTA, FLORIDA

GOAL

The Ann Goldstein Children's Rainforest Garden is a safe place for children and families to discover and develop a lifelong appreciation for the natural wonder of rainforest plants. Visitors experience the tropical landscape and rainforest displays through a series of elevated walkways that meander through the tree canopy. Marie Selby Botanical Gardens in vibrant downtown Sarasota, Florida, is a unique tropical, urban oasis set along Sarasota Bay and the Hudson Bayou. The garden was the original residence of philanthropist Marie Selby, who wanted to leave her property to the community as a botanical garden "for the enjoyment of the general public" (Marie Selby Botanical Gardens, n.d., "Facts"). The garden was named after Ann Goldstein by her husband, Al, both of whom were steadfast supporters of education and major benefactors to numerous universities.

Selby Gardens is a research center that focuses on education, research, and conservation. Hundreds of thousands of living and preserved plant collections are on the site. The Center for Tropical Plant Science and Conservation consists of the Bromeliad Identification Center, the Orchid Identification Center, and the Selby Gardens' Herbarium. The Ann Goldstein Children's Rainforest Garden embodies the mission of the Marie Selby Botanical Gardens by providing "an oasis of inspiration and tranquility, while furthering the understanding and appreciation of plants, especially epiphytes" (Marie Selby Botanical Gardens, n.d., "Mission").

Selby House

Moreton Bay fig

Service
area

Entrance

Pond

6

3

2

1

7

8

4

Amazon
Village

5

9

Hudson Bayou

2

11

10

Key
1   Banyan grove
2   Waterfall
3   Forest Pool
4   Epiphyte Canyon
5   Research station
6   Canopy Walk and Rope Bridge
7   Amphitheater
8   Village Shelter
9   Three huts
10   Horticulture research station
11   Lawn
12   Activity Trail

Office building

Illustrative plan by EDAW

Moreton Bay fig

CONCEPT

The idea of a children's garden was initiated in 2005 when the Selby Gardens' board of trustees began its initial exploration. Extensive planning and research took place between 2006 and 2008. Oasis Design Group developed early concept drawings with a focus on rainforests. This theme was chosen to educate visitors about where and how the plants grow and why the habitats need to be protected. In 2007, Herb Schaal, principal at EDAW/AECOM, was retained to lead the design process to further develop the theme. Schaal had a great deal of expertise, because he had designed more than twenty children's gardens by this time. He collaborated with the garden staff, board members, a contractor, and other interested parties through a weeklong design workshop. The workshop ratified the vision, mission, theme, audience, and project goals; proposed solutions to technical issues; investigated rainforest characteristics; and delineated program elements. This process led to a schematic plan that included the educational Waterfall and Forest Pool, the Canopy Walk and Rope Bridge, the Epiphyte Canyon, a research station, an amphitheater, and the Village Shelter. The schematic design also allowed establishing a budget. A model built under the supervision of Emmanuel Didier, associate landscape architect, was invaluable to the contractor in developing the construction working drawings. Under the direction of Tom Buchter, chief executive officer of Selby Gardens, construction of the project began in 2009 and was completed in 2013.

Banyan grove and Waterfall

Opposite: Entrance to Children's Garden

DESIGN

The 1-acre (0.4-hectare) Children's Rainforest Garden is southwest of the Selby House around the base of a very large, nearly one-hundred-year-old Moreton Bay fig tree (*Ficus macrophylla*, an evergreen banyan tree of the Moraceae family) planted by Marie Selby in the 1920s. Three key areas of the garden are described below.

Banyan Grove, Waterfall, and Forest Pool

Visitors enter the Children's Rainforest Garden via a narrow, gentle ramp, slowly rising and opening to a spectacular grove of banyan trees, the centerpiece of this garden. Under these majestic trees is a shaded deck, the 12-foot (3.6-meter) Waterfall, and the Forest Pool, which provide a comfortable seating area and activity spaces for children to learn about aquatic eco-systems and rainforest plants. The Waterfall cascades down a rock face covered with lush plants, emits delicate cooling mist, and enhances the rainforest ambiance. The Forest Pool provides hands-on discovery of an aquatic rainforest ecosystem.

From this main entry space, visitors can venture up to the Epiphyte Canyon, go down to the Amphitheater, Village Shelter, and Lawn, or go up to the Canopy and Rope Bridge by way of a ramp or lift.

Waterfall and Epiphyte Canyon

THE MAGIC OF CHILDREN'S GARDENS

Ann Goldstein Children's Rainforest Garden at Marie Selby Botanical Gardens

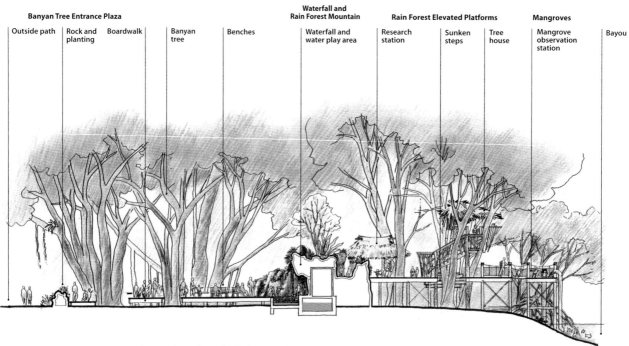

Banyan Tree Entrance Plaza

**Waterfall and
Rain Forest Mountain**

Rain Forest Elevated Platforms

Mangroves

Outside path | Rock and planting | Boardwalk | Banyan tree | Benches | Waterfall and water play area | Research station | Sunken steps | Tree house | Mangrove observation station | Bayou

Section through garden looking north

Waterfall

Epiphyte Canyon, Canopy Walk, and Rope Bridge

Rocks and unique epiphytic plants, which grow in the rocks, frame the winding corridor up to the top of Epiphyte Canyon, immersing visitors in the richness of the rainforest environment. At the top of the canyon, a thatched-roof research station hut allows children to explore and examine plants using field botany techniques and gadgets. Children can hide and play in the Canyon Cave. In the treetops, 27 feet (8.2 meters) in the air, the Canopy Walk and Rope Bridge provide children the opportunity to soak in the sights and sounds of the rainforest if they have dared to cross over the swinging bridge. Children learn fifty amazing facts about the rainforest. From the overlook atop the Epiphyte Canyon are great surrounding views of canopy treetops, blue waters of the Hudson Bayou, mangrove roots, and roaring sounds of the Waterfall below.

Amphitheater, Village Shelter, Lawn, and Activity Trail

The Amphitheater and Village Shelter are spaces for performances and special exhibits about life in a rainforest. The three huts along the edge of the rainforest represent the layers of the rainforest: the Canopy Café, the Understory Theater, and the Leafy Lair. Adjacent to this space is the Lawn—which is the sunniest spot in the garden and exposes children to common tropical food plants such as bananas, pineapples, and papayas. Three new features added in the summer of 2015 are the rainforest river, climbing forms painted by the Boruca indians of Costa Rica, and a raised-bed hands-on gardening area for children. In the adjacent Activity Trail beyond, children play hide-and-seek under the elevated decks and canyon base.

CONCLUSION

The Ann Goldstein Children's Rainforest Garden simulates one of the wildest places on earth—the tropical rainforest, home to half the world's known plant and animal species. The garden was designed to educate visitors about the rainforest and for children and families to connect, play, discover, and learn in a fun, safe, and natural environment.

Cave with ruins

THE MAGIC OF CHILDREN'S GARDENS

Activities at Epiphyte Canyon

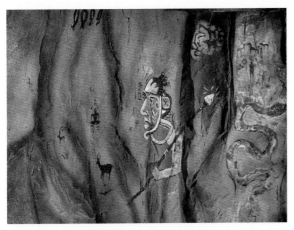

Paintings in Canyon Cave

Bromeliads on Epiphyte Canyon

Ann Goldstein Children's Rainforest Garden at Marie Selby Botanical Gardens

264   THE MAGIC OF CHILDREN'S GARDENS

Village shelter | Hut | Horticulture station | Hut | Amphitheater

Opposite: Research station with three huts and activities in lawn area

Top: Amphitheater with Village Shelter

Bottom: Amphitheater

2015 additions to village and lawn area
including wattle tunnel, frog sculptures,
Canopy Café, and tent

Moreton Bay fig along entrance to Children's Rainforest Garden

Selected plants in the garden

Acalypha hispida
Alpinia zerumbet 'Variegata'
Ananus comosus
Annona squamosa
Artocarpus heterophyllus
Averrhoa carambola 'Fwang Tung'
Bambusa vulgaris 'Wamin'

Bunchosia argentea
Carica papaya 'Red Lady'
Ceiba pentandra
Cocos nucifera
Codiaeum variegatum 'Mamey'
Codiaeum variegatum 'Revolutions'
Coffea arabica

Cordyline terminalis 'Black Magic'
Cyathea cooperi
Encyclia tampensis
Ficus altissima
Ficus macrophylla
Heliconia caribaea
Heliconia schiedeana 'Fire and Ice'
Hibiscus rosa-sinensis

Mangifera indica 'Haden'
Manihot esculenta
Musa spp.
Myrciaria cauliflora
Saccharum officinarum
Sterlitzia reginae
Trevesia palmata
Vanilla planifolia

Canopy Walk and Rope Bridge

Ann Goldstein Children's Rainforest Garden

Marie Selby Botanical Gardens

900 South Palm Avenue, Sarasota, FL 34236

941-366-5731   http://www.selby.org/the-gardens/childrens-rainforest-garden

Opening date: November 9, 2013

Project size: 1 acre (0.4 hectare) within Marie Selby Gardens' 16-acre (6.5-hectare) site

Design and Construction Team

Chief executive officer of Marie Selby Botanical Gardens (2009–2014): Tom Buchter

Marie Selby Botanical Gardens trustee and Hazeltine Nurseries chief executive officer: Stephen Hazeltine

Landscape architects:

 Final concepts and schematic design: EDAW/AECOM; Herb Schaal, principal landscape architect; Emmanuel Didier, associate landscape architect and project manager)

 Early design concepts: Oasis Design Group

Civil engineer: George F. Young

Electrical engineer: Crawford Williams Engineering

General contractor: Tandem Construction

Illustrator: Joe McGrane and Emmanuel Didier

Manufacturer of custom faux rock and water features: Certified Pool Mechanics

Owner's agent: Milton Shenk LLC

Project architect: Hazeltine Nurseries

Structural engineer: Stirling and Wilbur Engineering

Current Contacts

Marketing and communications director: Mischa Kirby

Interviews and Personal Communications

Tom Buchter, June 24, 2010; Mike McLaughlin, September 25, 2015; Jeannie Perales, September 25, 2015; Angelo Randaci, October 16, 2015; Herb Schaal, September 7, 2015

Art sculptures in the garden

Filling watering cans at a giant flower pot fountain

United States Botanic Garden Children's Garden

WASHINGTON, DC

GOAL

The United States Botanic Garden Children's Garden is part of a museum of living plants. It is small but unique and allows children to explore the garden through their senses, get hands-on experience using gardening tools to dig and plant, and simply get their hands dirty. The Children's Garden, originally installed during the garden's Conservatory restoration in 1997–2001, opened in May 2002.

CONCEPT

Measuring 65 by 50 feet (19.8 by 15.2 meters), the garden occupies the Conservatory's East Courtyard (open air although enclosed). According to Holly Shimizu, former director of the Botanic Garden, "The garden's emphasis was about how plants could be used to create an environment that would encourage children's interaction with plants, and [it] was designed so that what is in the garden could be experienced by the children on their own terms."

The initial program evolved from a collaborative effort involving Botanic Garden staff and Rodney Robinson Landscape Architects. This process later led to conceptualizing interpretive panels in the garden. Having had extensive experience with designs of children's environments and interpretive signage in zoo settings, Rodney Robinson had ample expertise to design the United States Botanic Garden Children's Garden. A multidisciplinary team of Botanic Garden staff and its government stakeholders were involved throughout the design process.

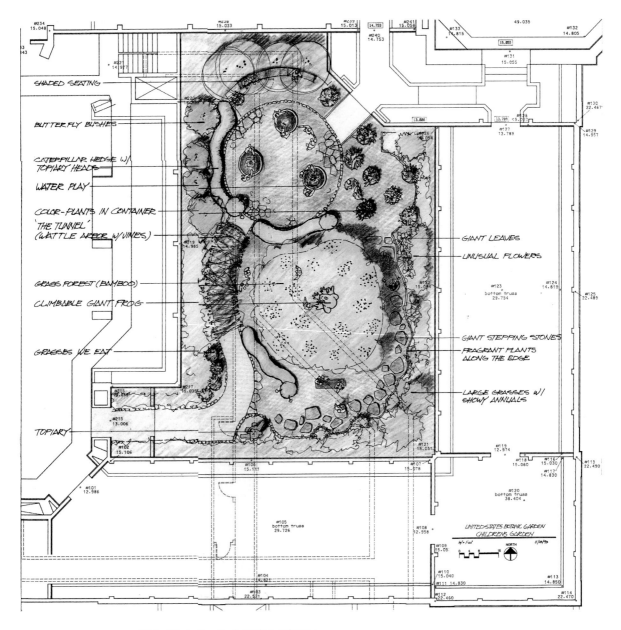

SHADED SEATING

BUTTERFLY BUSHES

CATERPILLAR HEDGE W/
TOPIARY HEADS

WATER PLAY

COLOR-PLANTS IN CONTAINER
'THE TUNNEL'
(WATTLE ARBOR W/ VINES)

GRASS FOREST (BAMBOO)

CLIMBABLE GIANT FROG

GRASSES WE EAT

TOPIARY

GIANT LEAVES

UNUSUAL FLOWERS

GIANT STEPPING STONES

FRAGRANT PLANTS
ALONG THE EDGE

LARGE GRASSES W/
SHOWY ANNUALS

UNITED STATES BOTANIC GARDEN
CHILDRENS GARDEN

NORTH

Original illustrative plan by Rodney Robinson
Landscape Architects. This concept predated
what was installed with the 1997–2001
renovation.

Opposite: Whimsy and mystery. Playing hide-
and-seek in the bamboo.

United States Botanic Garden Children's Garden

Running along the fieldstone path

Opposite left: Watering plants in the plant border

Opposite right: Whimsical planters and bird house
in the plant border

DESIGN

The garden is designed to allow children to engage all their senses and to touch, play, and run around. The main components in the garden are plants, water, interpretive panels, color, an arbor, and a maze. A variety of plants were integrated, including edible plants and herbs. The perimeter of the garden contains a border of shorter woody plants, including hydrangea, espaliered apples, bananas, and grasses for texture. Flowering bulbs in spring are followed by tropical summer displays. The glass wall of the Conservatory is the backdrop, with some borrowed views into the Conservatory. Mystery and whimsy are key elements in the design. The bamboo maze and the bean tunnel provide mystery, inviting children to play hide-and-seek within them. Face planters and giant planter fountains provide whimsical interests in the garden.

A circle motif was developed early in the design process and represents unity. It was an appropriate geometry to be used in a small space as it minimized sharp corners. The composition of formal and informal circles in the design organizes the 0.1-acre (0.04-hectare) space into several different spaces. Since the garden space is small, it needed sufficient paved area to accommodate crowds. A variety of paving materials—such as stepping-stones, mulch, Belgian block curb, and Fibar engineered wood fiber (ADA accessible)—provide interesting textures and control the speed of children's movement. For example, large Pennsylvania fieldstones slow children's movement to a rock hop along the perimeter adventure trail. The descriptive signs were collaboratively developed by the Botanic Garden staff. The signs were specifically designed to be changeable to accommodate new information throughout the seasons about plants, exhibits, and events. Much of the design details were refined during the construction drawings stage. The garden took less than six months to build.

Child-sized bean tunnel arbor

Opposite: Sketch of early arbor concept by
Rodney Robinson Landscape Architects

STEEL TRELLIS

24" HIGH WOOD BOX
(2', 4', 6', MODULE LENGTHS)
4" GRAVEL
EXIST. GRADE

United States Botanic Garden Children's Garden

Water-bell spray fountains in giant flower
pots and water pump in background

THE MAGIC OF CHILDREN'S GARDENS

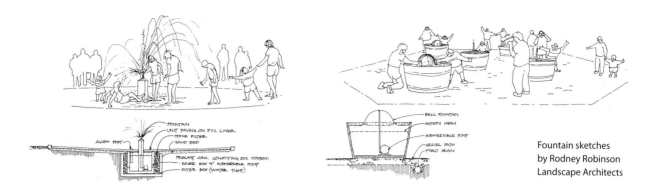

CONCLUSION

The United States Botanic Garden Children's Garden and all the programs evolved from a collaborative effort between the designers from Rodney Robinson Landscape Architects and the U.S. Botanic Garden staff. Continual improvements to the garden over time were made by the Botanic Garden staff, such as the addition of a cottage with a green roof and a new water pump feature. Exposing children to possibilities in the outdoor environment geared toward their experiences and preferences was always the primary intent. Ideas were generated on paper as well as on site. The Botanic Garden's Interpretive Master Plan served as a guide. According to Shimizu, "The goal was to encourage children to interact with the natural world through a space where connections with plants, soil, and the outdoors is freely accessible as a play experience that would allow children to have an emotional and lasting experience."

The Children's Garden is an extremely well-attended and popular area of the Botanic Garden. Years of heavy use resulted in the need to upgrade, reorganize, and refresh the area. Renovation planning took two years, and in summer 2015 the first phase of the renovation, designed by Deneen Powell Atelier, was opened to the public. The garden integrates the existing layout and adds paving, new mist poles, a tool shed trellis, and raised planters installed within the core of the garden. The new water features were designed to be more durable, require less maintenance, and conserve water. The mist poles are motion activated, adding an element of surprise. The new design adds more usable space and pathways accessible by wheelchairs. To minimize disturbance, the full renovation is planned as a series of small projects that can be implemented over a number of years. Work will be executed each winter and spring so that the garden can be open to the public during the warmest months. The garden has remained a botanically oriented educational play experience, incorporating plant interaction, water play, digging, planting, and exploration.

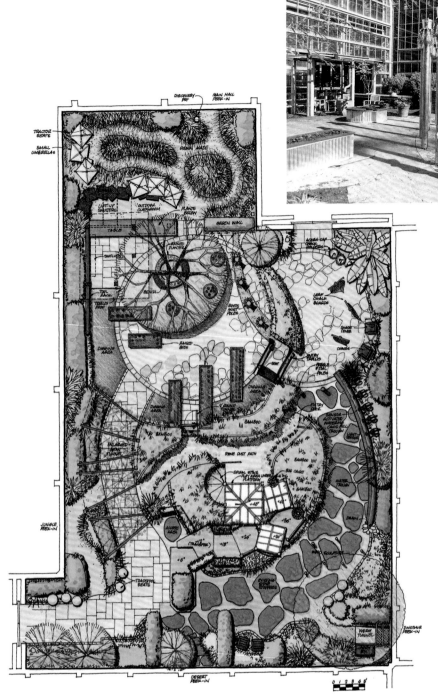

Top: A portion of the renovated garden recently completed and opened to the public in summer 2015

Bottom: Garden renovation by Deneen Powell Atalier

Opposite top: Getting dirty and getting clean

Selected plants in the garden

Acanthus mollis
Actinidia chinensis
Canna × generalis 'Wyoming'
Dahlia 'Bishop of Canterbury'
Ficus carica 'Brown Turkey'
Fargesia sp. 'Scabrida'
Hakonechloa macra 'Aureola'

Hydrangea quercifolia 'Pee Wee'
Lavandula × intermedia 'Provence'
Lonicera sempervirens
Malus domestica 'Co-op 32'
Musa 'African Rhino Horn'
Salvia guaranitica 'Black and Blue'
Salvia hybrida 'Wendy's Wish'

United States Botanic Garden Children's Garden

245 First Street SW, Washington, DC 20024

202-225-8333 http://www.usbg.gov/growing-children's-imaginations

Opening date: May 2002

Project size: 0.1 acre (0.04 hectare) within U.S. Botanic Garden Conservatory's 7-acre (2.8-hectare) site

2002 Design and Construction Team

United States Botanic Garden director and project leader: Holly Shimizu
Landscape architect: Rodney Robinson Landscape Architects Inc.
Architect: DMJM Architects
General contractor: Clark Construction

2015 Design and Construction Team

United States Botanic Garden project leader and landscape architect: Nick Nelson
Landscape architect: Deneen Powell Atelier
General contractor for phase I: Centennial Construction

Current Contacts

United States Botanic Garden executive director: Ari Novy
United States Botanic Garden landscape architect: Nick Nelson

Interviews and Personal Communications

Nick Nelson, August 1, 2014; Rodney Robinson and Allan Summers at Rodney Robinson Landscape
Architects, February 20, 2015; Holly Shimizu, February 27, 2015

Dragonfly Pond and views of straw-bale
building and living roof

18

Children's Discovery Garden
at Wegerzyn Gardens MetroPark

DAYTON, OHIO

GOAL

The Children's Discovery Garden introduces young children to the natural world around them. The goal is to immerse visitors within the native Dayton, Ohio, landscapes of woodlands, caves, streams, wetlands, ponds, and prairie and to promote healthy youth gardening through hands-on planting opportunities. The garden was also designed to inspire caregivers with ideas to create their own affordable do-it-yourself nature play spaces in backyards and schoolyards.

CONCEPT

The site selected for the Children's Discovery Garden was a long and narrow multipurpose lawn within Wegerzyn Gardens MetroPark. Creating a place with a sense of magic that would be enticing to children was a challenge on this site. To add variety and interest, Cindy Tyler, while a partner with Marshall Tyler Rausch, designed this garden and incorporated unique features. A loop pathway around the Dragonfly Pond provides views at different vantage points. Planted berms add a landform dimension while screening the adjacent parking lot. Openings through the hedge create window views toward the eastern side of the garden. A series of garden rooms throughout the garden provides a sense of enclosure, making the overall garden appear much larger.

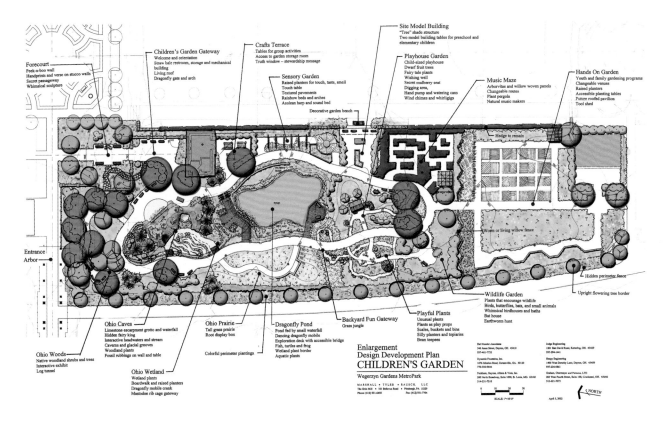

Forecourt
Peek-a-boo wall
Handprints and verse on stucco walls
Secret passageway
Whimsical sculpture

Children's Garden Gateway
Welcome and orientation
Straw bale restroom, storage and mechanical building
Living roof
Dragonfly gate and arch

Crafts Terrace
Tables for group activities
Access to garden storage room
Truth window – stewardship message

Sensory Garden
Raised planters for touch, taste, smell
Touch table
Textured pavements
Rainbow beds and arches
Aeolian harp and sound bed

Decorative garden bench

Site Model Building
"Tree" shade structure
Two model building tables for preschool and elementary children

Playhouse Garden
Child-sized playhouse
Dwarf fruit trees
Fairy tale plants
Wishing well
Secret mulberry seat
Digging area,
Hand pump and watering cans
Wind chimes and whirligigs

Music Maze
Arborvitae and willow woven panels
Changeable routes
Plant pergola
Natural music makers

Hands On Garden
Youth and family gardening programs
Changeable venues
Raised planters
Accessible planting tables
Future roofed pavilion
Tool shed

Hedge to remain

Worm or living willow fence

Hidden perimeter fence

Upright flowering tree border

Entrance Arbor

Ohio Woods
Native woodland shrubs and trees
Interactive exhibit
Log tunnel

Ohio Caves
Limestone escarpment grotto and waterfall
Hidden fairy king
Interactive headwaters and stream
Caverns and glacial grooves
Woodland plants
Fossil rubbings on wall and table

Ohio Wetland
Wetland plants
Boardwalk and raised planters
Dragonfly mobile crank
Mastodon rib cage gateway

Ohio Prairie
Tall grass prairie
Root display box

Colorful perimeter plantings

Dragonfly Pond
Pond fed by small waterfall
Dancing dragonfly mobile
Exploration deck with accessible bridge
Fish, turtles and frog
Wetland plant border
Aquatic plants

Backyard Fun Gateway
Grass jungle

Playful Plants
Unusual plants
Plants as play props
Scales, buckets and bins
Silly planters and topiaries
Bean teepees

Wildlife Garden
Plants that encourage wildlife
Birds, butterflies, bats, and small animals
Whimsical birdhouses and baths
Bat house
Earthworm hunt

Enlargement
Design Development Plan
CHILDREN'S GARDEN
Wegerzyn Gardens MetroPark

MARSHALL • TYLER • RAUSCH, LLC
The Orbit Mill • 101 Bellevue Road • Pittsburgh, PA 15229
Phone: (412) 931-6455   Fax: (412) 931-7764

Earl Reader Associates
348 Jones Street, Dayton, OH 45410
937-461-7752

Dynamic Fountains, Inc.
1676 Mission Road, Greenville, GA 30120
770-356-9646

Peckham, Guyton, Albers & Viets, Inc.
200 North Broadway, Suite 1909, St. Louis, MO 63102
314-231-7318

Judge Engineering
1201 East David Road, Kettering, OH 45429
937-294-1441

Heapy Engineering
1400 West Dorothy Lane, Dayton, OH 45409
937-224-0861

Graham, Obermeyer and Partners, LTD
205 West Fourth Street, Suite 100, Cincinnati, OH 45202
513-621-7073

SCALE: 1"=10'-0"   April 3, 2002

NORTH

Top: Study model of Ohio Caves
Bottom: Design development plan by Cindy Tyler
Opposite: Early conceptual master plan

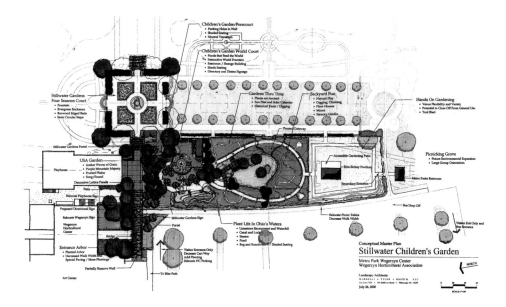

DESIGN

The Discovery Garden is organized into four zones:

1. **Forecourt and gateway:** welcome and orientation
2. **Ohio Habitat:** re-creations of key western Ohio landscape typologies
   - Dragonfly Pond
   - Ohio Caves, Prairie, and Woods
3. **Backyard Fun:** inspiration for caregivers
   - Playful Plants
   - Playhouse Garden
   - Wildlife Garden
   - Music Maze
   - Build-Your-Own-Garden modeling table
4. **Skeeter's Garden:** hands-on gardening

A series of pocket nature gardens of Dayton landscapes fill the spaces within the Ohio Habitat zones. The Crafts Terrace and Sensory Garden are garden spaces along the northeast side of the main loop pathway.

Two dominant features in this garden are the Dragonfly Pond and the Ohio Caves. The Dragonfly Pond and the naturalized wetlands around it are at the core of the garden and serve as a central and unifying element. Water is an extremely popular element for children in this garden, as they are drawn to the discovery of a vast array of diverse aquatic plants and wildlife. A low deck along the pond's southern edge allows children to touch the water, while a more elevated deck along the northern edge provides an expansive view of the garden.

Cave and tunnel elevation

Ohio Caves and stream

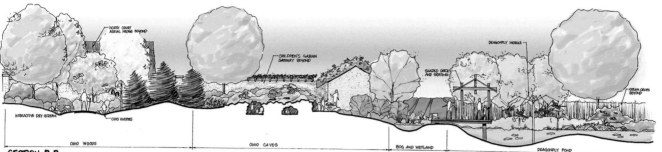

SECTION B·B

North–south section through garden

Ohio Caves

Children's Discovery Garden at Wegerzyn Gardens MetroPark

Top: Southern deck on Dragonfly Pond
Bottom: Northern deck on Dragonfly Pond
Opposite: Sensory Garden

THE MAGIC OF CHILDREN'S GARDENS

The Ohio Caves and grotto waterfall located near the entrance of the garden were designed to be reminiscent of the ever-present water system in southwestern Ohio. As visitors approach the cave, an interactive stream and caverns appear in the landscape, much like the southwestern Ohio spring that flows and disappears in caverns, taking the shape of waterfalls, pools, and meandering streams. Adjacent to this area are the Ohio Prairie and Woods.

The design and construction of this cave was one of the most challenging components of the Children's Discovery Garden. The objective was to create a believable simulated limestone grotto on a flat site. Photographs of rock formations in the area, particularly around caves, provided by Five Rivers MetroParks served as inspiration. Various grotto sketches were drawn. Clay models helped to determine the grotto heights, configuration, plant intensity, and ways to nestle this mound into the landscape. "Once we arrived at a solution we all loved, we photographed the results from many angles to share with [Five Rivers MetroParks]. The photos of the model and the real-life limestone grotto that was our inspiration were both included in the construction document set," says Cindy Tyler, now the owner of Terra Design Studios. The general contractor enlisted a subcontractor with experience in concrete sculpture, who then prepared a mockup of the cultured limestone façade, stalagmites, streambed, and natural boulders. Once the mockups were approved by the design and construction team, the subcontractor began construction of the life-size installation. The team reviewed and provided comments during the process, including during the formwork, the first coat of concrete, and concrete theme painting in final stages of construction. "It was very much a long, collaborative, and rewarding process," remarks Tyler.

Again working collaboratively, Tyler developed the schematic design for the planting while Wegerzyn Gardens' horticultural staff chose species to meet design goals. Many plant materials were chosen for immediate landscape effect on opening day. "Without any existing trees to offer shade, we strategically placed shade structures and playhouses throughout the Children's Discovery Garden until the overhead canopy matured," Tyler adds.

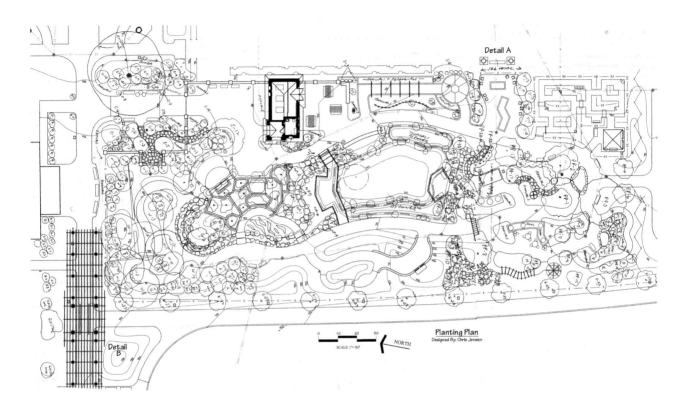

Planting Plan
Designed By: Chris Jensen

SCALE 1"=30'

NORTH

Detail A

Detail B

Selected plants in the garden

Native plants

Asarum canadense
Asclepias tuberosa
Asimina triloba
Conoclinium coelestinum
Echinacea paradoxa
Eryngium yuccifolium
Passiflora incarnata
Rudbeckia maxima
Sambucus canadensis
Solidago ohioensis
Spigelia marilandica

Playful plants

Allium 'Globemaster'
Asparagus verticillatus
Campanula punctata 'Pink
  Octopus'
Eryngium × *planum* 'Sapphire Blue'
Hibiscus moscheutos 'Summer
  Storm
Humulus lupulus 'Aureus'
Mentha arvensis 'Banana'
Mentha rotundifolia
Mimosa pudica

Morus alba 'Pendula'
Platycodon grandiflorus 'Komanchi'
Rudbeckia subtometosa 'Henry
  Eliers'
Senna didymobotrya

Opposite top: Main entrance
Opposite middle: Planting plan
by Chris Jensen, horticulture staff
Right: Child-scaled gate at main entrance

CONCLUSION

Before establishment of the Children's Discovery Garden, Wegerzyn Gardens was a sleepy and seldom-visited part of the MetroParks system. This garden struck a chord with its visitors. Today, the Children's Discovery Garden welcomes an average of three hundred people per day during spring, summer, and autumn months.

Children's Discovery Garden
Wegerzyn Gardens MetroPark
1301 E. Siebenthaler Avenue, Dayton, OH 45414
937-277-6545   http://www.metroparks.org/discovery-garden

Opening date: 2006
Project size: 1 acre (0.4 hectare) within Wegerzyn Gardens MetroPark's 31-acre (12.5-hectare) site

Design and Construction Team
Five Rivers MetroParks director: Charlie Shoemaker
Wegerzyn Gardens MetroPark horticulturist: Chris Jensen
Landscape architect: Terra Design Studios (Cindy Tyler, principal and lead designer; Eric Walsnovich, project director)
Architect: Earl Reeder Associates
Civil engineer: Judge Engineering Company
Electrical engineer: Heapy Engineering LLC
Structural engineer: Graham, Obermeyer, and Partners Ltd.
Water feature design: Dynamic Fountains Inc.

Current Contacts
Five Rivers MetroParks director: Rebecca Benna
MetroParks director of marketing: Trish Butler

Interviews and Personal Communications
Gita Michulka, December 2, 2015; Cindy Tyler, December 1, 2015

Faerie Cottage

19

Enchanted Woods at Winterthur Museum, Garden, and Library

WILMINGTON, DELAWARE

GOAL

Enchanted Woods is a special fairy-tale children's garden at Winterthur with a charming collection of magical outdoor spaces. Created to be in complete harmony with Winterthur's 1,000-acre (404.7-hectare) estate, it was built under an existing mature woodland canopy in a style appropriate to the historic Winterthur garden, with subtle colors in the hardscape and plantings with sweeps of color. The theme developed for the garden was based on the history of Winterthur. The design team's intention to reuse materials from the estate, garden, and farm aligns with Winterthur's guidelines "to retain and preserve historic features and materials," according to Linda Eirhart, Winterthur's plants curator.

CONCEPT

The Winterthur design team, under the leadership of Denise Magnani, curator and director of the landscape division, decided on the name and theme of Enchanted Woods—thus, the atmosphere for the children's garden. Landscape architect W. Gary Smith took these initial ideas and developed the design and the atmosphere further by using literary and artistic references related to enchantment, fairies, and mythology. He also drew from his own childhood experiences. Together with a design team of horticulturists, arborists, and curators, Smith incorporated the goals of the original owner, Henry Francis du Pont, who wanted visitors to find enjoyment and inspiration in the beauty of the naturalistic landscape garden. Du Pont had learned much about gardening by growing up with flowers. The design team's goal was for the new garden to be a place where children would be encouraged to use their imagination and enjoy the beauty of a naturalistic garden. Enchanted Woods was designed to be a garden rather than a playground. Different from many high-tech, high-energy, and exciting gardens, this was to be a quiet place where calm children could find refuge and enjoyment.

Kurume azaleas with bluebells

Back pond and fields

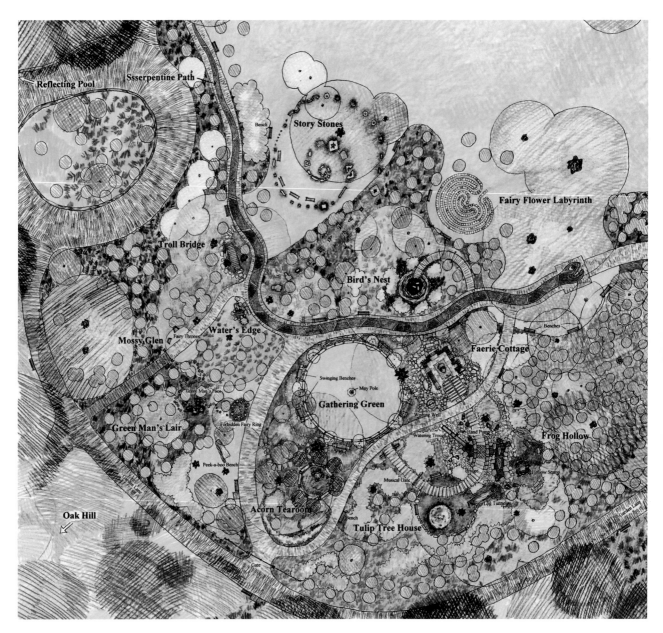

Illustrative plan by W. Gary Smith Design Inc.

The following labels appear on the map:

Reflecting Pool

Ssserpentine Path

Story Stones

Bench

Fairy Flower Labyrinth

Troll Bridge

Bird's Nest

Water's Edge

Mossy Glen

Fairy Thrones

Benches

Faerie Cottage

Swinging Benches

May Pole

Gathering Green

Green Man's Face

Wishing Well

Frog Hollow

Green Man's Lair

Forbidden Fairy Ring

Watering Trough

Hand Pump

Hollow Stump

Bridge

Peek-a-boo Bench

Log Tunnel

Musical Gate

Garden Lane

Oak Hill

Acorn Tearoom

Bench

Tulip Tree House

Garden Lane

Gate

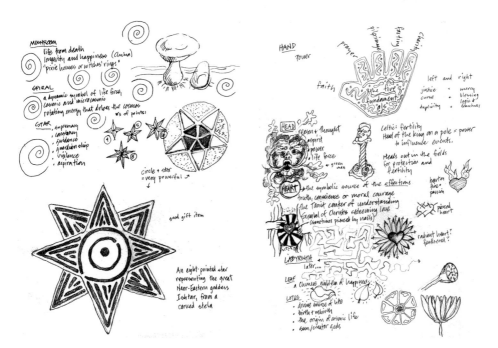

Sketches of magical symbols

During the research phase, the design team studied how children learn and play. They visited other children's gardens and interviewed other institutions that were planning gardens. They also solicited help from parents and teachers and polled almost every child with whom they came in contact. The Enchanted Woods team was fortunate to also have the results of Longwood Gardens' extensive focus group discussions for its new children's garden.

The team learned of three basic elements that children wanted in the garden: water, places to hide and pretend, and discovery on their own. The team considered the design for an environment that would be fun and also provide opportunities for creative play and contact with nature, encourage different experiences in the landscape, provide stimulation of all the senses, accommodate different ages and activity levels, provide space for special programs, ensure safety, and address needs of parents and guardians.

DESIGN

The Faerie Cottage is in the center of the garden, nestled among great oaks and tulip-poplars, and is the main unifying element of the garden. An imprint of a smiling snake on the S-s-serpentine Path greets visitors at the entry and forms the main pedestrian spine. This idea was inspired by Smith's childhood experiences and his love of such wildlife.

Access from the main garden at Winterthur to Enchanted Woods is by way of existing paths. On arrival, the paths change from asphalt to cobblestone and alert visitors that they are in a different space. Along the Enchanted Woods paths, children encounter garden rooms that delight them.

S-s-serpentine Path

THE MAGIC OF CHILDREN'S GARDENS

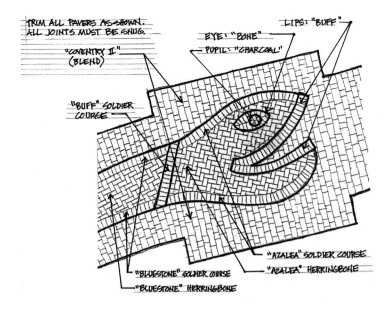

The following garden rooms were especially designed for the children's enjoyment:

- Acorn Tearoom
- Green Man's Lair
  - Forbidden Fairy Ring
  - Green Man's Face
- Frog Hollow
- Story Stones
- Tulip Tree House
- Bird's Nest
- Fairy Flower Labyrinth
- Troll Bridge
- Gathering Green
- Water's Edge

The rooms are sited with relationship to each other as well as to the greater context of Winterthur. Where appropriate, visual connections between the new garden and existing views and vistas are maintained.

The Fairy Flower Labyrinth, for example, was sited on the edge of Enchanted Woods specifically so that it would not be visible. It is partially surrounded by later-flowering azaleas. It has views of the Sundial garden, the meadow, and the woodlands beyond. However, because of its elevation and location, it is not visible from a distance and does not impose on the Winterthur Garden.

Plants are the main emphasis of the Winterthur Garden, but they also define spaces, paths, and views. To maintain the garden experience without interruption, it was important to keep as many of the existing plants as possible. For example, the lavender Winterthur azalea flowers that bloom in mid-May are the backdrop for the Fairy Ring, and the seasonal colors direct visitors along different paths during the year.

THE MAGIC OF CHILDREN'S GARDENS

Enchanted Woods was designed with broad sweeps of related plants within a select color palette that complements and builds on du Pont's theme of summer colors and extended season of bloom. Concentrated in the landscape are hydrangeas, clethras, and hostas with a white, lavender, and blue theme and a touch of pink. Plants were added from surrounding garden areas to tie Enchanted Woods to the main garden. Sweeps of August-blooming *Hosta* 'Royal Standard' and September-blooming *Aster divaricatus* were duplicated in Enchanted Woods. Planted along the S-s-serpentine Path are continuous clusters of *Hosta ventricosa* that bloom in July throughout the garden. "More bulbs will be added to echo the millions of spring bulbs in the area referred to as the March Bank," remarks Linda Eirhart. Every effort was made to retain the integrity of the garden and to maintain a place that appears as if it had always been there.

CONCLUSION

By staying true to the history, the site, and the design style, the design team created a magical space within a magnificent woodland setting. Today, children continue to enjoy Enchanted Woods. A ten-year-old visitor perhaps put it best when he stated simply, "It's cool here. I like it!" Enchanted Woods stirs the imagination of a new generation and helps children and adults appreciate the beauty, wonder, and power of nature.

Sketch of Faerie Cottage by W. Gary Smith Design Inc.

Top: Faerie Cottage thatched roof construction

Middle: Faerie Cottage front view

Bottom: Faerie Cottage interior, niche, and fireplace

Enchanted Woods at Winterthur Museum, Garden, and Library

Frog Hollow Bridge

Watering trough and hand
pump in Frog Hollow

Enchanted Woods at Winterthur Museum, Garden, and Library

COWSLIP

OAK

FOXGLOVE

FERN

LILY-OF-THE-VALLEY

TOADSTOOL

Top: Sketches of plants inscribed on stepping-stones in Fairy Flower Labyrinth

Centerfold: Running around the Fairy Flower Labyrinth

Left and right: Story Stones

Enchanted Woods at Winterthur Museum, Garden, and Library

Top: Forbidden Fairy Ring
Bottom: Green Man's Face

Gathering Green in full bloom with *Cercis canadensis* f. *alba*, *Cercis canadensis*, *Rhododendron* 'Firefly', and *Rhododendron* 'Snow'

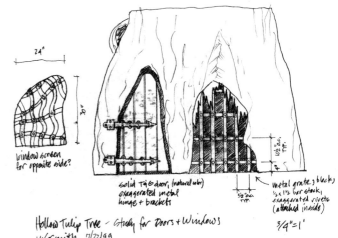

24"

window screen
for opposite side?

solid T&G door (natural color)
exaggerated metal
hinge + brackets

metal grate (black)
½ x 1½ bar stock,
exaggerated rivets
(attached inside)

3/4" = 1'

Hollow Tulip Tree — Study for Doors + Windows
WCGsmith 7/22/99

Opposite top: Detail sketch of the door on the Tulip Tree House

Opposite bottom: Sketch of tulip tree house by W. Gary Smith Design Inc.

Top left and right: Transporting and reusing the tulip tree

Bottom: Tulip Tree House in Enchanted Woods

Top: Pretending to be fairies in the Acorn Tearoom

Bottom: Acorn Tearoom construction details

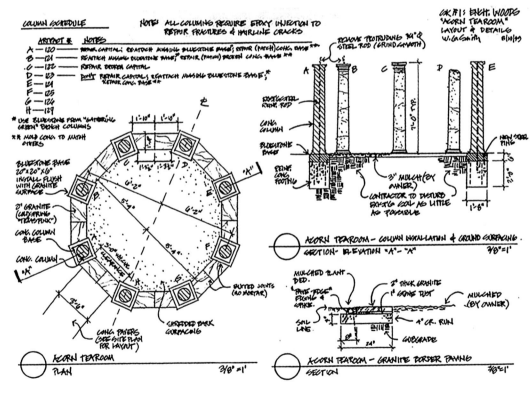

Bird's Nest

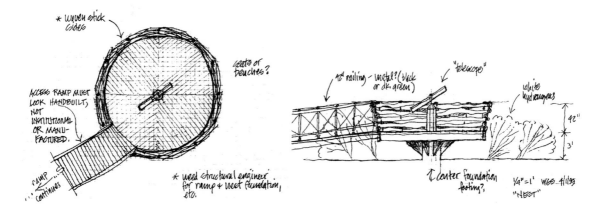

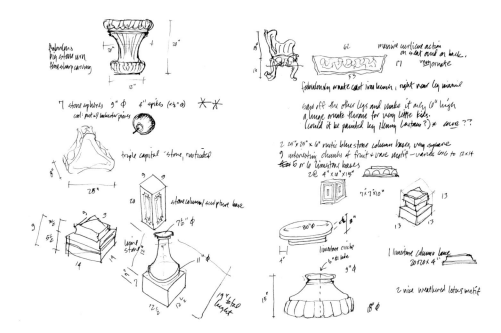

Top: Detail study sketches
Bottom: Water's edge

Rhododendron obtusum
(Kurume azaleas)

Hydrangea arborescens 'Grandiflora'
(smooth hydrangea)

Lilium hansonii
(Japanese Turk's cap lily)

Hydrangea quercifolia (oakleaf hydrangea)

Begonia grandis (hardy begonia)

Aster divaricatus (white wood aster)
and *Actaea japonica* (bugbane)

Major plants around each feature

Acorn Tearoom

Dryopteris spp.
Viburnum dilatatum

Bird's Nest

Hydrangea arborescens
 'Grandiflora'
Liriodendron tulipifera
Rhododendron kaempferi hybrid

Faerie Cottage

Clethra barbinervis
Helleborus cvs.
Hosta cvs.
Hydrangea involucrata
Rhododendron carolinianum

Fairy Flower Labyrinth

Liriodendron tulipifera
Quercus alba
Rhododendron kaempferi
 hybrid

Frog Hollow

Hosta cvs.
Hydrangea quercifolia cvs.
Liriodendron tulipifera
Quercus alba
Rhododendron 'Alight'
Rhododendron 'Caronella'
Rhododendron 'Firefly'

Gathering Green

Cercis canadensis f. *alba*
Epimedium × *versicolor*
 'Sulphureum'
Galanthus elwesii
Hosta 'Royal Standard'
Hosta ventricosa
Hydrangea 'Preziosa'
Mertensia virginica
Rhododendron 'Elizabeth'

Green Man's Lair

Fagus grandifolia

Halesia diptera var. *magniflora*
Hydrangea arborescens
 'Grandiflora'
Quercus alba
Rhododendron mucronatum
 'Winterthur'

S-s-serpentine Path

Actaea japonica
Aster divaricatus (syn. *Eurybia*
 divaricata)
Begonia grandis
Begonia grandis 'Alba'
Hosta cvs.
Hydrangea spp. and cvs.
Rhododendron cvs.

Story Stones

Asimina triloba
Diospyros virginiana
Hydrangea arborescens
 'Grandiflora'

Quercus alba
Rhododendron kaempferi
 hybrid

Troll Bridge

Liriodendron tulipifera
Polystichum acrostichoides
Rhododendron kaempferi
 hybrid
Sarcococca hookeriana var.
 humilis

Tulip Tree House

Crataegus spp.
Hydrangea quercifolia cvs.
Rhododendron 'Firefly'
Rhododendron 'Snow'

Upside-Down Tree

Crataegus spp.
Hosta cvs.
Rhododendron 'Firefly'

Enchanted Woods at Winterthur Museum, Garden, and Library

Swing bench

Stone bench

Tree stump bench

Faux bois bench donated by Currey and Company

Fairy thrones benches

Metal benches made specifically for Enchanted Woods by Paul Lashua

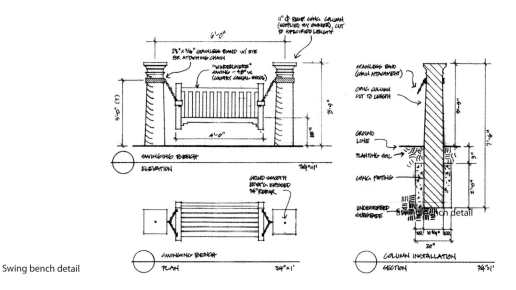

Swing bench detail

Enchanted Woods

Winterthur Museum, Garden, and Library

5105 Kennett Pike, Wilmington, DE 19735

302-888-4600   http://winterthur.org/?p=671

Opening date: Father's Day 2001

Project size: 3 acres (1.2 hectare) within Winterthur's 1,000-acre (404.7-hectare) site

Design and Construction Team

Winterthur:

 Landscape Division curator and director and project manager: Denise Magnani

 Associate curators of landscape: Pam Allenstein, Joseph Lazorchak

 Plants curator: Linda Eirhart

 Arborist supervisor: Randy Fisher

 Garden programs and events coordinator: Laura Payne

 Horticulturist: Brian Phiel

 Horticulture supervisor: Jim Smith

Landscape architect: W. Gary Smith Design Inc.

Civil engineer: Apex Engineering Inc.

Construction management and architecture: Buck Simpers Architect and Associates Inc. (David P.
   Mengers, project architect)

General contractor: Construct Con Inc. (Frank Patille Jr. and Frank Patille III, principals)

Mechanical and electrical engineer: Furlow Associates Inc.

Current Contact

Winterthur plants curator: Linda Eirhart

Interviews and Personal Communications

Linda Eirhart, August 12, 2014; Denise Magnani, 2005; Gary Smith, December 9, 2015

Atlanta Botanical Garden Gainesville Children's Garden

1911 Sweetbay Drive, Gainesville, GA 30501

404-888-4760   http://atlantabg.org/visit/gainesville

Opening date: Fall 2016

Project size: 2.5 acres (1 hectare) within Atlanta Botanical Garden Gainesville's 12-acre (4.8-hectares) site

Design and Construction Team

Atlanta Botanical Garden Gainesville:

    Chief operating officer, project manager: Arthur Fix

    Vice president, horticulture, and garden director: Mildred Fockele

    The Anna and Hays Mershon president and chief executive officer ex-officio: Mary Pat Matheson

    Vice president, institutional advancement: Leslie Myers

    Vice president, programs: Tracy McClendon

Landscape design and planning manager, lead designer: Tres Fromme

Landscape architect of record: Spurlock Poirier

Master planner and concept designer: Herb Schaal

Civil engineer: Rochester Engineering

Architect: Smith Dalia Architects

General contractor: Genoa Construction

Conclusion

Atlanta Botanical
Garden, Gainesville:
Dragon Grotto

The creative design process generates inspiring and magical children's garden spaces that are appealing to children and draw them to happily interact in these spaces. Engagement with nature and outdoor environments is crucial for children. Studies have shown that children benefit in all aspects of physical, mental, emotional, and social well-being (Kellert and Derr 1998).

The gardens display assorted themes, hardscape materials, plants, and special features with varying emphasis on concepts of play, education, and environmental sustainability. However, the gardens all share elements that are essential to the design of a children's garden. Safety, stimulation, and development are key principles in designing these special garden spaces. The gardens have elements that appeal to all five senses, and they incorporate scale, water, heights, plants, wildlife, enclosure and retreat, construction with loose parts, and games of make-believe that involve active and creative play, all of which provide opportunities for discovery (Dannenmaier 1998).

In 2014, the Brooklyn Botanic Garden's Children's Garden celebrated its one-hundred-year anniversary. However, devoted interest to the design of children's gardens in the United States is a fairly recent trend. Since the establishment of the Michigan 4-H Children's Garden in 1993, numerous children's gardens have entered the design, renovation, or new-construction phase.

In summer 2015, Brooklyn Botanic Garden celebrated the grand opening of its new Discovery Garden, United States Botanical Garden completed the first phase of its renovated Children's Garden, and San Antonio Botanical Garden started construction on its Family Adventure Garden, anticipated to open in 2017. In spring 2016, Atlanta Botanical Garden's Children's Garden reopened as the Lou Glenn Children's Garden after undergoing major renovation. Bok Tower Garden's Hammock Hollow Children's Garden and Santa Fe Botanical Garden's Ojos y Manos (Eyes and Hands) Children's Garden both opened in fall 2016. At the same time, McKee Botanical Garden completed the conceptual design phase of its new children's garden; Tower Hill Botanical Garden began the design development phase of its children's garden, the Ramble; and Houston Arboretum and Nature Center completed construction documents on its Children's Discovery Garden and Nature Playground. In addition, the Desert Botanical Garden started its planning process. New York Botanical Garden anticipates completing major renovations of its Everett Children's Adventure Garden by late 2018.

It is evident that new children's gardens are on the rise, although no comprehensive data show the rate of increase. *Designing Outdoor Environments for Children*, published ten years ago, notes 81 children's gardens in the United States. My own recent survey found 152 children's gardens. Hence, on average, seven new children's gardens have been gained each year in the past decade, which shows a significant increase in interest in children's gardens.

As the population of children living in urban settings grows, we need to continue to create more gardens. Children need spaces of their own to play, learn, think, laugh, move, and socialize. When nature no longer occurs naturally for children, we need to provide well-designed outdoor spaces to give them the freedom to experience nature, explore life, and develop into healthy, well-rounded, and unique individuals.

Atlanta Botanical Garden Lou Glenn Children's Garden

1345 Piedmont Avenue, Atlanta, GA 30309

404-876-5859   http://atlantabg.org/explore/children-s-garden

Opening date: Memorial Day weekend 2016

Project size: 2 acres (0.8 hectare) within Atlanta Botanical Garden's 30-acre (12-hectare) site

Design and Construction Team

Atlanta Botanical Garden:

    Display gardens manager: Amanda Bennett

    Chief operating officer, project manager: Arthur Fix

    Youth program manager: Kathryn Masuda

    The Anna and Hays Mershon president and chief executive officer ex-officio: Mary Pat Matheson

    Vice president, programs: Tracy McClendon

Landscape design and planning manager, lead designer: Tres Fromme

Landscape architects of record: Deneen Powell Atelier

Civil engineer: Long Engineering

Architect: Smith Dalia Architects

General contractor: Genoa Construction

References

Atlanta Botanical Garden: The Splash

American Association of Botanical Gardens and Arboreta, ed. 2001. *Reaching Out to the Garden Visitor: Informal Learning and Biodiversity*. Kennett Square, PA: American Association of Botanical Gardens and Arboreta.

American Horticultural Society. n.d. "AHS in a Nutshell." Available at http://ahs.org/about-us (accessed August 9, 2016).

———. n.d. "Children's Garden." Available at http://www.ahs.org/about-river-farm/virtual-tour/childrens-garden (accessed September 19, 2016).

———. n.d. "Our Mission." Available at http://www.ahs.org/about-us/what-we-do (accessed September 17, 2016).

———. 1993a. "Children's Gardens Take Shape at River Farm." *American Horticulturist* 72 (5): 11–14.

———. 1993b. "Designers Help AHS 'Plant the Future.'" *American Horticulturist* 72 (3): 18.

———. 1993c. "Hobhouse Designs AHS Children's Garden." *American Horticulturist* 72 (7): 20–23.

———. 1994. "Children's Garden Designs." *American Horticulturist* 73 (7): 43–45.

American Public Gardens Association. n.d. "Naples Botanical Garden." Available at https://public gardens.org/about-public-gardens/gardens/naples-botanical-garden (accessed September 29, 2016).

ASLA (American Society of Landscape Architects). 2012. "The Indoor Children's Garden at Longwood Gardens." July 11. Available at http://thefield.asla.org/2012/07/11/a-post-occupation-evaluation-of-the-indoor-childrens-garden-at-longwood-gardens/.

Bennett, P. 1998. "Landscape for Learning." *Landscape Architecture* 88 (7): 70–101.

Bilski, N. 1994. "The Best Children's Gardens in the World." *American Horticulturist* 73 (7): 26.

Black, A. n.d. "The Monsters of Bomarzo: A 16th-Century Horror Show Built in a Lovely Italian Garden." *Atlas Obscura*. Available at http://www.atlasobscura.com/places/the-monsters-of-bomarzo (accessed August 9, 2016).

Bok Tower Gardens. n.d. "Hammock Hollow Children's Garden." Available at https://boktower gardens.org/tower-gardens/hammock-hollow-childrens-garden (accessed September 16, 2016).

———. n.d. "Our History." Available at https://boktowergardens.org/tower-gardens/our-history (accessed September 16, 2016).

Botanica Wichita. n.d. "Downing's Children's Garden." Available at http://www.botanica.org/gardens/downing-childrens-garden (accessed August 9, 2016).

Boyer, J. 2014. "Scientific Adventure in a Children's Garden." *Public Garden* 28 (3): 8–9.

Brooklyn Botanic Garden. n.d. "Children's Garden." Available at http://www.bbg.org/discover/gardens/childrens_garden (accessed August 9, 2016).

———. n.d. "New Discovery Garden." Available at http://www.bbg.org/discover/new_discovery_garden (accessed August 9, 2016).

———. 2013. "Mission and Reports." Available at http://www.bbg.org/about/mission.

———. 2014. "Brooklyn Botanic Garden's Children's Garden Celebrates 100th Anniversary." February 21. Available at http://www.bbg.org/press/bbg_childrens_garden_celebrates_100th_anniversary.

———. 2015a. "New Discovery Garden for Children Opens at BBG!" Available at http://www.bbg.org/
press/new_discovery_garden_for_children_opens_at_bbg.

———. 2015b. "The New Discovery Garden Opens, Inspiring Kids to Explore." June. Available at http://
nextcentury.bbg.org/news/the_new_discovery_garden_opens_inspiring_kids_to
_explore.

Byrd, R., M. T. Haque, L. Tai, G. McLellan, and E. J. Knight. 2007. "Designing a Children's Water
Garden as an Outdoor Lab for Environmental Education." *Applied Environmental Education and
Communication* 6 (1): 39–47.

Camden Children's Garden. n.d. "Welcome to Camden Children's Garden." Available at http://www
.camdenchildrensgarden.org/ (accessed August 9, 2016).

Campbell, A. 2016. "Atlanta Botanical Garden Updates Children's Garden." *Upstate Parent*, June 1.
Available at http://www.upstateparent.com/story/travel/destinations/2016/06/01/atlanta
-botanical-garden-updates-childrens-garden/85241408.

Central Texas Gardener. 2014. "Luci and Ian Family Garden, Lady Bird Johnson Wildflower Center."
YouTube, April 24. Available at https://www.youtube.com/watch?v=xzJmz5UzdP8.

Chawla, L. 1988. "Children's Concern for the Natural Environment." *Children's Environments Quarterly*
5 (3): 13–20.

Cheyenne Botanic Gardens. n.d. "About the Gardens: Mission and Statistics." Available at http://www
.botanic.org/about-us-mission-statistics/about-us-mission-statistics (accessed September 28,
2016).

———. n.d. "Paul Smith Children's Village." Available at http://www.botanic.org/discover/childrens
-village/ (accessed August 9, 2016).

Chicago Botanic Garden. n.d. "Grunsfeld Children's Growing Garden." Available at http://www
.chicagobotanicgardens.org (accessed August 30, 2016).

City of Albuquerque. 2016. "Children's Fantasy Garden." Available at https://www.cabq.gov/cultural
services/biopark/garden/exhibits/childrens-fantasy-garden.

Cleveland Botanical Garden. n.d. "Step Inside a Storybook." Available at http://www.cbgarden.org/
come-visit/collection-gardens/hershey-childrens-garden.aspx (accessed August 9, 2016).

Coastal Maine Botanical Gardens. n.d. "A Garden for Children." Available at http://www.maine
gardens.org/blog/a-garden-for-children (accessed August 9, 2016).

Cobb, E. 1993. *The Ecology of Imagination in Childhood*. 2nd ed. Dallas, TX: Spring.

Collins, A. 1993. *Design Issues for Learning Environments*. New York: Bank Street College of Education.

Creasy, R. 2010. *Edible Landscaping*. San Francisco: Sierra Club Books.

Dallas Arboretum and Botanical Garden. n.d. "Rory Meyers Children's Adventure Garden." Available at
http://www.dallasarboretum.org/named-gardens-features/the-rory-meyers-childrens
-adventure-garden (accessed August 9, 2016).

Daniel Stowe Botanical Garden. n.d. "Lost Hollow: The Kimbrell Children's Garden." Available at
http://www.dsbg.org/lost-hollow/ (accessed August 9, 2016).

Danks, S. 2010. *Asphalt to Ecosystems: Design Ideas for Schoolyard Transformation*. Oakland, CA: New
Village Press.

Dannenmaier, M. 1998. *A Child's Garden*. Portland, OR: Timber Press.

Denver Botanic Gardens. n.d. "Mordecai Children's Garden." Available at http://www.botanicgardens
.org/york-street/mordecai-childrens-garden (accessed August 9, 2016).

Didier Design Studio. 2012. *Fossil Narrative, Children's Garden: The Arboretum at Penn State*. Fort
Collins, CO: Didier Design Studio.

Dobbs, V. 2009. "Paradise Found: A New Tropical Garden," *Public Garden* 24–25 (4): 28–29.

Dorf, Philip. 1956. *Liberty Hyde Bailey: An Informal Biography*. Ithaca, NY: Cornell University Press.

Dudek, M., ed. 2005. *Children's Spaces*. Boston: Architectural Press.

Earthplay. n.d. "Who Is Earthplay?" Available at http://earthplay.net/category/who-is-earthplay (accessed September 23, 2016).

Eberbach, C. 2001. "The Children's Adventure Project." In *Reaching Out to the Garden Visitor: Informal Learning and Biodiversity*, edited by American Association of Botanical Gardens and Arboreta, 71–74. Kennett Square, PA: American Association of Botanical Gardens and Arboreta.

EDAW. 2004. *Morton Arboretum Children's Garden: Schematic Design Report*. Fort Collins, CO: EDAW.

———. 2006a. *Cheyenne Botanic Gardens Children's Sustainable Village for Sustainable Living: Schematic Design Report*. Fort Collins, CO: EDAW.

———. 2006b. *Naples Botanical Gardens Children's Garden: Schematic Design Report*. Fort Collins, CO: EDAW.

———. 2007. *Marie Selby Botanical Gardens Children's Rainforest Garden: Schematic Design Report*. Fort Collins, CO: EDAW.

EDAW/AECOM. 2012. *Nit-a-Nee Glen Children's Garden, Penn State University*. Fort Collins, CO: EDAW/AECOM.

Folsom, J. 2014. "From Concept to Concrete." *Public Garden* 28 (3): 21.

Fromme, T., M. Allinson, and B. Ney. 1999. "Longwood Gardens: Opening the Garden to Children." Paper presented at the Youth Gardening Symposium, Denver, CO, July 22–24.

The Gardens on Spring Creek. n.d. "The Children's Garden." Available at http://www.fcgov.com/gardens/our-gardens/childrens-garden (accessed August 9, 2016).

Gill, T. 2007. *No Fear: Growing Up in a Risk Averse Society*. London: Calouste Gulbenkian Foundation.

Haque, M., L. Tai, D. Ham, D. Mizejdewski, and National Wildlife Federation. 2002. *National Wildlife Federation's Tree Conservation and Home Site Development Guide*. Reston, VA: National Wildlife Federation.

Hershey Gardens. n.d. "The Children's Garden at Hershey Gardens." Available at http://hershey gardens.org/attractions/childrens-garden (accessed August 9, 2016).

———. 2005. *The Children's Garden $1.5 Million Campaign: A Garden to Sweeten the Imagination*. Hershey, PA: Hershey Gardens. Pamphlet.

Houston Arboretum and Nature Center. n.d. "Master Plan." Available at http://houstonarboretum .org/support/master-plan (accessed September 19, 2016).

Hwang, H. I. 2007. "Drooling Dragon Has Children Dreaming: A Children's Garden, Loaded with Fountains, Is Set to Open at Longwood." *Philly.com*, October 25. Available at http://articles .philly.com/2007-10-25/news/25233056_1_longwood-gardens-new-fountains-water-jets.

The Huntington. n.d. "About the Huntington." Available at http://www.huntington.org/about (accessed September 28, 2016).

———. n.d. "Children's Garden." Available at http://www.huntington.org/WebAssets/Templates/content.aspx?id=486 (accessed August 9, 2016).

International Play Organization. n.d. "The Child's Right to Play." Available at http://ipaworld.org/childs-right-to-play/the-childs-right-to-play (accessed September 17, 2017).

Ithaca Children's Garden. n.d. "Inspiring the Next Generation of Environmental Stewards." Available at http://ithacachildrensgarden.org (accessed August 9, 2016).

Jekyll, G. 1982. *Children and Gardens*. Woodbridge, UK: Antique Collectors' Club.

Jensen, J. 2014. "The Garden of Monsters." *Italian Ways*, January 23. Available at http://www.italian ways.com/the-garden-of-monsters.

Johnson, S. 2015. "Chicago Botanic Garden Breaks Ground on New $26 Million Campus." *Chicago Tribune*, April 22. Available at http://www.chicagotribune.com/entertainment/museums/ct-botanic-garden-campus-20150422-column.html.

Jost, D. 2010. "Humanizing the Botanical Garden." *Landscape Architecture* 100 (5): 100–115.

Keeler, Wendy. 2011. "Lee and Jane Taylor: Cape Elizabeth's Own 'Mr. and Mrs. Plant.'" *Cape Courier*, May 4, pp. 1, 18.

Kellert, S. R., and V. Derr. 1998. *National Study of Outdoor Wilderness Experience*. New Haven, CT: Yale School of Forestry and Environmental Studies.

Kessler, A. 2009. "Seeds Are Sown for Grand Opening at the Naples Botanical Garden." *Naples Florida Weekly*, June 4. Available at http://naples.floridaweekly.com/news/2009-06-04/arts_and _entertainment_news/063.html.

Kwon, M. H., C. Seo, J. Kim, M. Kim, C. H. Pak, and W. K. Lee. 2015. "Current Status of Children's Gardens within Public Gardens in the United States." *HortTechnology* 23 (5): 671–680.

Lady Bird Johnson Wildflower Center. n.d. "About Us." Available at https://www.wildflower.org/about (accessed September 28, 2016).

———. n.d. "Family Garden." Available at http://www.wildflower.org/family_garden/ (accessed August 9, 2016).

———. n.d. "Plant Selection: Luci and Ian Family Garden." Available at https://www.austintexas.gov/ sites/default/files/files/Watershed/growgreen/2016LPT/Plant-Selection-DeLong-Amaya.pdf (accessed September 12, 2016).

———. 2014. *Map and Guide: Welcome to Nature's Kaleidoscope*. Austin, TX: Lady Bird Johnson Wildflower Center. Pamphlet.

Lewis Ginter Botanical Garden. n.d. "Children's Garden." Available at http://www.lewisginter.org/ visit/gardens/garden-descriptions/childrens-garden/ (accessed August 9, 2016).

"List of Botanical Gardens and Arboretums in the United States." 2016. *Wikipedia*, August 7. Available at https://en.wikipedia.org/wiki/List_of_botanical_gardens_and_arboretums_in_the_United _States.

Long Engineering. 2016. "The Lou Glenn Children's Garden at Atlanta Botanical Garden." May 25. Available at https://longengineering.wordpress.com/2016/05/25/the-lou-glenn-childrens -garden-at-atlanta-botanical-garden.

Longwood Gardens. n.d. "Children's Corner." Available at http://longwoodgardens.org/gardens/ childrens-corner (accessed August 9, 2016).

———. n.d. "Indoor Children's Garden." Available at http://www.longwoodgardens.org/gardens/ indoor-childrens-garden (accessed August 9, 2016).

———. n.d. "1916–1926: Grand-Style Gardening." Available at http://longwoodgardens.org/history/ 1916-1926 (accessed September 29, 2016).

———. 2007. *Longwood Gardens Kids' Map and Guide*. Kennett Square, PA: Longwood Gardens. Pamphlet.

Louv, R. 2005. *Last Child in the Woods: Saving Our Children from Nature-Deficit Disorder*. Chapel Hill, NC: Algonquin Books.

Lovejoy, S. 1999. *Roots, Shoots, Buckets and Boots: Gardening Together with Children*. New York: Workman.

Magnani, D. 2001. *Discover Enchanted Woods: A Fairy-Tale Garden at Winterthur*. Winterthur, DE: Henry Francis du Pont Winterthur Museum.

Marie Selby Botanical Gardens. n.d. "Ann Goldstein Children's Rainforest Garden." Available at http:// selby.org/the-gardens/childrens-rainforest-garden/ (accessed August 9, 2016).

———. n.d. "Facts about Marie Selby Botanical Gardens." Available at http://selby.org/press-room/ fact-sheet (accessed September 17, 2017).

———. n.d. "Mission, Vision, Values" Available at http://selby.org/about/mission-vision-values (accessed September 17, 2017).

———. 2014. *Selby Gardens: A Tropical Urban Oasis.* Sarasota, FL: Carlson Studio Marketing. Pamphlet.

McGuire, L. 2006. "The Best Backyard in the World." *LandscapeOnline*, February. Available at http://landscapeonline.com/research/article.php/6509.

Memphis Botanic Garden. 2011. "My Big Backyard Map." Available at http://www.memphisbotanicgarden.com/mbb-map (accessed September 17, 2016).

Miavitz, E. 2006. "Down to Earth." *Naples Daily News*, July 8. Available at http://www.naplesnews.com/lifestyle/home-and-garden/down_earth.

Michael Van Valkenburgh Associates. n.d. "Brooklyn Botanic Garden." Available at http://www.mvvainc.com/project.php?id=47&c=cultural (accessed August 9, 2016).

Michigan State University. n.d. "Help Us Grow." Available at http://4hgarden.cowplex.com/Help_us_Grow/Our_Growth (accessed October 3, 2016).

———. n.d. "Information." Available at http://4hgarden.cowplex.com/Information (accessed September 17, 2016).

Milazzo, B. 2014. "Finishing Touches Put on Childhood Gate Children's Garden at PSU Arboretum." *Centre Daily Times*, July 3. Available at http://www.centredaily.com/news/article42856461.html.

Milton Hershey School. n.d. "School History." Available at http://www.mhskids.org/about/school-history (accessed September 17, 2016).

Moore, R. C. 1993. *Plants for Play: A Plant Selection Guide for Children's Outdoor Environments.* Berkeley, CA: Mig Communications.

———. 1997. "The Need for Nature: A Childhood Right." *Social Justice* 24 (3): 203–220.

Morton Arboretum. n.d. "Children's Garden." Available at http://www.mortonarb.org/visit-explore/activities-and-exhibits/childrens-garden (accessed September 17, 2016).

"The Morton Arboretum." 2015. *LandscapeOnline*. Available at http://www.landscapeonline.com/research/article.php/12484.

Na 'Aina Kai Botanical Gardens and Sculpture Park. n.d. "Welcome to Na 'Aina Kai ('Lands by the Sea') Botanical Gardens, Sculpture Park and Hardwood Plantation." Available at http://naainakai.org (accessed September 17, 2016).

Nabhan, G. P., and S. Trimble. 1994. *The Geography of Childhood: Why Children Need Wild Places.* Boston: Beacon Press.

Naples Botanical Garden. n.d. "Garden Mission." Available at https://www.naplesgarden.org/gardens/about-the-garden/ (accessed September 17, 2016).

New York Botanical Garden. n.d. "Everett Children's Adventure Garden." Available at http://www.nybg.org/gardens/adventure-garden/index.php (accessed August 9, 2016).

———. n.d. *Guide to the Everett Children's Adventure Garden.* Bronx, NY: New York Botanical Garden. Pamphlet.

———. 2002. *School Programs for Grades Pre-K through 8 and Teachers, 2002–2003.* Bronx, NY: New York Botanical Garden. Brochure.

Nixon, W. 1997. "How Nature Shapes Childhood: Personality, Play and Sense of Place." *Amicus Journal* 19 (2): 31–35.

North Shore Elementary School. 2013. "75th Anniversary Keynote Event: Jane Taylor on Children's Gardening and Outdoor Education." *Facebook*, August 3. Available at https://www.facebook.com/events/402741756498538/.

Oregon Garden. n.d. "Children's Garden." Available at http://www.oregongarden.org/gardens/childrens-garden/ (accessed August 9, 2016).

Orr, D. W. 2002. "Political Economy and the Ecology of Childhood." *In Children and Nature: Psychological, Sociocultural and Evolutionary Investigations*, edited by P. H. Kahn Jr. and S. R. Kellert, 279–304. Cambridge: Massachusetts Institute of Technology.

Peters, F., ed. 2011. *Edible Gardens*. Brooklyn, NY: Brooklyn Botanic Garden.

———. 2014. "A Lasting Harvest: A Century of Children's Education at BBG." Brooklyn Botanic Garden, March 16. Available at http://www.bbg.org/news/a_lasting_harvest.

Raver, A. 2015. "Brooklyn Botanic's New Discovery Garden, Not Just for Kids." *New York Times*, June 11. Available at http://www.nytimes.com/2015/06/12/arts/design/brooklyn-botanics-new -discovery-garden-not-just-for-kids.html.

Red Butte Garden. n.d. "Youth and Family." Available at http://www.redbuttegarden.org/youth-family (accessed August 9, 2016).

Rotary Botanical Gardens. n.d. "Children's Garden." Available at http://www.rotarybotanicalgardens .org/gardens/childrens-garden/ (accessed August 9, 2016).

San Antonio Botanical Garden. n.d. "Children's Vegetable Garden Program." Available at http://www .sabot.org/education/childrens-education/childrens-vegetable-garden-program/ (accessed August 9, 2016).

Schmidt, S. 2015. "Discovery Garden Sneak Peak." *Garden News Blog*, June 5. Available at http://www .bbg.org/news/discovery_garden_sneak_peek.

Selby Gardens. 2013. "New Rainforest Garden for Children and Families to Open in Sarasota." *Tampa Bay Times*, November 5. Available at http://www.tampabay.com/prlink/stories/New-Rainforest -Garden-for-Children-and-Families-to-Open-in-Sarasota,59638.

Smith, G. W. 2010. *From Art to Landscape: Unleashing Creativity in Garden Design*. Portland, OR: Timber Press.

———. 2014. "Enchanted Woods: A Garden of Fairies and Woodland Spirits." *Public Garden* 28 (3): 17–18.

Smith, M. 2015. "The Benefits of Playing in Nature." *Garden News Blog*, April 8. Available at http:// www.bbg.org/news/the_benefits_of_playing_in_nature.

Sobel, D. 2002. *Children's Special Places: Exploring the Role of Forts, Dens and Bush Houses in Middle Childhood*. Detroit: Wayne State University Press.

Sustainable Sites Initiative. n.d. "SITES Is the Most Comprehensive System for Developing Sustainable Landscapes." Available at http://www.sustainablesites.org (accessed August 9, 2016).

Tai, L., M. Haque, G. McClellan, E. Jordan-Knight. 2006. *Designing Outdoor Environments for Children*. New York: McGraw-Hill.

Taylor, Jane. 1994. "In a Child's Garden . . . Imagination Grows." *American Horticulturist* 73 (7): 24–26.

Tepe, E. 2012. *The Edible Landscape: Creating a Beautiful and Bountiful Garden with Vegetables, Fruits and Flowers*. Minneapolis, MN: Voyageur Press.

———. Fromme Design. n.d. "Smithgall Woodland Garden Children's Garden (Atlanta Botanical Garden Gainesville)." Available at http://www.3frommedesign.com/childrens_atlanta_gaines ville.html (accessed August 9, 2016).

Tower Hill Botanic Garden. n.d. "History." Available at http://www.towerhillbg.org/history-and -mission (accessed September 16, 2016).

Tyler Arboretum. n.d. "Totally Terrific Treehouses." Available at https://www.tylerarboretum.org/visit/ things-to-do/kids-and-families/ (accessed August 9, 2016).

United Nations. 2014. "Sustainable Urbanization." Available at http://www.un.org/en/ecosoc/ integration/pdf/fact_sheet.pdf.

United Nations Secretary-General. 2005. *World Demographic Trends: Report of the Secretary-General*. New York: UN Economic and Social Council.

United States Botanic Garden. n.d. "Growing Children's Imaginations." Available at https://www.usbg .gov/growing-children%E2%80%99s-imaginations (accessed August 9, 2016).

U.S. Fish and Wildlife Service. 2014. "Hands-on-Nature Anarchy Zone." Available at https://www.fws .gov/northeast/nyfo/HONAZ.htm.

U.S. Green Building Council. n.d. "Better Buildings Are Our Legacy." Available at http://www.usgbc
.org/LEED/ (accessed August 9, 2016).

Weeks, A. 2015. "The South Garden Transformed: Q&A with Landscape Architect A. Paul Seck."
Garden News Blog, April 3. Available at http://www.bbg.org/news/the_south_garden
_transformed_qa_with_landscape_architect_a._paul_seck.

Weigel, G. 2014. "Penn State Opens New Children's Garden: George Weigel." *PennLive*, July 25.
Available at http://blog.pennlive.com/gardening/2014/07/penn_state_opens_new_childrens
.html.

W. Gary Smith Design. n.d. "The Luci and Ian Family Garden." Available at http://wgarysmith.com/
projects/the-luci-and-ian-family-garden/ (accessed August 9, 2016).

Winterthur. n.d. "Enchanted Woods." Available at http://winterthur.org/?p=671 (accessed August 9,
2016).

Downing Children's Garden,
Botanica, the Wichita Gardens,
Kansas

Bibby and Harold Alfond Children's Garden,
Coastal Maine Botanical Gardens, Maine

Opposite: Children's Garden, Red Butte Garden,
Colorado

Resources

Alabama

Huntsville Botanical Garden
Children's Garden
4747 Bob Wallace Avenue SW
Huntsville, AL 35805
256-830-4447
http://hsvbg.org/childrens-garden

Alaska

Georgeson Botanical Garden
University of Alaska, Fairbanks
Babula Children's Garden
117 West Tanana Drive
Fairbanks, AK 99775
907-474-7222
https://www.uaf.edu/campusmap/
    buildings/georgeson

Arizona

Boyce Thompson Arboretum
Children's Garden
37615 E. U.S. Highway 60
Superior, AZ 85173
520-689-2723
http://arboretum.ag.arizona.edu

Tohono Chul
Bank of America Garden for Children
7366 North Paseo del Norte
Tucson, AZ 85704
520-742-6455
http://www.tohonochul.org/gardens

Tucson Botanical Gardens
Children's Discovery Garden
2150 North Alvernon Way
Tucson, AZ 85712
520-326-9686
https://tucsonbotanical.org/visit

Arkansas

Garvan Woodland Gardens
University of Arkansas
Evans Children's Adventure Garden
550 Arkridge Road
Hot Springs National Park, AR 71913
501-262-9300
http://garvangardens.org/the_gardens/
    evans_adventure_garden/default
    .aspx

California

Alta Vista Gardens
Children's Garden
1270 Vale Terrace Drive
Vista, CA 92084
760-945-3954
http://altavistagardens.org/html/
    children-s_garden.html

Balboa Park
WorldBeat Center
Children's Ethnobotany Garden
2100 Park Boulevard
San Diego, CA 92101
619-230-1190
http://balboapark.org/in-the-park/
    childrens-ethnobotany-garden

Conejo Valley Botanic Garden
Kids' Adventure Garden
400 West Gainsborough Road
Thousand Oaks, CA 91360
805-494-7630
http://conejogarden.com/KidsGarden

Fullerton Arboretum
Children's Garden
1900 Associated Road
Fullerton, CA 92831
657-278-3407
http://fullertonarboretum.org/edu
    _programs_childrens_garden.php

Huntington Botanical Gardens
Helen and Peter Bing Children's Garden
1151 Oxford Road
San Marino, CA 91108
626-405-2100
http://Huntington.org/WebAssets/
    Templates/general.aspx?id=16566

Kidspace Children's Museum
Outdoor Learning Environments
480 North Arroyo Boulevard
Pasadena, CA 91103
626-449-9144
http://kidspacemuseum.org/exhibits/
    outdoor-play

San Diego Botanic Garden
Hamilton Children's Garden
230 Quail Gardens Drive
Encinitas, CA 92024
760-436-3036
http://sdbgarden.org/hcg-home.htm

San Francisco Botanical Garden at
    Strybing Arboretum
Children's Garden
Golden Gate Park
Corner of 9th Avenue and Lincoln Way
San Francisco, CA 94122
415-661-1316
http://sfbotanicalgarden.org

Mordecai Children's Garden, Denver Botanical Gardens, Colorado

Children's Garden, Gardens on Spring Creek, Colorado

San Luis Obispo Botanical Garden
Children's Garden
3450 Dairy Creek Road
San Luis Obispo, CA 93405
805-541-1400
http://slobg.org /our-gardens/childrens
-garden/

South Coast Botanic Garden
Children's Garden
26300 Crenshaw Boulevard
Palos Verdes Peninsula, CA 90274
310-544-1948
http://southcoastbotanicgarden.org

Turtle Bay Exploration Park's
McConnell Arboretum and Botanical
Gardens
Children's Garden
844 Sundial Bridge Drive
Redding, CA 96001
530-243-8850
http://turtlebay.org/gardens

Colorado

Betty Ford Alpine Gardens
Children's Garden
522 South Frontage Road
Vail, CO 81657
970-476-0103
http://bettyfordalpinegardens.org

Denver Botanical Gardens
Mordecai Children's Garden
1007 York Street
Denver, CO 80206
720-865-3500
http://botanicgardens.org/york-street/
mordecai-childrens-garden

The Gardens on Spring Creek
Children's Garden
2145 Centre Avenue
Fort Collins, CO 80526
970-416-2486
http://fcgov.com/gardens/our-gardens/
childrens-garden

Western Colorado Botanical Gardens
Children's Secret Garden
641 Struthers Avenue
Grand Junction, CO 81501
970-245-3288
http://wcbotanic.org

Delaware

Delaware Center for Horticulture
1810 North Dupont Street
Wilmington, DE 19806
302-658-6262
http://thedch.org/what-we-do/
community-gardens-urban%20agri
culture/our-gardens/hedgeville
-childrens-garden

Winterthur Museum, Garden, and
Library
Enchanted Woods
5105 Kennett Pike
Winterthur, DE 19735
302-888-4600
http://winterthur.org/?p=671

District of Columbia

United States Botanic Garden
Children's Garden
100 Maryland Avenue, SW
Washington, DC 20001
202-226-8333

https://www.usbg.gov/growing
-children's-imaginations

United States National Arboretum
Children's Garden
Washington Youth Garden
3501 New York Avenue, NE
Washington, DC 20002
202-245-2709
http://usna.usda.gov/Gardens/
collections/youth.html

Florida

Bok Tower Gardens
Hammock Hollow Children's Garden
1151 Tower Boulevard
Lake Wales, FL 33853
863-676-1408
https://boktowergardens.org/tower
-gardens/hammock-hollow
-childrens-garden

Flamingo Gardens
Children's Garden
3750 South Flamingo Road
Davie, FL 33330
954-473-2955
http://www.flamingogardens.org/
botanical-gardens.html

Florida Botanical Gardens
Children's Trail
12520 Ulmerton Road
Largo, FL 33774
727-582-2100
http://flbg.org/childrens_trail.htm

Children's Garden,
Oregon Garden, Oregon

Heathcote Botanical Gardens
Children's Garden
210 Savannah Road
Fort Pierce, FL 34982
772-464-4672
http://heathcotebotanicalgardens.org/
   garden-rooms/childrens-garden

McKee Botanical Garden
Children's Garden (in planning)
350 U.S. Highway 1
Vero Beach, FL 32962
772-794-0601
http://mckeegarden.org

Mounts Botanical Garden of Palm
   Beach County
Children's Maze
531 N. Military Trail
West Palm Beach, FL 33415
561-233-1757
https://www.mounts.org/our_garden/
   the-maze-2

Naples Botanical Garden
Vicky C. and David Byron Smith
   Children's Garden
4820 Bayshore Drive
Naples, FL 34112
239-643-7275
http://naplesgarden.org/garden/
   childrens-garden

Marie Selby Botanical Gardens
Ann Goldstein Children's Rainforest
   Garden
900 South Palm Avenue
Sarasota, FL 34236
941-366-5731
http://selby.org/the-gardens/
   childrens-rainforest-garden

Georgia

Atlanta Botanical Garden
Lou Glenn Children's Garden
1345 Piedmont Avenue NE
Atlanta, GA 30309
404-876-5859
http://atlantabg.org/explore/
   children-s-garden

Atlanta Botanical Garden, Gainesville
Smithgall Woodland Garden Children's
   Garden (in planning)
1911 Sweetbay Drive
Gainesville, GA 30501
404-888-4760
http://atlantabg.org

Botanic Garden at Georgia Southern
   University
Children's Learning Garden
1505 Bland Avenue
Statesboro, GA 30460
912-478-4636
http://academics.georgiasouthern.edu/
   garden/education/childrens
   -learning-garden

Callaway Gardens
Discovery Center and Day Butterfly
   Center
17800 U.S. Highway 27
Pine Mountain, GA 31822
706-663-6799
http://callawaygardens.com

Dauset Trails Nature Center
Children's Garden
360 Mount Vernon Road
Jackson, GA 30233
770-775-6798
http://dausettrails.com/childgarden
   .htm

Hawaii

Lyon Arboretum
University of Hawaii at Mānoa
Children's Garden
3860 Mānoa Road
Honolulu, HI 96822
808-988-0456
http://manoa.hawaii.edu/lyonarbo
   retum/visit/gardens/childrens-garden

Na ʻĀina Kai (Lands by the Sea)
   Botanical Gardens, Sculpture Park,
   and Hardwood Plantation
Under the Rainbow Children's Garden
4101 Wailapa Road
Kilauea, HI 96754
808-828-0525
http://naainakai.org

Idaho

Idaho Botanical Garden
Children's Adventure Garden
2355 Old Penitentiary Road
Boise, ID 83712
208-343-8649
http://idahobotanicalgarden.org/
   gardenfeature/childrens-adven
   ture-garden

Illinois

Cantigny Park
Just for Kids
1S151 Winfield Road
Wheaton, IL 60189
630-668-5161
http://cantigny.org/visit/just-for-kids

Children's Fantasy Garden,
ABQ BioPark Botanic Garden,
New Mexico

Camden Children's Garden,
New Jersey

Chicago Botanic Garden
Regenstein Learning Campus
Grunsfeld Children's Growing Garden,
    Kleinman Family Cove, and Nature
    Play Garden
1000 Lake Cook Road
Glencoe, IL 60022
847-835-5440
http://chicagobotanic.org/education/
    campus

Lloyd C. Erickson Park
Elwood Children's Garden
801 North Chicago Street
Elwood, IL 60421
815-423-6112
http://villageofelwood.com/161/
    Childrens-Garden-Project-of
    -Elwood

Garfield Park Conservatory
Elizabeth Morse Genius Children's
    Garden
300 North Central Park Avenue
Chicago, IL 60624
312-746-5100
http://garfieldconservatory.org/gardens
    -collections/elizabeth-morse-genius
    -childrens-garden

Klehm Arboretum and Botanic Garden
Nancy Olsen Children's Garden
2715 South Main Street
Rockford, IL 61102
815-965-8146
http://klehm.org/nancy-olson
    -childrens-garden/#.V79auJhrg2w

Luthy Botanical Garden
Children's Garden
2520 North Prospect Road
Peoria, IL 61603
309-686-3362
http://peoriaparks.org/gardens

Morton Arboretum
Children's Garden
4100 Illinois Route 53
Lisle, IL 60532
630-968-0074
http://mortonarb.org/visit-explore/
    activities-and-exhibits/childrens
    -garden

Quad City Botanical Center
Children's Garden
2525 4th Avenue
Rock Island, IL 61201
309-794-0991
http://qcgardens.com/gardens.html

Indiana

Foellinger-Freimann Botanical
    Conservatory
1100 S. Calhoun Street
Fort Wayne, IN 46802
260-427-6440
http://botanicalconservatory.org

Garfield Park Conservatory and Sunken
    Garden
Children's Garden
2505 Conservatory Drive
Indianapolis, IN 46203
317-327-7183
http://garfieldgardensconservatory.org

Taltree Arboretum and Gardens
Adventure Garden
450 West 100 North
Valparaiso, IN 46385
219-462-0025
http://taltree.org/around-the-arboretum/
    gardens/childrens-adventure-garden

Iowa

Brenton Arboretum
O'Brien Nature Play Area
25141 260th Street
Dallas Center, IA 50063
515-992-4211
http://thebrentonarboretum.org/
    NaturePlay.asp

Cedar Valley Arboretum and Botanic
    Gardens
Children's Garden
1927 East Orange Road
Waterloo, IA 50701
319-226-4966
http://cedarvalleyarboretum.org/
    the-gardens/children-s-garden

Dubuque Arboretum
McGreger's Children's Garden
3800 Arboretum Drive
Dubuque, IA 52001
563-556 2100
http://www.dubuquearboretum.com/
    gardens

Iowa Arboretum
1875 Peach Street
Madrid, IA 50156
515-795-3216
http://iowaarboretum.org/our
    -collections/childrens-garden

Hershey Children's Garden,
Cleveland Botanical Garden,
Ohio

Reiman Gardens
Iowa State University
Patty Jischke Children's Garden
1407 University Boulevard
Ames, IA 50011
515-294-2710
http://www.reimangardens.com/
    plan-your-visit/spaces-to-visit/patty
    -jischke-childrens-garden

Kansas

Botanica, the Wichita Gardens
Downing Children's Garden
701 Amidon Street
Wichita, KS 67203
316-264-0448
http://botanica.org/gardens/
    downing-childrens-garden

Overland Park Arboretum and
    Botanical Gardens
Children's Discovery Garden
8909 West 179 Street
Overland Park, KS 66013
913-685-3604
http://opkansas.org/things-to-see
    -and-do/arboretum-and-botanical-gar
    dens/botanical-gardens-and-exhibits

Kentucky

Arboretum, State Botanical Garden of
    Kentucky
University of Kentucky
Kentucky Children's Garden
500 Alumni Drive
Lexington, KY 40503
859-257-6955
http://arboretum.ca.uky.edu/gardens/
    childrens

Boone County Arboretum
Children's Garden
9190 Camp Ernst Road
Union, KY 41091
859-384-4999
http://bcarboretum.org

Western Kentucky Botanical Garden
Children's Garden
25 Carter Road
Owensboro, KY 42301
270-852-8925
http://wkbg.org

Louisiana

Longue Vue House and Gardens
Discovery Garden
7 Bamboo Road
New Orleans, LA 70124
504-488-5488
https://longuevue.com/learn

Maine

Coastal Maine Botanical Gardens
Bibby and Harold Alfond Children's
    Garden
132 Botanical Gardens Drive
Boothbay, ME 04537
207-633-8000
http://mainegardens.org

Maryland

Adkins Arboretum
Children's Funshine Garden
12610 Eveland Road
Ridgely, MD 21660
410-634-2847
http://adkinsarboretum.org/visit_us/
    funshine_garden.html

Brookside Gardens Children's Garden
1800 Glenallan Avenue
Wheaton, MD 20902
301-962-1453
http://www.montgomeryparks.org/
    brookside/virtual_tour.shtm
    #childrens

Massachusetts

Berkshire Botanical Garden
Children's Garden
5 West Stockbridge Road
Stockbridge, MA 01262
413-298-3926
http://berkshirebotanical.org

Elm Bank Horticulture Center
Massachusetts Horticultural Society
Weezie's Garden for Children
900 Washington Street
Wellesley, MA 02482
617-933-4900
http://masshort.org

New England Wildflower Society
Garden in the Woods
Family Activity Area
180 Hemenway Road
Framingham, MA 01701
508-877-7630
http://newfs.org/visit/Garden-in-the
    -Woods/for-families.html

Tower Hill Botanic Garden
The Ramble (in design development)
11 French Drive
Boylston, MA 01505
508-869-6111
http://towerhillbg.org

Lost Hollow, Kimbrell Children's Garden, Daniel Stowe Botanical Garden, North Carolina

Michigan

Dow Gardens
Children's Garden
1809 Eastman Avenue
Midland, MI 48640
989-631-2677
http://dowgardens.org/gardens

Fernwood Botanical Garden and Nature
    Preserve
Children's Nature Adventure Garden
13988 Range Line Road
Niles, MI 49120
269-695-6491
http://fernwoodbotanical.org/gardens/
    discovery-garden-railway-garden.html

Frederik Meijer Gardens and Sculpture
    Park
Lena Meijer Children's Garden
1000 East Beltline NE
Grand Rapids, MI 49525
888-957-1580
http://meijergardens.org/attractions/
    childrens-garden

Leila Arboretum Society
Children's Garden
928 West Michigan Avenue
Battle Creek, MI 49037
269-969-0270
http://lasgarden.org/children.html

Matthaei Botanical Gardens and Nichols
    Arboretum
University of Michigan
Gaffield Children's Garden
1800 N. Dixboro Road
Ann Arbor, MI 48105
734-647-7600
http://www.lsa.umich.edu/mbg/see/
    gaffield.asp

Michigan State University
Michigan 4-H Children's Garden
1066 Bogue Street
East Lansing, MI 48824
517-353-5191 ext. 1-327
http://4hgarden.cowplex.com

Otsego County Alternative Landscaping
Demonstration Gardens and Conserva-
    tion Forest
800 Livingston Boulevard
Gaylord, MI 49735
989-732-4021
http://otsegocd.org/otsego-county
    -demo-garden.html

Slayton Arboretum
Children's Garden
Hillsdale College
33 East College Street
Hillsdale, MI 49242
517-607-2241
https://www.hillsdale.edu/about/
    facilities/slayton-aboretum

Minnesota

Minnesota Landscape Arboretum
Marion Andrus Learning Center and
    Sally Pegues Oswald: A Growing
    Place for Kids
3675 Arboretum Drive
Chaska, MN 55318
952-443-1400
http://www.arboretum.umn.edu/
    history.aspx

Theodore Wirth Regional Park
JD Rivers' Children's Garden
2900 Glenwood Avenue
Minneapolis, MN 55405
612-499-9248
https://www.minneapolisparks.org/
    parks__destinations/gardens__bird
    _sanctuaries/jd_rivers_childrens
    _garden

Mississippi

Crosby Arboretum
Mississippi State University
Children's Garden/Butterfly Garden
370 Ridge Road
Picayune, MS 39466
601-799-2311
http://crosbyarboretum.msstate.edu

Missouri

Missouri Botanical Garden
Doris I. Schnuck Children's Garden
4344 Shaw Boulevard
St. Louis, MO 63110
314-577-5100
http://missouribotanicalgarden.org/
    learn-discover/youth-families/just
    -for-kids/doris-i.-schnuck-childrens
    -garden.aspx

Montana

Tizer Botanic Gardens and Arboretum
Children's Garden
38 Tizer Road
Jefferson City, MT 59638
406-933-8789
http://tizergardens.com/gardens
    .html#children

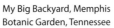
Bee-aMazed Garden,
Longwood Gardens,
Pennsylvania

My Big Backyard, Memphis
Botanic Garden, Tennessee

Nebraska

Arbor Day Farm Tree Adventure
National Arbor Day Foundation
2611 Arbor Avenue
Nebraska City, NE 68410
402-873-8717
http://arbordayfarm.org/attractions/
    tree-adventure.cfm

Lauritzen Gardens
Omaha's Botanical Center
Children's Garden
100 Bancroft Street
Omaha, NE 68108
402-346-4002
https://www.lauritzengardens.org/Visit/
    Gardens/Childrens_Garden

New Hampshire

Robert Frost Homestead
Summer Children's Garden
Route 28
Derry, NH 63038
603-432-3091
http://derrygardenclub.org/activ.html

New Jersey

Camden Children's Garden
3 Riverside Drive
Camden, NJ 08103
856-365-8733
http://camdenchildrensgarden.org

Frelinghuysen Arboretum
353 East Hanover Avenue
Morris Township, NJ 07962
973-326-7601
http://www.arboretumfriends.org/
    content/about-frelinghuysen-arbo
    retum

Wagner Farm
Children's Garden
197 Mountain Avenue
Warren, NJ 07059
908-350-7383
http://wfafnj.org/the-gardens/childrens
    -garden

New Mexico

ABQ Biopark Botanic Garden
Children's Fantasy Garden
2601 Central Avenue NW
Albuquerque, NM 87104
505-768-2000
http://cabq.gov/culturalservices/
    biopark/garden/exhibits/childrens
    -fantasy-garden

Santa Fe Botanical Garden
Ojos y Manos (Eyes and Hands)
    (opening October 22, 2016)
725 Camino Lejo, Suite E
Santa Fe, NM 87505
505-471-9103
http://santafebotanicalgarden.org/
    ojos-y-manos-grand-opening-cele
    bration

New York

Brooklyn Botanic Garden
Children's Garden and Discovery
    Garden
1000 Washington Avenue
Brooklyn, NY 11225
718-623-7200
http://bbg.org/collections/gardens/
    childrens_garden
http://www.bbg.org/collections/
    gardens/discovery_garden

Buffalo and Erie County Botanical
    Gardens
Wegman's Family Garden and Outdoor
    Children's Garden
2655 South Park Avenue
Buffalo, NY 14218
716-827-1584
http://www.buffalogardens.com/pages/
    our-gardens

Genesee Country Village and Museum
Children's Garden
1410 Flint Hill Road
Mumford, NY 14511
585-538-6822
https://www.gcv.org/Historic-Village/
    Heirloom-Gardens-and-Farms

Ithaca Children's Garden
Taughannock Boulevard and Cass Park
    Access Road
Ithaca, NY 14850
607-272-2292
http://ithacachildrensgarden.org

New York Botanical Garden
Everett Children's Adventure Garden
Ruth Rea Howell Family Garden
2900 Southern Boulevard
Bronx, NY 10458
718-817-8700
http://nybg.org/gardens/adventure
    -garden/index.php
http://www.nybg.org/gardens/
    family-garden/index.php

Meyer's Children's Adventure Garden, Dallas Arboretum and Botanical Garden, Texas

NYU Rusk Institute
Glass Garden
Children's PlayGarden
400 East 34th Street
New York, NY 10016
212-263-605
http://med.nyu.edu/glassgardens/
    about/facility.html

Queens Botanical Garden
43–50 Main Street
Flushing, NY 11355
718-886-3800
http://queensbotanical.org/programs/
    gardenprogramsforkids

North Carolina

Cape Fear Botanical Garden
Children's Garden
536 North Eastern Boulevard
Fayetteville, NC 28301
910-486-0221
http://capefearbg.org

Sandhills Horticultural Gardens
Children's Garden
3395 Airport Road
Pinehurst, NC 28374
910-695-3882
http://sandhillshorticulturalgardens
    .com/childrensgarden.htm

Daniel Stowe Botanical Garden
Lost Hollow: Kimbrell Children's Garden
6500 South New Hope Road
Belmont, NC 28012
704-825-4490
http://www.dsbg.org/lost-hollow

North Dakota

Northern Plains Botanic Garden Society
Children's Garden and Children's
    Museum (in master plan)
1201 28th Ave North
Fargo, ND 58102
701-281-2568
http://www.npbotanicgarden.com/
    gardens

Ohio

Cleveland Botanical Garden
Hershey Children's Garden
11030 East Boulevard
Cleveland, OH 44106
216-721-1600
http://cbgarden.org/come-visit/
    collection-gardens/hershey
    -childrens-garden.aspx

Cox Arboretum MetroPark
6733 Springboro Pike
Dayton, OH 45449
937-434-9005
http://www.metroparks.org/places
    -to-go/cox-arboretum

Inniswood Metro Gardens Sisters'
    Garden
940 South Hempstead Road
Westerville, OH 43081
641-895-6216
http://inniswood.org

Lorain County Metro Parks
Schoepfle Children's Garden
11106 Market Street
Birmingham, OH 44816
440-965-7237
http://metroparks.cc/schoepfle_garden
    .php

Wegerzyn Gardens MetroPark
Children's Discovery Garden
1301 East Siebenthaler Avenue
Dayton, OH 45414
937-277-6545
http://www.metroparks.org/discovery
    -garden

Oklahoma

Botanical Garden and Arboretum at
    Oklahoma State University
3425 West Virginia
Stillwater, OK 74078
405-744-5404
http://botanicgarden.okstate.edu/
    gardens-and-grounds/childrens
    -garden

Myriad Botanical Gardens
Children's Garden
301 West Reno Avenue
Oklahoma City, OK 73102
405-445-7080
http://myriad.gardenexplorer.org

Tulsa Botanic Garden
Children's Discovery Garden
3900 Tulsa Botanic Drive
Tulsa, OK 74127
918-289-0330
http://tulsabotanic.org/content/
    childrens-discovery-garden-0

Oregon

Oregon Garden
Children's Garden
879 W. Main Street
Silverton, OR 97381
503-874-8100
http://oregongarden.org/gardens/
    childrens-garden

Children's Garden, Lewis Ginter Botanical Garden, Virginia

Under the Rainbow Children's Garden, Na 'Aina Kai Botanical Gardens, Sculpture Park, and Hardwood Plantation, Hawaii

Pennsylvania

Arboretum at Pennsylvania State University
Childhood's Gate Children's Garden
Park Avenue and Bigler Road
University Park, PA 16802
814-865-9118
https://arboretum.psu.edu/gardens/gardens-groves

Awbury Arboretum
Francis Cope House
1 Awbury Road
Philadelphia, PA 19138
215-849-2855
http://awbury.org

Bartram's Garden
5400 Lindbergh Boulevard
Philadelphia, PA 19143
215-729-5281
http://bartramsgarden.org

Clarion County Park
Children's Creativity Garden
41 Clarion County Park
Shippenville, PA 16254
814-226-4000 ext. 2854

Hershey Gardens
Children's Garden
170 Hotel Road
Hershey, PA 17033
717-534-3492
http://hersheygardens.org/attractions/childrens-garden

Longwood Gardens
Indoor Children's Garden and Bee-aMazed Children's Garden
1001 Longwood Road
Kennett Square, PA 10458
610-388-1000
http://longwoodgardens.com/gardens/indoor-childrens-garden

Phipps Conservatory and Botanical Gardens
Children's Discovery Garden
1 Schenley Park
Pittsburgh, PA 15213
412-622-6914
https://phipps.conservatory.org/visit-and-explore/explore/online-tour-and-history/childrens-discovery-garden

Pittsburgh Botanic Garden
Children's Garden (in master plan)
799 Pinkerton Run Road
Oakdale, PA 15071
412-444-4464
http://pittsburghbotanicgarden.org/sensory-garden
http://pittsburghbotanicgarden.org/about-us-2/plan

John J. Tyler Arboretum
515 Painter Road
Media, PA 19063
610-566-9134
http://tylerarboretum.org/visit/things-to-do/kids-and-families

South Carolina

Linky Stone Park
Greenville Children's Garden
City of Greenville, Parks and Recreation
24 Reedy View Drive
Greenville, SC 29601
864-467-4355
http://greenvillesc.gov/333/Public-Gardens

Sandhills Research and Education Center
Clemson University
For Kids Only
900 Clemson Road
Columbia, SC 29229
803-788-5700
http://clemson.edu/public/rec/sandhill/kids.html

Philip Simmons Children's Garden
727–729 East Bay Street and Blake Street
Charleston, SC 29403
843-724-7350
http://www.charlestonparksconservancy.org/parkDetail/5l1nYW2yGs2EAsmWmAqSwc/philip-simmons-childrens-garden

South Carolina Botanical Garden
Children's Garden
150 Discovery Lane
Clemson, SC 29631
864-656-3405
http://www.clemson.edu/public/scbg/visiting/sights1/gardens

Nancy Yahr Memorial
Children's Garden, Rotary
Botanical Gardens, Wisconsin

South Dakota

Kuhnert Arboretum
Children's Play Garden (in master plan)
17th Avenue SE
Aberdeen, SD 57401
605-626-7015
http://www.aberdeen.sd.us/238/
    Kuhnert-Arboretum

McCrory Gardens
Children's Maze
South Dakota State University
631 22nd Avenue
Brookings, SD 57006
605-688-6707
http://www.mccrorygardens.com/#!the
    -childrens-maze/cmmo

Tennessee

Memphis Botanic Garden
My Big Backyard
750 Cherry Road
Memphis, TN 38117
901-636-4100
http://memphisbotanicgarden.com/
    mybigbackyard

Texas

Aransas/San Patricio County Master
    Gardener Association
Green Acres Demonstration Gardens
Children's Discovery Garden
611 East Mimosa
Rockport, TX 78382
361-790-5456
http://txmg.org/aransas/kids-garden
    ing/kids-gardening-events-games

Clark Gardens Botanical Park
567 Maddux Road
Weatherford, TX 76088
940-682-4856
http://clarkgardens.org

Dallas Arboretum and Botanical Garden
Rory Meyers Children's Adventure
    Garden
8525 Garland Road
Dallas, TX 75218
214-515-6615
http://dallasarboretum.org/named
    -gardens-features/the-rory-meyers
    -childrens-adventure-garden

Houston Arboretum and Nature Center
Nature Playground and Discovery
    Garden (in construction documen-
    tation)
4501 Woodway Drive
Houston, TX 77024
713-681-8433
http://houstonarboretum.org

Lady Bird Johnson Wildflower Center
University of Texas at Austin
Luci and Ian Family Garden
4801 La Crosse Avenue
Austin, TX 78739
512-232-0100
http://wildflower.org/family_garden

Riverside Nature Center
150 Francisco Lemos Street
Kerrville, TX 78028
830-257-4837
http://riversidenaturecenter.org

San Antonio Botanical Garden
Children's Garden (under construction
    to open spring 2017)
555 Funston Place
San Antonio, TX 78209
210-207-3250
http://sabot.org

Shangri La Botanical Gardens and
    Nature Center
Here We Grow! Children's Garden
2111 West Park Avenue
Orange, TX 77630
409-670-9113
http://starkculturalvenues.org/shan
    grilagardens

South Texas Botanical Gardens and
    Nature Center
Children's Play Area
8545 South Staples Street
Corpus Christi, TX 78413
361-852-2100
http://www.stxbot.org/stxbot_exhibits
    .html

Zilker Botanical Garden
Children's Garden
2220 Barton Springs Road
Austin, TX 78746
512-477-8672
http://zilkergarden.org/gardens/
    childrens.html

Utah
Red Butte Garden
University of Utah
Children's Garden
300 Wakara Way
Salt Lake City, UT 84108
801-585-0556
http://redbuttegarden.org

Downing Children's Garden, Botanica, the Wichita Gardens, Kansas

Thanksgiving Point
Children's Discovery Garden
3003 North Thanksgiving Way
Lehi, UT 84043
801-768-2300
http://thanksgivingpoint.org

Vermont

Vermont Community Garden Network
Gardens for Learning
12 North Street
Burlington, VT 05401
802-861-4769
http://vcgn.org/gardens-for-learning

Virginia

Lewis Ginter Botanical Garden
Children's Garden
1800 Lakeside Avenue
Richmond, VA 23228
804-262-9887
http://lewisginter.org/visit/gardens/
    garden-descriptions/childrens
    -garden

Norfolk Botanical Garden
World of Wonders Children's Garden
6700 Azalea Garden Road
Norfolk, VA 23518
757-441-5830
http://norfolkbotanicalgarden.org/
    explore/wow-childrens-garden

George Washington's River Farm
American Horticultural Society
Children's Garden
7931 East Boulevard Drive
Alexandria, VA 22308
703-768-5700
http://ahs.org/about-river-farm/
    virtual-tour/childrens-garden

Washington

Raab Park Community Garden
18349 Caldart Avenue NE
Poulsbo, WA 98370
360-779-9898
http://extension.wsu.edu/kitsap/2014/
    01/raab-park-community-garden

West Virginia

West Virginia Botanic Garden
Children's gardening programs
1061 Tyrone Road
Morgantown, WV 26508
304-322-2093
http://www.wvbg.org/index.php/
    activities-events/school-programs

Wisconsin

Field of Dreams Community Garden
3003 30th Avenue
Kenosha, WI 53403
262-857-2945
http://garden.org/regional/report/
    arch/inmygarden/1725

Green Bay Botanical Garden
Gertrude B. Nielsen Children's Garden
2600 Larsen Road
Green Bay, WI 54303
920-490-9457
http://gbbg.org/gardens

Rotary Botanical Gardens
Nancy Yahr Memorial Children's
    Garden
1455 Palmer Drive
Janesville, WI 53545
608-752-3885
http://rotarybotanicalgardens.org/
    gardens/childrens-garden

University of Wisconsin–Madison
    Arboretum
Wisconsin Native Plant Garden
Homeowner's Demonstration and
    Children's Garden
1207 Seminole Highway
Madison, WI 53711
608-263-7888
http://arboretum.wisc.edu/explore/
    gardens

Wyoming

Cheyenne Botanical Gardens
Paul Smith Children's Village
710 South Lion Park Drive
Cheyenne, WY 82001
307-637-6458
http://botanic.org/discover/childrens
    -village

Children's Healthcare of Atlanta
Children's Garden, Atlanta
Botanical Garden, Georgia, 2006

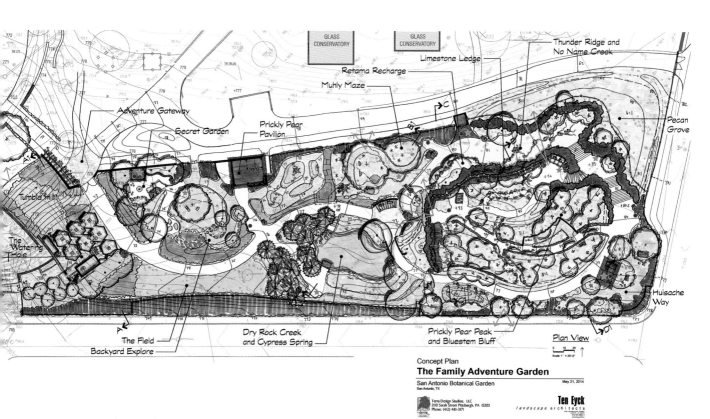

Concept Plan
The Family Adventure Garden
San Antonio Botanical Garden
San Antonio, TX

May 21, 2014

Terra Design Studios, LLC
210 Sarah Street Pittsburgh, PA 15203
Phone: (412) 481-3171

Ten Eyck
landscape architects

Family Adventure Garden at San Antonio Botanical Garden

555 Funston Place, San Antonio, TX 78209

210-536-1400   http://www.sabot.org/grow/family-adventure-garden

Opening date: Spring 2017

Project size: 2.5 acres (1 hectare) on San Antonio Botanical Garden's 38-acre (15.4-hectares) site

Design and Construction Team

San Antonio Botanical Garden executive director: Bob Brackman

Landscape architects:

    Concept design: Terra Design Studios (Cindy Tyler, principal and lead designer; Rob Thompson, project director)

    Landscape architect of record: Ten Eyck Landscape Architects

Child-learning consultant: Natural Learning Initiative

General contractor: Kopplow Construction Co.

Illustration Credits

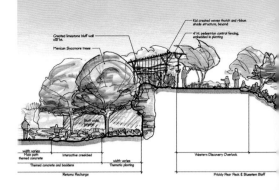

San Antonio Family
Adventure Garden

ABQ BioPark Botanic Garden: 336 (left)

Dave Allen, courtesy of Brooklyn Botanic Garden: 6 (left side), 7 (right side)

American Horticultural Society: 244, 245, 246, 247 (left), 248 (middle left, bottom), 249 (middle right, bottom right), 250 (left)

Arboretum at Penn State: 230 (bottom right), 240 (right), 241 (bottom)

Atlanta Botanical Garden: 320, 321, 324, 325

Todd Bennitt: 80 (top), 84, 90, 91 (bottom), 93, 95, 96

Lisa Blackburn: 81, 87, 94 (top), 97 (top middle)

Botanica, the Wichita Gardens: 331, 343 (top)

Brooklyn Botanic Garden: 4 (bottom), 5 (right), 6 (top middle), 7 (top middle), 12 (top), 13 (bottom middle)

Louise Buhle, courtesy of Brooklyn Botanic Garden: 2, 4 (top), 5 (left), 6 (top left)

Dave Burbank: 98

Scott Byron: 34, 59 (bottom)

Rob Cardillo, courtesy of Winterthur Museum, Garden, and Library: 292

David Cavagnaro: 157 (right), 162 (right), 163 (right)

Fred Charles: 208, 214 (top right, middle right), 215 (bottom left and middle), 218, 224

Chicago Botanic Garden: 35 (right), 36–37, 38, 39, 40 (bottom right), 41 (top left), 42, 44, 48 (top right), 53 (left), 58

Herb Crossan, courtesy of Winterthur Museum, Garden, and Library: 313 (bottom)

Lisa Delplace, courtesy of Oehme, van Sweden and Associates: 47, 48 (bottom)

Didier Design Studio: 228, 230 (top, middle, bottom left), 231, 232, 234, (top, middle left), 235, 236, 237, 238 (top left, middle, bottom), 239, 240 (left), 241 (top), 254, 259, 260

W. Rich Dunoff, courtesy of Winterthur Museum, Garden, and Library: 298, 310 (bottom)

Marcia Eames-Sheavly: 104

Linda Eirhart, courtesy of Winterthur Museum, Garden, and Library: 300, 305 (bottom), 311, 317 (top middle, bottom)

Sheri Elderson, courtesy of the Arboretum at Penn State: 234 (right side)

Stacilyn Feldman, courtesy of Oehme, van Sweden and Associates: 49

Tres Fromme: 127 (top)

James Gagliardi, courtesy of American Horticultural Society: 247 (right)

Caitlin Garvey, courtesy of American Horticultural Society: 251 (top)

Ellin Goetz: 200, 202–203

Glass House USA: 233, 234 (bottom left)

Michael Gunselman, courtesy of Winterthur Museum, Garden, and Library: 306–307 (bottom)

Booth Hansen, courtesy of Chicago Botanic Garden: 32 (top)

Philip Hawk, courtesy of the Arboretum at Penn State: 238 (top right)

Hitchcock Design Group: 166, 174 (top, bottom left), 175, 176 (bottom), 180 (top), 181 (left), 187 (top left)

Huntington: 82, 83, 85

Ithaca Children's Garden: 101 (top), 103 (top left, right middle and bottom), 105, 107 (bottom)

Susan Jacobson: 178 (bottom), 179 (bottom), 182, 183, 186 (bottom left)

Chris Joob: 53 (right)

Deb Kinney, courtesy of Division of Campus Park and Planning, Michigan State University: 152 (top)

Mikyoung Kim: 32 (bottom), 50, 51

Mark Kosmos: 22, 23 (bottom), 24, 26 (top left, bottom), 27 (bottom), 29 (bottom), 31 (top middle)

M. S. Hershey Foundation: 60, 62, 63, 64–65, 67, 68, 69, 70, 71, 72, 73, 74, 75

Lady Bird Johnson Wildflower Center: 112 (top), 113 (top), 114 (bottom), 118 (bottom), 119 (bottom), 120 (top), 121

Longwood Gardens: 124, 126, 127 (bottom), 128 (bottom), 129 (left), 130, 132–133, 134 (top), 136, 137 (bottom), 140 (bottom right), 141, 142 (left), 143 (top), 144 (bottom right), 145, 146, 149 (top left), 339 (left)

Norm Lownds: 152 (bottom), 155, 157 (left), 158, 159, 160, 161, 162 (left), 163 (left, middle), 164 (bottom), 165 (bottom left)

Ray Magnani: 309 (top), 310 (top), 315 (top)

Rick Manning: 100, 102

Marie Selby Botanical Gardens: 255, 261, 262 (top), 263 (top), 265, 268

Leslie Martin, courtesy of Chicago Botanic Garden: 45

Michael Van Valkenburgh Associates Inc.: 10, 11, 12 (bottom left), 13 (top), 14 (right), 15 (top, bottom left), 17, 19 (top)

MKW and Associates: 210, 212 (middle left, bottom), 213 (left), 215 (top), 217, 222, 223, 225, 226, 340

Na ʻAina Kai Botanical Gardens and Sculpture Park: 341 (right)

Nick Nelson, courtesy of United States Botanic Garden: 270, 273 (top), 274, 276, 280 (right), 281 (top)

New York Botanical Garden: 212 (top), 213 (right), 214 (middle left, bottom), 216, 219, 220, 221, 227

Tim O'Connell: ii, 128 (top), 129 (right), 131, 134 (bottom left), 137 (top), 139 (bottom right), 142 (right), 144 (bottom left), 147 (top), 149 (bottom)

Oehme, van Sweden and Associates: 43, 46

Oregon Garden: 335

L. Patrick, courtesy of Brooklyn Botanic Garden: 13 (bottom right), 15 (bottom right)

Jeannie Perales: 266

Eileen Prendergast, courtesy of Chicago Botanic Garden: 40 (bottom left), 41 (top right)

Scott Preston: 57 (top right)

Rodney Robinson Landscape Architects: 272, 273 (bottom), 277, 279

Antonio Rosario, courtesy of Brooklyn Botanic Garden: 7 (top left and right)

Rotary Botanical Garden: 342

Terry Ryan, courtesy of Jacobs/Ryan Associates: 52, 54, 56, 57 (top left, bottom), 59 (top left)

Herb Schaal: 20, 23 (top), 25, 26 (top right) 29 (top middle and right), 30 (middle), 31 (top right, bottom), 168, 169, 170, 171, 172, 173, 174 (bottom right), 176 (top), 177, 178 (top), 179 (top), 180 (bottom), 181 (right), 184, 185, 186 (top, middle, bottom right), 187 (top middle and right), 188, 190, 192, 193 (left), 195, 196 (bottom), 197 (bottom), 198 (bottom), 199 (bottom), 204, 205, 206, 207 (top), 258, 264 (bottom), 332, 333

S. Schmidt, courtesy of Brooklyn Botanic Garden: 18 (top)

James Schneck, courtesy of Winterthur Museum, Garden, and Library: 295, 305 (top)

W. Gary Smith: cover, 108, 110, 111, 114 (top), 115, 118 (top), 119 (top), 120 (bottom), 122, 123, 294, 296, 297, 299, 301, 302, 304, 306 (top), 307 (top), 308, 312, 313 (top right), 314, 315 (bottom), 316 (top), 319, 338

Jim Sohn, courtesy of American Horticultural Society: 242, 248 (middle right), 249 (bottom left), 250 (right)

Bonnie Tai: 348, 349, 359

Kuang-Ming Tai: v

Lolly Tai: vi, xiv, 6 (top right), 7 (bottom), 14 (left) 18 (bottom), 19 (bottom), 27 (top), 28, 29 (top left), 30 (left and right), 31 (top left), 35 (left), 40 (top), 41 (bottom left), 48 (top left and middle), 76, 78, 79, 80 (bottom), 86, 88, 89, 91 (top), 92, 94 (bottom), 97 (top left and right, bottom), 101 (bottom), 103 (top right, right top), 112 (bottom), 113 (bottom), 116–117, 134 (bottom middle and right), 138, 139 (top, bottom left), 140 (top, middle, bottom left), 143 (bottom), 144 (top), 147 (middle, bottom), 148, 149 (top right), 187 (bottom), 191, 193 (right), 194, 196 (top), 197 (top), 198 (top), 199 (top), 201, 207 (middle, bottom), 211, 212 (middle right), 214 (top left), 215 (bottom right), 248 (top), 249 (top, middle left), 251 (bottom), 252, 256, 257, 262 (bottom), 263 (bottom), 264 (top), 267, 269, 275 (right), 281 (bottom), 282, 286 (bottom), 287 (bottom left), 288, 289, 290 (top right), 291, 303 (middle, bottom), 309 (bottom), 315 (middle), 316 (bottom), 318, 323, 334, 336 (right), 337, 341 (left), 343 (bottom), 351, 353, 354

Luther Tai: xi

Lee Taylor: viii, 150, 153, 154, 156, 164 (top), 165 (top, bottom right)

Terra Design Studios: 284, 285, 286 (top), 287 (top, bottom right), 290 (top left, bottom), 339 (right), 344, 345

United States Botanic Garden: 275 (left), 278, 280 (left)

Lexi Van Valkenburgh: 8, 12 (bottom right), 13 (bottom left)

Amy Wells, courtesy of Chicago Botanic Garden: 41 (bottom right)

Whitman Planning and Design: 106, 107 (top)

Toni Wierig, courtesy of Chicago Botanic Garden: 59 (top right)

Winterthur Museum, Garden, and Library: 303 (top), 313 (top left), 317 (top left and right)

Mary Yee: 250 (middle)

Index

Crooked Goblin Shack at Tyler
Arboretum, Pennsylvania

Playing in the Crooked Goblin
Shack at Tyler Arboretum

Looking out of the Crooked Goblin
Shack at Tyler Arboretum

About the Author

Lolly Tai is an educator and a licensed landscape architect. She is a professor of landscape architecture at Temple University, where she was formerly Senior Associate Dean of the School of Environmental Design and chair of the Landscape Architecture and Horticulture Department. She began her teaching career at Clemson University, where she also established her landscape architecture private practice. Before that, she was a landscape architect and project manager for Hart Howerton in New York City.

For nearly twenty years, her research focus has been on designing outdoor environments for children. It was sparked by the first schoolyard project she assigned her students at Clemson University. To her surprise, she found that little had been written about the topic. Since then, she has been passionate about exploring, learning, and writing about designing inspiring spaces for children.

She is a coauthor of the acclaimed book *Designing Outdoor Environments for Children* (2006). A Fellow of the American Society of Landscape Architects, she is also the recipient of the Bradford Williams Medal from the American Society of Landscape Architects, the Award of Distinction from the Council of Educators in Landscape Architecture, the Honor Award for Design from the National Landscape Association, and numerous other professional awards. She holds a B.S. from Cornell University, an M.S. from Harvard University, and a Ph.D. from Heriot-Watt University in landscape architecture.